The Cambridge Introduction to
Creative Writing

DAVID MORLEY

CAMBRIDGE
UNIVERSITY PRESS

CAMBRIDGE UNIVERSITY PRESS
Cambridge, New York, Melbourne, Madrid, Cape Town, Singapore, São Paulo

Cambridge University Press
The Edinburgh Building, Cambridge CB2 8RU, UK

Published in the United States of America by Cambridge University Press, New York

www.cambridge.org
Information on this title: www.cambridge.org/9780521547543

First published 2007

Printed in the United Kingdom at the University Press, Cambridge

A catalogue record for this publication is available from the British Library

Library of Congress Cataloguing in Publication data
Morley, David, 1964–
The Cambridge introduction to creative writing / David Morley.
    p.   cm. – (Cambridge introductions to literature)
Includes bibliographical references and index.
ISBN-13 978-0-521-83880-1 (hardback)
ISBN-10 0-521-83880-0 (hardback)
ISBN-13 978-0-521-54754-3 (pbk.)
ISBN-10 0-521-54754-7 (pbk.)
1. English language – Rhetoric – Problems, exercises, etc.   2. Creative writing – Problems,
exercises, etc.   3. Report writing.   I. Title.   II. Series.
PE1413.M583   2007
808'.042 – dc22
2006036851

ISBN 978-0-521-83880-1 hardback
ISBN 978-0-521-54754-3 paperback

To teachers

'several things dovetailed in my mind and at once it struck me, what quality went to form . . . Achievement especially in Literature & which Shakespeare possessed so enormously – I mean *Negative Capability*, that is when man is capable of being in uncertainties, Mysteries, doubts, without any irritable reaching after fact and reason.'

John Keats

'When it comes to atoms, language can be used only as in poetry. The poet, too, is not nearly so concerned with describing facts as with creating images.'

Niels Bohr

Contents

Preface

The purpose of this book is to introduce readers to the practice of creative writing. Equally, the purpose of this book is to introduce writers to the practice of creative reading. Writing and reading share an interdependent orbit around the open space of language.

This double helix of reading and writing makes you more alert to your potential as a reader and writer of yourself, of other people and of other writers. It also creates a discipline in your life that makes these acts of attention a way of life. It is then vital you learn to work alone and beyond your potential – writers and readers alike work beyond their own intelligence.

As this is an introduction to a discipline, we discuss where creative writing comes from, the various forms and camouflages it has taken and why we teach and learn it. I do not present you with an anatomy of the various histories of creative writing in higher education; there are fine examples available in print (Dawson, 2005; Myers, 1995).

The first five chapters explore principles and procedures of creative writing that apply generally to the writing and techniques of fiction, creative nonfiction, poetry and, to some extent, drama. Guests to this party include reading, criticism, vocation, influence, reflection, experience, play, publishing, editing, language, translation, imitation, experiment, design, form, quality, discipline, notebooks, working habits, fieldwork, composition, incubation, planning, fluency, finishing, rewriting, deadlines, precision, confidence, practice, audience, voice and selves. We look at the meaning and sound of language; the different states of mind we use for writing; the workshop in its various guises and disguises; and the enemies and allies of creativity. I also explore the characteristics of mind by which we might develop writerly stamina.

The first five chapters concern the generics; Chapters Six to Nine introduce important genres. They present some of the techniques and practice for fiction, poetry and the international supergenre, creative nonfiction. However, not all creative writers write for the page. We look at creative writing as a verbal art in performance; as hybrid with public and visual art; and as electronic literature. I argue that none of these is at odds with the making of books; they are all spaces open to creative literary practice. Chapter Ten looks at writing as an act of community; I then attempt to speculate modest engagements for creative writing in the creative academy, for example within science.

For experts in this field, all of what I have to say is rudimentary. This book is for creative writing students, beginning writers and new teachers of writing. The cast of this book is about the roots of creativity in writing, and the routes into the writing of fiction, creative nonfiction and poetry, rather than higher techniques. My reason for the book's architecture is to send you immediately into the action of writing, by offering a series of open spaces for discussion, reflection and practice. It has been argued that half the skills a writer needs to learn are skills of psychological sturdiness, and the other half are skills of literary craft (Bly, 2001: xix). I agree, and the book is designed to address these complementary phases of creative development.

This is an introduction, partial and selective. No book can, or should, cover everything. I think that you should be given open space to find your own way in these matters, and to argue back on points I take to extremes. Given its length, I centre on topics rather than texts, tempting though it was to select examples instead of moving forward single-handed. Guidance is offered through the lists of recommended reading, and by following up the next section on examples and sources. A book about creative writing requires lifetime subscription to The Alexandrian Library, and my recommended reading lists scan only the eye-level shelves. That said, 'A man will read a library to write just one book' – Dr Johnson. Those lists are starting points.

Since this is a book about, of all things, *creative* writing, I tried to keep my language open and personal, tuning out academic white noise – citations only when necessary, endnotes shown the door. I welcomed into the book subjective and general values like pleasure, passion, experience, love, intuition, hate, pain and playfulness. Moreover, the book is written to be read from beginning to end, as a story of learning. It is not a hoard of tips, or a compendium of games. I wanted to make a book that hits things fresh; one that is written from inside writing. While I do not disguise the difficulties of process, I celebrate its epiphanies, especially the euphoria of reading. Reading and writing are never-ending journeys. I wanted to remind myself of how it feels to be beginning as a writer, the first excitements of reading, the waking in created countries.

Creative writing – even clear writing – closes distances between us. It makes us wake up. What this book offers you is an introduction and an invitation. Think of it as a miniature stage: the matters that are closest to the covers are your entrances and exits. What is in the middle is *play*, where you are both the players and – with your acceptance of this invitation – those upon whom ideas and language play.

I gathered the arguments and discussions from my own reading but also from others more deeply and widely read than myself. I took examples of practice from hundreds of discussions with contemporary writers about their philosophies, influences and craft. I reflected on my own teaching of creative writing in universities, adult education, communities and schools; and co-teaching and observing teaching in the English-speaking world, especially the United States, Canada and in Europe. Writing this book has been a chastening personal experience, and my admiration for writers and teachers has increased inestimably. Errors in this book are my responsibility.

Examples and sources for writers

Readers who wish to become writers find resonance – even purpose – in statements on the writing process made by authors who have lived their lives by the word. I pepper the text with examples, and attempt to synthesise some of the best standard guidance. When thinking about the aims and processes of creative writing, literary biographies and autobiographies are a useful place to begin to find out about a writer's working methods and philosophy. The *Paris Review* interviews, downloadable at the journal's website, remain the best resource for testimonies by writers about their practice. There are other rich sources for this type of material (Allen, 1948; Brown and Paterson, 2003; Burke, 1995; Haffenden, 1981; Harmon, 2003; Herbert and Hollis, 2000).

In writing, what we leave half-said is as significant as what we spell out. I signal a variety of key works and further reading that amplify, or exemplify, matters that need your closer attention, especially in regard to writing fiction, creative nonfiction and poems. There are several superb technical books on imaginative and formal writing (Behn and Twichell, 1992; Bernays and Painter, 1991; Burroway, 2006; Fussell, 1979; Koch, 1990; Matthews and Brotchie, 1998; Novakovich, 1995; Padgett, 2000; Steele, 1999; Stein, 1995; Strand and Boland, 2000); on the practical and philosophical processes of writing fiction, poetry or creative nonfiction (Addonizio and Laux, 1997; Boisseau and Wallace, 2004; Brande, 1981; Burroway, 2003; Dillard, 1989; Eshleman, 2001; Gardner, 1983, 1985; Gutkind, 1997; Hughes, 1967; Hugo, 1979; King, 2000; Kinzie, 1999; Kundera, 2000; Lamott, 1995; Lodge, 1992; Oliver, 1994; Packard, 1992; Sansom, 1994; Stein, 1995; Zinsser, 1976); on creative writing, revision and rewriting (Anderson, 2006; Bell and Magrs, 2001; Browne and King, 2004; Le Guin, 1998; Mills, 2006; Ostrom et al., 2001; Schaefer and Diamond, 1998); and on the nature of creativity and the psychology of writing (Boden, 2004; Hershman and Lieb, 1998; Hunt and Sampson, 2006; Koestler, 1975; Lakoff and Johnson,

1980; Pfenninger and Shubik, 2001; Pope, 2005; Turner, 1996). On questions of style, you will find your own answers as you read and practise. Be sure to pack *The Elements of Style* (Strunk and White, 2000) with you on the journey; it will take little room compared to what it offers so generously.

Extensive quotation of primary texts is, unfortunately, expensive in permissions. I offer examples in the main text and epigraphs to chapters, but guide readers towards literature within commonly used anthologies, as widespread in public libraries as they are on international university reading lists. You need not possess those anthologies to use this book. This is the key:

NA1
The Norton Anthology of American Literature, 6th edition/package 1: vols. A and B. General editor: Nina Baym, Norton, 2003.
NA2
The Norton Anthology of American Literature, 6th edition/package 2: vols. C, D and E. General editor: Nina Baym, Norton, 2003.
NE1
The Norton Anthology of English Literature, 7th edition/vol. 1. General editors: M. H. Abrams and Stephen Greenblatt, Norton, 2000.
NE2
The Norton Anthology of English Literature, 7th edition/vol. 2. General editors: M. H. Abrams and Stephen Greenblatt, Norton, 2000.
NP
The Norton Anthology of Poetry, 5th edition. Editors: Margaret Ferguson, Mary Jo Salter and Jon Stallworthy, Norton, 2005.

Writing Games

Writing creatively can feel a little like working out logistical, even mathematical, challenges. Writing Games provide this elegant calculus in taut form. A bare page can terrify; a game simulates the real thing, or is a means of keeping your hand in, almost like playing scales. With practice, simulations can become the real thing. No writer creates a book at one sitting; they write it in stages, as passages, scenes and stanzas, and each stage requires several drafts. Writing Games clone this process, and are often true to the natural rhythm of literary production in that technique and style are often learned on the job. There are many creative writing projects embedded in the text, as well as ideas and suggestions that students and teachers can use as starting points for games. Within the body of each chapter, I offer some self-standing games that help you explore its issues. Each project has an aim for judging progress.

Acknowledgements

My wife Siobhan Keenan provided wonderful support, ideas and criticism. I thank my colleagues at the University of Warwick – above all, Jeremy Treglown, who took on all of my administrative and managerial duties during the period of composition; and my friend Peter Blegvad, whose drawings are a much-needed parallel world for the reader. Peter Blegvad, with Maureen Freely, led me towards authors I simply would not have come across, left to my own devices. Thanks are due to the University of Warwick for research leave, and for a Warwick Award for Teaching Excellence, the proceeds of which were spent researching this book. Thanks to those who made life easier during the time of writing this book, especially Peter Mack and Thomas Docherty.

My thanks to those who discussed some of these ideas, or who, over the years, were teachers or co-teachers: Anne Ashworth, Susan Bassnett, Jonathan Bate, Richard Beard, Mike Bell, Jay Boyer, Zoe Brigley, Andy Brown, Elizabeth Cameron, Ron Carlson, Peter Carpenter, Nina Cassian, Jonathan Coe, Peter Davidson, Douglas Dunn, Brian Follett, Maureen Freely, Dana Gioia, Jon Glover, David Hart, Miroslav Holub, Ted Hughes, Russell Celyn Jones, Stephen Knight, Doris Lessing, Denise Levertov, Emma McCormack, Paul Muldoon, Les Murray, Bernard O'Donoghue, Maggie O'Farrell, Melissa Pritchard, Al Purdy, Jewell Parker Rhodes, Jane Rogers, Carol Chillington Rutter, William Scammell, Michael Schmidt, Jane Stevenson, George Szirtes, Michelene Wandor; and to the following institutions where thinking took place: the Arvon Foundation, the University of Warwick, National Association of Writers in Education and the Virginia Piper Center for Creative Writing at Arizona State University. I field-tested many of the Writing Games in the United States, Europe and China. I thank the thousands of members of the public, students, school pupils, medical workers, teachers – and writers – who let me play. Finally, thanks to my former teacher, Charles Tomlinson, who taught me that the first cause of creative writing is creative reading.

Extracts and versions of this text appeared in a slightly altered form in *Anon Magazine* (Edinburgh), the *Guardian* and *Poetry Review* (London).

Writing Game

IN YOUR END IS YOUR BEGINNING

Write a 500-word introduction to your own imaginary collected poems or complete stories. Assume your working life has undergone a struggle, from obscurity to hard-won fame. This is your final opportunity to say something *wise* to your readers and critics. What were your strengths; and why did your audience first ignore your writing, then welcome it? Do you have any literary or personal debts outstanding? Now you can settle them publicly. State what you think the future holds for your work.

AIM: Writers feel intense dissatisfaction. Learn to wait, and work at it; get used to that feeling of being perpetually dissatisfied with your abilities, achievements and the mercury-movement of language as you try to control it:

> Trying to use words, and every attempt
> Is a wholly new start, and a different kind of failure
> Because one has only learnt to get the better of words
> For the thing one no longer has to say

T. S. Eliot, *The Four Quartets* (1943)

Chapter 1

Introducing creative writing

If you wish to be brief, first prune away those devices that contribute to
an elaborate style; let the entire theme be confined within narrow limits.
Do not be concerned about verbs; rather, write down with the pen of the
mind only the nouns . . . follow, as it were, the technique of the
metalworker. Transfer the iron of the material, refined in the fire of the
understanding, to the anvil of the study. Let the hammer of the intellect
make it pliable; let repeated blows of the hammer fashion from the
unformed mass the most suitable words. Let the bellows of the mind
afterwards fuse those words, adding others to accompany them, fusing
nouns with verbs, and verbs with nouns, to express the whole theme.
The glory of a brief work consists in this: it says nothing either more or
less than is fitting.

GEOFFREY DE VINSAUF, *Poetria Nova* or *The New Poetics*
(c. 1210)

An open space

Think of an empty page as open space. It possesses no dimension; human
time makes no claim. Everything is possible, at this point endlessly possible.
Anything can grow in it. Anybody, real or imaginary, can travel there, stay put,
or move on. There is no constraint, except the honesty of the writer and the
scope of imagination – qualities with which we are born and characteristics
that we can develop. Writers are born and made.

We could shape a whole world into that space, or even fit several worlds,
their latitudes and longitudes, the parallel universes. Equally, we could place
very few words there, but just enough of them to show a presence of the life of
language. If we can think of the page as an open space, even as a space in which
to play, we will understand that it is also Space itself.

By choosing to act, by writing on that page, we are creating another version
of time; we are playing out a new version of existence, of life even. We are
creating an entirely fresh piece of space-time, and another version of your *self*.

1

The iceberg

Space-time is a four-dimensional space used to represent the Universe in the theory of relativity, with three dimensions corresponding to ordinary space and the fourth as time. I mean the same when thinking about creative writing. Writing a poem, a story or a piece of creative nonfiction, is to catalyse the creation of a four-dimensional fabric that is the result when space and time become one.

Every event in the universe can be located in the four-dimensional plane of space and time. Writing can create personal universes in which this system of events within space-time operates for the reader; the reader is its co-creator. Writing and reading are collaborative acts in the making and performance of space-time. Readers participate; they become, partly, writers. They will take part, consciously and unconsciously, in a literary creation, and live their life in that moment and at that speed – while they are reading. You make the words; they make the pictures. The reader lives their reading-time in a kind of psychological fifth dimension, where the book takes them, where the reader places themselves. A novel or poem is the visible part of an iceberg. As Ernest Hemingway put it, the knowledge a writer brings to the creation of that novel or poem is the unrevealed submerged section of that same iceberg. This book dives under that iceberg.

The writer weaves a certain degree of sparseness into their final text. If matters are left unexplained, untold, or the language of a poem is elliptically economical without becoming opaque, then inquiring readers will lean towards that world. Readers fill in the gaps for themselves, in essence, writing themselves into that small universe, creating that fifth dimension, and their experience of that dimension. The reader is active, as a hearer and a witness.

Moreover, if they are reading aloud to others, that piece of space-time will attract and alter several lives simultaneously. Some readers may be affected for the rest of their lives, loving that space so much they return to that work repeatedly, and even act out their own lives differently, in their own worlds, once they have put down the book. A well-drawn character in fiction or poetry, say, may find their actions and language imitated by readers simply because of the creative radiation of that fictional self, and the accuracy of the writing. Think about the force and precision behind the creation of fictional or dramatic characters we admire or cherish.

New worlds

Stories, like dreams, have a way of taking care of people, by preparing them, teaching them. I argue that, although there is an inherent simplicity to this, it is not simple as a practice. With dreams come responsibilities, and the created worlds of a book require a vocation of trust between the writer and reader. It is that vocation, how we create ourselves as writers – never forgetting that we are also readers – that is the subject of the final part of this chapter. We will none of us become a good writer unless we become a great reader, of more matter than just books. We must also learn to become shapers of language and, in that way, shapers of the small, new worlds that take the form of poems or novels, each of them a piece of fresh space-time, remembering itself. Hemingway, writing of the practice of fiction, states:

> You have the sheet of blank paper, the pencil, and the obligation to invent truer than things can be true . . . to take what is not palpable and make it completely palpable and . . . have it seem normal . . . so that it can become a part of the experience of the person who reads it.
> (Phillips, 1984: 16)

Writing can change people, for writing creates new worlds and possible universes, parallel to an actual. At best, creative writing offers examples of life, nothing less. To some, writing remains an artifice, a game even, and it is – as most things are, as all of us are – something made or played upon. However, when nurture builds carefully on nature, then life is not only made well, it can be shaped well and given form.

Why we write

Writing is so absorbing and involving that it can make you feel more alive – concentrated yet euphoric. The process focuses at the same time as it distracts; the routine of its absorptions is addictive. It can also recreate in you something you may have lost without noticing or glimpse when you are reading a rewarding book: your sense for wonder. Certainly, the process of writing is often more rewarding than the outcome, although, when you capture something luminous, that sense of discovery and wonder swims through the words and leaps in the page. There is a pleasure in precision; in solving and resolving the riddles of your syntax and voice; and in the choices of what to lose and what to allow.

However, while creative writing is no panacea, some writers find its practice therapeutic; and some teachers of writing believe that writing is a powerful aid to various types of therapy, from the treatment of depression to social reha- bilitation. More accurately, writing may contribute towards self-development and self-awareness (see Hunt, 2000; Sampson, 2004). Writing wakes you up – it forces you beyond your intelligence and quotidian attention – and anything that makes you think and perceive more clearly and expansively may assist you with finding perspectives on yourself and others. Research has shown that we are never happier than when we are working towards some objective, and the spaces we work, and within which we work, are open enough to provoke surprise in ourselves.

What I must add is that writers invest a lot of time in getting the opposite results – storm-blind language, stillborn literature – in order to travel through darker space towards pleasure. Most days, this feels more like anti-therapy than art-therapy. Writers must journey into an abyss in themselves to make truth through fiction and form. Such journeys can be unforgiving rather than consoling. They can even lead to a sense of worthlessness and loss of direction. But, as the poet Richard Hugo advises writing students, 'isn't it better to use your inability to accept yourself to creative advantage? Feelings of worthlessness can give birth to the toughest and most welcome critic within' (1979: 70). Good writers exercise a sharpened discrimination; very little of what they write will get past this acuity.

If – and this is the Mount Everest of ifs – you ever impress yourself as a writer, you are probably suffering a kind of artistic altitude sickness. Don't get me wrong: you may be right, but the feeling will pass as you descend to other work. Toughness and dissatisfaction over your own work is itself rewarding, but only with practice. It can also seem ruthless, not therapeutic. If writing is not subject to these tests and taut self-tests, then you cheat your devil of his pay. You cheat your writing, in fact. It is possibly more therapeutic to allow writing to become both a form of pleasure and a form of work, rather than an outlet exclusively for emotions and epiphanies.

A balance

Having created a life, the first duty of the writer is to give it away. So long as what we have written is well made, this is a huge gift. Generosity is one of the pleasures of invention, and a principle of human love: honest of itself, it must be given, or given away freely. Now, look at that blank page again. Hold in the mind for a moment that this is both a private and a public space. The first to know this space is you, the writer, and the next person to know that space is yourself, the reader; a balance of perception and self-perception. To move from 'this' to 'that' requires a process which is both creative and which requires work, work that is sometimes euphoric and easy, and sometimes difficult, jagged.

Sometimes you will write for weeks as though your mind itself is running and even flying, independent of your ability and knowledge. It will seem like the mind has mountains, that it can contain the world. Sometimes you will write as though you are stumbling through a dark forest; your thought is sheer plòd. Sometimes you will be completely helpless, as though language's light had never existed in you or for you. There are feasts and famines. Any new writer who fears that flow and ebb, who takes no pleasure or pain in it, who is incapable of studying their own flaws or the flaws of their writing too nearly, must try to find their own balance. Marianne Moore wrote in her poem 'Picking and Choosing' (1968: 45):

> Literature is a phase of life. If one is afraid of it,
> the situation is irremediable; if one approaches it familiarly,
> what one says is worthless.

But, for all that commitment or familiarity, creative writing is not a mystery. One of the purposes of the academic discipline of creative writing is to demystify itself without falsifying its intricacy. Creative writing can be opened and learned, like any craft, like any game of importance. 'You become a good writer just as you become a good carpenter: by planing down your sentences' – Anatole France.

As a writer, especially of fiction, you are obsessed by character. However, your own character has to be shaped and planed. *Writing is rewriting*, and the *character* of the writer is rewritten by the activity of writing and rewriting. If you are interested in the energies of language, rather than 'being a writer', then you stand a very good chance of becoming a writer. The character of the reader, your character – you as a writer – are central to that journey. Yet you do not need to write creatively if your ambition is to be a great reader. It is essential that you become a great reader if your purpose is to become a good writer. There is only dual citizenship on this continent. I hope you have already begun the journey. If so, then everything is possible, at this point endlessly possible. Think of that open space as an empty page.

Writing Game

THE WORD HOARD

Go to a shelf of books of fiction or poetry. Take one book at random. Close your eyes while opening that book and place your finger somewhere in it. Your finger will have landed on a word or words. Write the word down, as well as the three words preceding it and the three words following it in the text. You now have a seven-word phrase. Write this phrase in your notebook and, once you have written it, keep writing for five minutes. There are only two rules to this game: you must not stop writing; and you must not think. Try to write as fast as you can. You are not producing a work of art. After five minutes, you should have covered quite a lot of pages. Now read what you have written Read it forwards, then read through it, word for word, backwards. Underline one phrase that strikes you as possessing any *one* of the following qualities: it has energy; it surprises you; it has never been written before in your language. The phrase must make a kind of sense; it must possess its own inner sense at the very least. That is, it must not be completely opaque in meaning. It might be a whole sentence, or it might be the end of one sentence and the beginning of the next. Now, write a short story or poem in which this phrase occurs without it seeming in any way out of place. You might wish to place the phrase into the mouth of a speaker in the poem or story, for example.

AIM: When we strive to be original, we tend to get tongue-tied, for we have been long taught that originality is no longer possible. As we shall see in Chapter Four, this 'free-writing' exercise is effective for warming up for writing, but it is also effective at creating unusual phrases, ones that possess a surprising amount of personal linguistic energy. You are trying to capture ideas and sentences that you would not ordinarily come up with consciously. You should try to do this exercise every day, not only to keep your writing mind limber, but also to create a hoard of original and unusual phrases from which you can draw when you are writing. 'Word hoard' is a 'kenning' (a Norse poetic device; see Chapter Eight), meaning 'a supply of words', such as a book, or vocabulary itself.

Learning to write

A continent

Energy is eternal delight. There are as many energetic views on how to teach writing as there are university writing programmes, writing workshops, writing theorists, teachers of writing, books about writing – and writers. This variety is a cause for that delight, or it should be. Different exponents shade the discipline of creative writing according to their practice and aesthetics. Some use workshops, and some do not. Textbooks vary in the weight given to this or that topic, unlike, say, textbooks of biochemistry; and some writer-teachers never use textbooks relying on primary texts only.

The fact is that most writers develop haphazardly – we hit things fresh whatever level we reach, and work through problems in countless directions. There are no absolute solutions. What a writer is experimenting with is language. The fastest-evolving species of this world is language. Given that speed of evolution, there is no wrong or right about the pedagogy of writing – no frozen framework. It is more a case of what works for a time and what does not.

As language lives by evolving, so writers survive in its open space for their time, often influencing the successful mutations as well as bringing about (as well as preventing) extinctions. There are many literary theories of writing, but those theories are not within my remit. However, the quality of things being so various can be confusing for a new writer searching for models, or one searching for some philosophy of practice they can lean against, or into, while they develop. Since creative writing is such an open space, whom do you believe?

You will do well to start with yourself – by refining your own ability in order to be able to trust your own judgement. Literature is a continent that contains many countries, languages, and countless contradictions; it is large, it contains multitudes. Its citizenship used to consist of its writers. Now there is a dual citizenship: writer-as-reader, reader-as-writer. Whenever you encounter contraries and inconsistencies between the citizens of that continent, bear in mind that the opposite of contention can be collusion, and even a closing down or culling of fresh thoughts. There are many belief systems, and that creates some leeway for the evolution of ideas for writers.

All these viewpoints about teaching writing are all right so long as they work within their time, and so long as they are not disingenuous (creating promises they cannot keep) or dogmatic (creating premises you, the new writer, cannot keep). This book attempts to concentrate some of that collective and contending energy, although it is by no means a synthesis of ancient and modern thought on the how and why of the art form. Although it touches some of these spheres, it can only glance off them and at them.

First, two questions to be asked as we cross into that continent. Can creative writing be taught? Can creative writing be learned? They are really the same question, but you will often hear it posed 'as a challenge rather than a genuine enquiry; a challenge which threatens to damn the foundational premise of Creative Writing by daring the addressee to answer in the affirmative' (Dawson, 2005: 6). The novelist David Lodge concluded, 'Even the most sophisticated literary criticism only scratches the surface of the mysterious process of creativity; and so, by the same token, does even the best course in creative writing' (1997: 178). Lodge quotes Henry James's essay *The Art of Fiction*:

> The painter is able to teach the rudiments of his practice and it is possible, from the study of good work (granted the aptitude), both to learn how to paint and how to write. Yet it remains true . . . that the literary artist would be obliged to say to his pupil much more than any other, 'Ah well, you must do it as you can!' If there are exact sciences, there are also exact arts, and the grammar of painting is much more definite that it makes a difference.   (1997: 173)

So: you must do it as you can. Writing is not painting, neither is it a systematised knowledge. It is not empirical science; teaching and learning writing is not like teaching and learning medicine.

Here are some cards; here is my table. I think creative writing can be taught most effectively when its students have some talent and vocation for it. If a teacher can shape the talent and steer that vocation, and the students enjoy the shaping and steering, then I think creative writing should be taught as a craft. The whole point of teaching creative writing, however, is that students must learn to make and guide themselves, for writing is mostly a solitary pursuit, even when written collaboratively using electronic media.

I also believe creative writing could be taught within other disciplines, as an option alongside science and social science, if students of those disciplines have some desire to try it, and can take the practice of creative writing for what it is: a possible second string, or a second chance at something from which they gain pleasure. It does not have to contribute to the pursuit of their profession, so long as the pleasure principle is foremost. It might contribute at some point through creative nonfiction. The role of popular science in raising the public's awareness of science and technology is a delightful benefit we consider in Chapter Ten.

Imagination's talent

The pleasure of creativity illuminates aspects of knowledge that we regard as non-literary, especially if we begin to accept the arguments of cognitive science: that 'the literary mind is the fundamental mind', not a separate kind of mind. Alongside many other neuroscientists, Mark Turner contends, '*Story* is a basic principle of mind', and 'the parable is the root of the human mind – of thinking, knowing, acting, creating, and plausibly of speaking' (1996: 1).

Writing is an extreme act of attention and memory; it pleads with your brain cells to make new connections. As neuroscientists put it, neurons that fire together wire together, and inspiration could be more natural *to* and more nurtured *in* a writer because they simply read the world (and the world of literature) a little closer when they were children.

Your brain interacts with itself: *hearing* words, *seeing* words, *speaking* words and generating *verbs*. These functions occur in widely spaced sections of the brain. Creative writing 'commands' these different departments of self to start cooperating, and they will, by stretching out synapses over relatively huge neural distances, wiring up. What else are they going to connect with along the way? What monsters or angels might be imagined into being? This is how writers are *made*, how the nanotechnology of your imagination is intricately (and provisionally) constructed.

We are capable of developing complementary senses – sight with sound, taste with touch, *time* with hearing – or all senses simultaneously transmitted through the medium of one line of poetry, or one paragraph of description. This is how your imagination talks to itself, talks across itself even, and becomes ever more versatile. Writing rewires our brains – from our tongue to our eye to our hands. It encourages synaesthesia: one sense triggers an image or a sensation in another. When we stop paying attention to the world, we do ourselves great harm. It is like a slow suicide of thought with the senses. The imaginative gains of synaptic complication are always provisional.

We are neurologically *changed* by our experience of writing as much as we are by reading. For a writer, metaphor is an art of attention-seeking, of asking you to perceive some thing afresh. Creative writing is the art of defamiliarisation: an act of stripping familiarity from the world about us, allowing us to see what custom has blinded us to. It is no less than an act of revivification. Metaphor has power and permutation, almost like a magic force. Metaphor is 'a transfer of meaning in which one thing is explained by being changed either into another thing or into an emotion or idea' (Kinzie, 1999: 435). As Shelley wrote of poetry, it 'lifts the veil from the hidden beauty of the world, and makes familiar objects be as they were not familiar'. In *Metaphors We Live By*, Lakoff and Johnson contend that 'Metaphorical thought is normal and ubiquitous in our mental life, both conscious and unconscious. The same mechanisms of metaphorical thought used throughout poetry are present in our most common concepts: time, events, causation, emotion, ethics, and business, to name but a few' (1980: 244).

Scientific, philosophical and artistic breakthroughs often go through four stages of cognitive and creative process – attention to detail (of a problem) → translation to metaphor → defamiliarisation → receiving something at a different angle – in effect, perceiving it anew, as a child does. We now know a little more about the physiological and neural states that certain types of creativity take, as well as those phases which acts of creativity and metaphor engender in readers. The making of creative language and story is natural, and part of everybody's potential world. 'Inspiration' and fluency are aspects of our neural flexibility, and practice, endeavour and good perception make them so. As Flaubert claimed to Van Gogh, 'Talent is long patience, and originality an effort of will and of intense observation' (Oliver, 1994: 121).

A play of mind

So: is the literary mind the fundamental mind? Are we all born storytellers and metaphor-makers? In *The Seven Basic Plots*, Christopher Booker argues that there are seven standard storylines in the world that all fiction uses and recycles (see Chapter Six). He believes, 'The very fact that they follow such identifiable patterns and are shaped by such consistent rules indicates that the unconscious is thus using them for a purpose: to convey to the conscious level of our mind a particular picture of human nature and how it works' (2004: 553). This creates an interesting picture of the power and purpose of story, but is an impossible point either to prove or falsify.

It is important not to lie about creative writing. It is not in its nature. Yet, what is its nature – what is our nature – if not in the making of fictions and metaphors? What are our lives but stories we constantly rewrite? What are metaphors but fictions, doppelgängers, sculpted otherness? *Voice*, for example, sings within a writer's poems or stories. The poems and stories possess that voice, or are possessed by it. A writer's voice is a metaphor for spoken voice, but is not the voice of the poet or novelist.

We need to travel back in time. If we go back to the plausible origin of creative writing as a taught discipline, we open Aristotle's *Poetics*, and read that 'the standard of rightness is not the same in poetry as it is in social morality or indeed in any other art' (that is, poetry as an art of fiction and drama). We might conclude that same oscillating standard holds within creative writing. We could reason that it depends upon the position of the player; on a writer as player of language; on their play of mind on mind, and mind in mind. The craft of writing lies in the way the cards of language *are* played; the voice in how the cards become *your* choices.

Writing Game

DISCOVERING YOUR CONTINENT

Imagine a door. It could be a door in your own home, or room, or a door in a library or in a wilderness. Close your eyes and visualise this door. Write a few lines of prose or poetry describing it. What does the surface and the handle look like (use simile or metaphor)? In your mind's eye, open that door. What does the handle feel like? You step through. You have passed through a door in time and space. In front of you is a land you do not know. What are the first three things you notice, and what do they look like or even smell like? Now describe what is under your feet. You begin to hear two sounds in the distance. What do they sound like? You see some words; they could be on a sign, or a piece of paper. What do they say? What is the weather? Imagine this is part of a continent. Nobody knows about it except you – for now. You begin to explore the space around you. Write ten sentences or ten lines describing this exploration. Then you meet somebody. It could be somebody you know well, or somebody quite new. They say something to you. What do they say? You answer. What do you say? Use another ten sentences or ten lines to finish this writing. Then put it away for three weeks, after which revise it completely into a short story or poem.

AIM: We are making a new poem or story created from a combination of a dream-state and a prompted imagination using a method somewhat like self-hypnosis. It is a good idea to try these questions on yourself regularly, writing with your eyes closed while you are visualising the images in your mind's eye. Be sure to alter the part of the continent each time you try this. In Philip Pullman's trilogy, *His Dark Materials*, the protagonists pass through warps or doors in time and space. You are doing the same. What is behind the door is entirely up to your writing self. How far you wish to go is also up to you, but try to go a little bit further every time, and spend more time beyond that door. Learn the entrances, exits, contours, cities and citizens of your continent of writing.

A psychological apprenticeship

Hemingway again: 'We are all apprentices in a craft where no one ever becomes a master.' For any prospective writer, it helps to know who you are, what role you are playing and what you wish your language to perform. Many myths and metaphors swirl around the discipline of creative writing. A student is an apprentice to writing and, by innocent attachment, to those selfsame myths and lies. They rub off on them. It is hard for them to know who they are; if they are a writer at all; or whether they are somebody who has never really left the audience, who is still lost in a book.

Some students of creative writing know who they are already, and will have sensed this self-knowledge at some early stage of their lives. Infancy and child-hood are the most important periods for the 'making' of the writer: the making of their neural complexity. However, talent and vocation are not selfish genes unless constructive nurture in childhood makes them so. Talent and vocation are understandings that need to be then identified, encouraged and corrobo-rated by the external world: firstly by your parents very early on, then by friends and teachers; and later by your editors, publishers and readers. This is where the teaching of creative writing comes into its own. Your creative writing teachers are your first real readers, and they are editors of your writing. They are also to some extent editors of your character – as parents and teachers are – in this case the editor of *the character who writes*, for whom the creation of story, of metaphor, of played language, is already, unbreakably, a natural habit of mind. You need to possess a purpose for writing, and to learn to keep this purpose strong and supple.

If an apprentice of writing does not have some genuine aptitude for these skills, then their time may be better spent some other way. This has nothing to do with talent being mystically (or even genetically) innate. It has more to do with being trained, taught and encouraged in creative language and writing when you were a child. I believe, however, you can 'catch up' without early encouragement: many good writers were once autodidact teenagers, going it alone, teaching themselves, or taking up serious writers as mentors *in loco parentis*, becoming their protégés.

This argument for aptitude (rather than, say, desire) would be accepted for any other profession, and creative writing is no different. It is not some special world where miracles, cures and conversions happen. It may create illusion, it may even invite illusion, but it is both more and less ordinary. It may prove that you can take the lessons of creative writing into the world, and use them to help conduct creative lightning if you are lucky and talented, but that depends on several factors, including your willingness to face failure. And failure rides in the slipstream of so many actions that require vocation.

Passion

Some of what I have just said sounds like a call to vocation and, to some extent it is, but only because vocation is a wholly commonplace state of mind for many people, be they good designers, entrepreneurs or athletes. Vocation is not a holy calling; it is about the callings of skill and, surely, it is about passion for that skill. If you are going to write, at least find your passion for writing first. Passion emboldens you. Boris Pasternak defined talent as 'boldness in the face of the blank sheet'. A passion for language will push you through a wall of words, and a passion for writing will push up the temperature of your written voice. It will also smoulder beneath your syntax unnoticed by the reader but, if it is not present, the reader will recognise, unconsciously, its absence. I am sure you have read a book and have not been able to understand why it did not *quite* work. The answer is that it was an unwanted child; the author did not wish to write it at all. It does not possess what the Spanish poet Federico García Lorca called *duende*, its own blood-beat (see Chapter Four on 'Inspiration and *duende*'). There is nothing wrong with being passionate or even obsessive about creative writing; drivenness can oxygenate writing when technique is under pressure.

Vocation's providence

Vocation is important to many professions, including those of science and medicine. The impulse to write and the desire to be a writer are not the same thing, and a good reader knows this in the same way that the calling to be a doctor and the desire to be one would be a terrifying confusion – for the patient, anyway. However, you can possess more than one vocation. William Carlos Williams was a poet and a doctor. The poets John Donne, George Herbert and Gerard Manley Hopkins were men of the church, although the tradition of the writer as an actual believer is thorny and interesting since some writers seem to require a structured belief system in order to write (or their books create belief systems for their reader, as in the work of J. R. R. Tolkien). Some believe that creative writing and belief are callings that sit all too shakily on the scales of responsibility and guilt. Does one finally outweigh the other? Do they circle each other like opposing magnets?

Some writers can be preachy, especially the godless ones. If that ossifies into a pose, that pose arises from their conception that creative writing is hieratic. This is false. If vocation is thought of as belonging to somebody who places importance on acquiring and developing literary skills, then creative writing is a vocation, humanly commonplace in its constituency. It is delusive to suppose writers are anything at all like priests or shamans. Readers are not congregations, nor are they tribes for whom writers act as walking, talking language-purifying plants.

If you possess a vocation in addition to writing, you may wish to consider the demands on your time and mind before you commit to both. At best, the other vocation offers language, philosophy and material *to* the vocational practice of writing. Please think about these issues both by the terms of your own character and motivations. Be warned that top-heavy seriousness can create a very disabling tension, putting too much pressure on yourself, expecting miracles of composition – the result is creative constipation. We make our own providence as writers, and there is nothing more spoiling to providence than pomposity; or programmatic ideas about writing; or outlandish measures of our importance. We can take ourselves far too seriously; we can regard our purpose over-earnestly. We over-prepare, over-think, and then under-shoot all our objectives in our desire to be taken seriously. It can also make our writing itch with puppy-fat self-consciousness and self-importance, both of which are unattractive qualities for many readers.

Writing Game

OBSESSIVE SERMONS
Playfully, write a 500-word monologue spoken by an authority figure (who should be somebody known by everybody in your group). Imitate their speech patterns in your prose. Use an obsessive subject (and keep to it unwaveringly), such as 'counting ants', 'skyscraper-hugging', 'mouse breath', 'invisible friends', etc. Read these aloud, and guess who is being parodied.

AIM: Parody makes for effective exercises in style, but often ends up saying more about the writer. Becoming aware of the tropes of language used by the powerful allows you to exploit them in creating believable character dialogue.

Honesty of the amateur

As Charlie Chaplin says in *Limelight*, 'We are all amateurs. We don't live long enough to be anything else.' There is much to be said for holding on to the mentality of being an amateur or apprentice. Knowing you have a lot to prove means you are freer to play and make errors (and accidental successes). If you go about the business of writing in the mask of The Professional, then you remove most of the fun from the natural guesswork of writing, and stymie your chances at finding your luck or voice. You end up prizing technical *ability* at the price of your imaginative *facility*.

Nothing kills the energy in prose or poetry like conscious professionalism or mere technical skill. Of course, in your dealings with the world of workshops and publishing, you should act professionally, but you can leave that persona, along with your ego, at the door of your writing room and the workshop room. There is no wrong in being serious or earnest. *Playfulness*, however, tends to produce honesty, providence and surprise in your work – and closer audiences. Try to view writing as something of a daily habit, rather than a moral activity. You will very likely achieve more by taking the pressure off yourself. Vocation should have the quality of being commonplace, even light-hearted, like having a daily working job, which – lucky us – is to write what we like.

Purposes

Creative writing is a discipline with many apprentices, but one that respects the fact that, at whatever stage we reach, in the Writing Game we are all beginners. This apparent modesty of self-perception could seem otherworldly to some people. Language *is* a little like a shifting belief system in which you settle, uncomfortably enough beside its many apostates and revisionists. Thus, writing seems a sharper vocation than most because of the unsettled and unsettling material with which it deals.

You live with that by finding your habit for expression. The Irish poet Seamus Heaney, writing of T. S. Eliot, believes 'vocation entails the disciplining of a habit of expression until it becomes fundamental to the whole conduct of life' (2002: 38). Getting to this point involves errors as well as epiphanies. You will know yourself better through failure and retrial, however tortuous the process, and learn more about yourself than others would have you know, by going beyond your own intelligence in language and writing. You will acquire different and oscillating rationalisations for your writing: from Jane Austen's miniaturist conception of painting upon two inches of ivory, to Franz Kafka's yearning to smash the frozen sea inside us.

We must never confuse literary vocation with literary or personal ambition. Although they wear a similar face, ambition is a mask and vocation is skin. As the writer Cynthia Ozick says, 'One *must* avoid ambition *in order to* write. Otherwise something else is the goal: some kind of power beyond the power of language. And the power of language . . . is the only kind of power a writer is entitled to' (Plimpton, 1989: 301). Self-belief is a quality of mind that arrives with time, however waveringly – it allows you to become driven. In the end, much good writing is gained by practice, by knowing your objectives and knowing how to achieve them in language. You just have to know what this means, and that you must put in the time. As the renowned novelist and creative writing teacher John Gardner states in *The Art of Fiction*:

> most of the people I've known who wanted to become writers, knowing what it meant, *did* become writers. About all that is required is that the would-be writer understand clearly what it is that he wants to become and what he must do to become it.   (1983: ix)

Whatever your approach to the continent of writing, you may find yourself serving an audience, sometimes by serving their consciences on their behalf, or by creating work that is entertaining or consoling. Most writing is an argument – and a working affair – between you and words. You write it for yourself, in a room, alone. Your first purpose should be to surprise yourself; and other people, second. 'No tears in the writer, no tears in the reader. No surprise for the writer, no surprise for the reader. For me the initial delight is in the surprise of remembering something I didn't know I knew' – Robert Frost (quoted in Barry, 1973: 126).

Creative writing in time

Some people believe there is something new or untested about the discipline of creative writing, and nowhere is this debate more volatile than in some departments devoted to the study of literature. Rare forests of paper are given over to compacted debate, the heart of which comes down to an argument between two vested interests: a desire for a mystification of the process of writing by some writers, and a covetousness of that privilege, that process, by some critics. What is clear to many writers is that creative writing, and its teaching, never really left the university building.

Inventions of creative writing

The modern version of the discipline of creative writing begins in 1940 with the foundation of the Iowa Writer's Workshop, although there were precursors, including George Baker's '47 Workshop' at Harvard from 1906 to 1925. The discipline can be seen partly as a reinvention of two great grainy wheels: ancient dramatic teaching and Renaissance rhetorical exercises in composition. Creative writing's tale begins in Athens, with Aristotle (384–322 BC). It originates before that because Aristotle's *Poetics* is an account of creative practices accepted and used for years, and is no more than a fragment of the knowledge he gathered for study. Aristotle tells his class what to seek and what to shun in the composition of poetic dramas; the outcome at which such dramas aim; how the achievement of that aim governs the form of the drama; by what means that aim is realised and by what defects a dramatist may fail to realise it. However, Aristotle's work goes further, for it has a moral aim, and creative writing teaching inherits this aim to some extent. For example, Carol Bly's *Beyond the Writers' Workshop* (2001) went as far as to include an 'Ethics Code' for creative writing teachers and students.

Reflecting his society, Aristotle is concerned with the effects of human conduct. The playwright Ben Jonson commented on this in *Timber or Beliefs* as 'how we ought to judge rightly of others, and what we ought to imitate specially in ourselves'. The practice of creative writing is as personal as he says. Aristotle uses the theatre as a means to an end: the players are the people, and the playhouse the world in which they live and die. He is anxious to show that the effect of tragedy upon spectators is good for them. It teaches civic and human conduct. Aristotle wants to move people to strong emotion through rhetorical and dramatic strategies. He shows his students the techniques for manipulating an audience – the *human body* as a reader of the drama of itself.

His former mentor, Plato, thought ill of the enterprise, urging emotional restraint: 'Poetry waters what we ought to let wither.' There is a moral dimension to creative writing; it is one of the reasons it troubles its detractors as well as its advocates. What does poetry 'water' in today's creative writing classes, and what might wither otherwise? What does the teaching of creative writing do to, or with, its small society when it goes beyond teaching mere technique? Is creative writing about more than just new writers, streaming into formation behind their teachers like a self-invading squadron?

A pedagogical mega-virus, Aristotle's teaching transmitted and mutated itself into later centuries by circuitous geographical routes and several translations through language, space and time (the earliest authentic version is in Arabic). It whispers in quotation in Chaucer's *Canterbury Tales*. It beaches itself within the body of theory about literature and poetry that formed and informed the Renaissance. Writers leaned into it for their own philosophy of practice. Time-travelling, the Aristotelian mind made itself felt in the work of many writers and their critics. Speaking and writing were seen as art, and rhetoric (from the Greek *rhetor*, 'public speaker') taught the means to speak and write effectively to persuade an audience and bind a society. The practice is as old as it is new. Step aboard the time machine of this book, and travel back in time to the Middle Ages to take part in a class taught in the thirteenth century.

Rhetoric's play

How would you feel if your creative writing teacher asked you to write a story or poem that personified 'the cross lamenting its captivity under non-Christian rule and urging a crusade'? This exercise comes from Geoffrey de Vinsauf's *Poetria Nova* or *The New Poetics*, published around 1210 AD. It is a manual of writing instruction, a casebook on style. Unlike any contemporary book on composition, *Poetria Nova* is a metrical composition of 2,000 Latin hexameter lines. An ambitious masterstroke, de Vinsauf teaches by example.

But what drives *Poetria Nova* deep into memory is its playful delight in restrictive and thematic creative writing. A stanza is a room, and a poem a house containing many lit rooms:

> If a man has a house to build, his hand does not rush, hasty, into the very doing: the work is first measured out with his heart's inward plumb-line, and the inner man marks out a series of steps beforehand, according to a definite plan; his heart's hand shapes the whole before his body's hand does so, and his building is a plan before it is an actuality.

Imagine yourself a student of creative writing in the thirteenth century. Our teacher instructs his students to write from the point of view of *a worn-out tablecloth*, or *an angry French fortress*. He urges us to compose a digression from the subject of *two lovers about to be separated* to a *description of springtime as the sexual union of air and earth*; and, for homework, an abbreviated version of *the anecdote of the adulterous mother, the vindictive father, and the snow-child*. Most demanding of all is to make a poem that is to be a 'Set Piece using the nineteen figures of thought (with fourteen sub-categories) on the Pope's responsibility with regard to clerical wrongdoing'.

I have tried some of these exercises in class. Oddly enough, they work. They represent an inventive pedagogy, daring in their feel for new shapes, forms, themes, even for anti-narrative. Our teacher is an expert on drafting too (read the epigraph of this chapter), with an endearingly human touch and a taste for

extended metaphor: 'I have given you a comb, with which, if they be combed, your works may gleam . . . My own way to polish words is by sweating: I chastise my mind, lest it stagnate by resting in one technique.' I would love to sign up for his creative writing class, but I am 800 years late.

Rhetoricians taught technique, style and rewriting using imitation and exemplification. The most effective teachers of creative writing teach wide, deep reading and the value of trying on voices, strategies and styles. They teach the techniques, forms, measures and metrics of writing, and their associated counter-practices. If time allows, they show the pleasures and imaginative challenges of translation and experiment. I would call this a basic curriculum. If these basics engage and delight the students in class, then the teacher has become a powerful alchemist of thought and practice.

During the Renaissance, rhetoric was taught to students when old universities were there to serve and teach the articulate and deserving poor. It was field-knowledge for the whole curriculum – lessons for survival through manipulation of, and skill with, language:

> For it happeneth verye sildome, that a man not exercised in writinge,
> how learned so euer he be, can at any tyme know perfectly the labour
> and toile of writers, or taste of the sweetnes and excellencye of styles, and
> those wiser observations that often times are found in them of olde tyme.
> (From Baldassare Castiglione's *The Courtier*, trans. Thomas Hoby, 1561)

It was granite knowledge upon which every subject grew by degrees, and by which language lived and played at the time. Drama was a branch of rhetoric, whose pedagogical purpose was to sharpen the skills of the future preacher and statesman by reading, imitation and compositional practice. Rhetoric was the vehicle for what we call now active learning, such as writing exercises; practising verbal gymnastics within incredible linguistic or formal constraints (anticipating the OuLiPo; see Chapter Three); and creating arguments and compositions in face-to-face competitions (what we would call slams). The poet John Milton taught rhetoric in the school he set up within his own home. If students were good, they were allowed a little original composition at the end of the curriculum. Romantic critics (not Romantic practitioners) teased and blasted this rhetorical tradition. To some of them it seemed artificial, or a petrifaction: language could not flourish among such ordered stones.

There was something in this, but it was taken to extremity. Many wrought and serious matters were tamed in the process. Aspects of the old teaching went to sleep in Europe one century; they woke up in America in the next, in safer hands, in a newer form called Creative Writing. Back in Europe, the sublime came into its thin inheritance; ideas of inspiration rose to their feet and walked away pocketing notions of deliberation, intelligence and practice. Writing gained an image, it even gained a kind of audience or celebrity, but it lost the ability to hear part of its history with reason and clarity.

A tradition of revolution

We lost something almost as valuable: not just the idea, but also the practical reality, that authors 'can be made', and that the further business of making (composition, technique, drafting) – what Scots and medievalists call being a 'makar' – is as worthy a living as being a maker of sculpture, of paintings, of music, of performance. Who begrudges the art school its students, the music school its composers, or the academies of dramatic art their young actors? I do not think anyone would question the necessity for serious painters, composers or actors to teach a rising generation, nor do we question their need for designated and secure space, and for qualifications to attach to their achievements before they enter the world to do it on their own.

This is tradition: a tradition of revolution, of revelation. Most iconoclasts go through mentoring; they learn, at the very least, technique. Structures and models must be known intimately if they are to be altered and renewed with precision. The rise of creative writing has reinstated a reality to one aspect of higher education and the writer's place within it. Now it needs to synthesise the teaching of 'making' with ensuring that we can do so with the respect – and understanding – of our fellow teachers and fellow students both inside and outside the academy. How we do that depends on how far we want to go, and on the standards we intend to set. It also depends on the seriousness of that intent, and on how serious the writers and poets are who do the teaching.

Writing Game

RECREATING THE SNOW-CHILD
Write a very short poem from the point of view of a worn-out tablecloth, or an angry French fortress. Then compose a playful short story about two lovers about to be separated in which you incorporate a description of springtime as the sexual union of air and earth. Write a longer and darker story in which you include the following characters (without naming their qualities): an adulterous mother, a vindictive father and the snow-child. Call the story 'The Snow-Child'.

AIM: These are very early examples of compositional exercises. Their very strangeness allows you a great deal of freedom of interpretation and expression. You may wish later to use these examples to create a story set in the Middle Ages, in which such a writing class took place.

The school of wildness

Creative writing has been looked upon with intellectual suspicion, or dismissed as a school for amateurism and wildness. Yet, the relation of university-based criticism and scholarship to contemporary writing and poetry has been affected by the redevelopment of creative writing, and always has been. The past few decades have seen a rapid flourishing of the subject, not only in number but also in the diversity of approach towards its teaching, and the use of such techniques in so-called 'academic' courses, including those *outside* humanities. The school of wildness is on the prowl; it has new purposes and territories and a motto of its own: 'If I chance to talk a little wild, forgive me' – Shakespeare.

Courses in which creative writing is part of learning need not have the purpose of only turning out better writers of poetry, fiction, drama, nonfiction and children's literature. They may have the purpose of creating better *readers* of these genres, more informed and sensitive *scholars* of these genres and keener *teachers* of the literary arts. Since the literary mind may prove to be the natural mind, such courses may even create better communicators of other disciplines, such as the sciences or business. However, one of our main purposes is the one we never talk of openly except in the company of other wolves: our role in helping the strange come to life through language.

Necessary wildness

Coleridge wrote that there is no great art without *strangeness*. Einstein believed that a sense for the *mysterious* was 'the fundamental emotion which stands at the cradle of true art and true science'. Harold Bloom names one of the characteristics of great literature as its downright *weirdness*. In *On Becoming a Novelist*, John Gardner claims, 'Strangeness is the one quality in fiction that cannot be faked'; its presence in writing reveals 'the very roots of the creative process' (1985: 57). I am not saying we can legislate for *wildness*, nor draw up a curriculum in which we teach *weirdness* on one day and *strangeness* on another. However, we can create conditions in which these qualities will not be immediately cornered and killed.

A good writer can scent creative wildness and will know, from their own experience, how best to develop and direct it toward a constructive target, without taming. Writers make for sympathetic teachers of writing because they are familiar with the weird and wayward process of making literature. They know the differing cages of form that allow a new writer to draw closer to the creature inside them.

Writers are as diverse as things are various. The teaching of writing is an ancient discipline but there cannot be a narrow 'modernising-standardising' of its pedagogies. Creative writing will not lend itself to systemisation or to blasé compositional step-by-steps. Systems curb experiments in teaching; in the evolution of the discipline. They tame the possibility of learning through failure and risk. Creative writing schools provide an open spatial structure in which learning basic principles goes hand in hand with a certain amount of wildness and invention. They foster a habit of mind that John Keats called negative capability, when a writer is 'capable of being in uncertainties, mysteries, doubts, without any irritable reaching after fact and reason'.

What wildness is shaping

The redevelopment of creative writing has now changed the composition of some Literature faculties. This provides a powerful dimension for creative writing, and for the art form's development. Serious writers are employed to teach writing. They work alongside literary critics and scholars, sometimes comfortably, sometimes at an angle. Many combine critical and creative work in a way that presents a distinctive opportunity for research, linking a writer's knowledge of literature, gained through practice, with perspectives developed by criticism, theory and scholarship. This is having a profound effect on the development of literary *study* within universities. It appears to be creating – I would say, recreating – a synthesis between work in universities and the non-academic professions of writing.

There have been mistakes made along the way, not least our allowing the perception that creative writing is some adjunct or educational tool *to* literary studies. There will always be theoreticians who patrol the approach roads to creative writing, setting up signs and limit-markers in their own unintelligible jargons. They need their epiphanies to live by, just like everybody. It is also a significant error to suppose that creative writing *needs* to take place in higher education when it already has a strong life outside it, in schools, libraries, literary festivals and communities. Neither does it matter greatly if some imaginative writers create a parallax view of writing within the academy: a view judged by intuitive laws and standards of literary achievement and craft, rather than one informed by an academic's antennae for the lattices of power and history that the new work's language is 'performing'.

Students are sharp enough to recognise a difference in depth, one that works both ways sometimes, depending on the talents of the teachers. 'Ignorant men of genius are constantly rediscovering "laws" of art which the academics had mislaid or hidden' – Ezra Pound (1960: 14). Let it lie; nobody expects perfection either way. The very finest practices in creative writing deliver strong literary achievement *and* incisive critical reflection on the social and historical context of the new work; our best writers are our most incisive critics and self-critics.

A total process

Creative writing rightly has its doubters among practising authors. In the words of the novelist Flannery O'Connor (an Iowa graduate), 'I am often asked if universities stifle writers. My view is that they don't stifle enough of them.' She had a point. It is important to learn what we *cannot* do. A writing course will usefully teach a would-be writer that they cannot, and do not want to, write creatively. Not everything we learn is the means for self-progress. We do not always 'win' through knowledge; sometimes it is better and wiser to lose. Creativity is not compulsory, nor is it a human right to create and publish imaginative literature. In fact, it is difficult, even terrifying, because it is a total and a totalling process.

To paraphrase Ben Jonson, language most shows a person. Writing requires nerve, stamina and long listening – as well as talent, and editorial discrimination. As Donald Hall lamented, writing workshops sometimes trivialise the art by minimising that terror of total process. Although learning to write creatively can be fun, *becoming and being* a writer is a far more ruthless, wilder game, and creative writing teachers should make no secret of this or try to disguise the true nature of this endeavour.

A course might indeed teach people to do something else, find some other focus for their latent creativity, equally life-affirming. None of us wants to make a counterfeit self-dedication, committing the rest of our time to what will amount to, at best frustration, at worst bitterness and falsified vocation. Writing teachers try to be the opposite of deceivers, even when it hurts the student or even when it hurts the tutor to tell the truth. That level of trust requires very good teachers, but it also requires rigour.

Rigorous teaching methods for writing courses and degrees fuse reading and critical discussion with concentrated practical work in a way that creates progression. We must be honest about our own development as writers and teachers; we must acknowledge that progression does not necessarily mean *progress*. As with the teaching of other art forms, this honesty about development and progress is the main reason that literary practitioners should teach creative writing, and not be teachers of technique or theoreticians of pedagogy. The presence of writers can lead to other outcomes just as valuable, such as creative communities.

Creative communities

Rigour wins respect, widens and deepens the knowledge base of writers, and helps create cultural centres of excellence in which new writers apprentice themselves yearly to more experienced writers. The initial group grows every year in number and diversity. One of the practical benefits of creative writing is that new and supportive communities and constituencies of writers are created and nurtured – real rooms with real writers in them. Teachers and students then begin to learn from each other, look after each other, set up enterprises such as magazines, presses and web journals, and receive help for these enterprises from that slightly apologetic patron of new writing: the university.

An impartial, supportive patron is worth more than the money that might flow from that relationship. It is more to do with creating opened spaces in which writers can work, in which literature is discussed, read *and* made. This applies as much to emerging writers as it does to professionals. It is worth my stating here that many communities of people in Britain perceive a connection with a university as something culturally and socially valuable, something tangible, which validates their efforts.

For example, women from Asian communities in the Midlands, and children from inner-city schools in our region, are given free space in the Humanities Building of the University of Warwick and Warwick Arts Centre in England to develop their creative work. For some, this is an opportunity beyond price. They enjoy, quoting most of the schoolchildren, a wonderful time, too. Some of them have become writers and publishers. All are better readers and thinkers, 'better' solely by their own idea of what that word means. Some have used their experience to travel into other subjects, even into work areas not usually associated with creative writing, such as science, technology and business.

Taught with ambition (and risking both hubris and envy), creative writing can teach us how to travel into our own potentialities; it can create Renaissance people. As I suggest in Chapter Ten, the discipline of creative writing is not the reserve of humanities but can be multidisciplinary. It is our job to stress the importance of practice, reading, criticism, drafting, as well as the poet-scientist Miroslav Holub's liberating notions of 'serious play', and the OuLiPo school's conception and creation of 'potential literature' that cuts across mathematics, the sciences and writing in the same way as rhetoric. We should be bolder and say that all writing, when well made, is creative. We are all wilder than we pretend.

The sister arts

We do not burden other taught art forms with the first name 'creative'. We do not talk of going to classes in Creative Music, Creative Painting, Creative Dance, Creative Film or Creative Acting. We think it implicit. We would feel that teachers were selling their students short if they were not teaching elements and techniques of creativity specific to those art forms during classes or workshops. We have no problem that these taught art forms carry examinations that test the acquisition and application of these elements and techniques. It is helpful if the students of these art forms have an interest in which talent might flicker, or be breathed into flame by a teacher – *always* a practitioner of that art form. The talent that students bring might simply be an inclination *for* practice, to try things out day after day. As the theatre director Peter Brook comments (1990: 34):

> scales don't make a pianist nor does fingerwork help a painter's brush: yet a great pianist practises finger exercises for many hours a day, and Japanese painters spend their lives practising to draw a perfect circle . . . without constant schooling, the actor will stop halfway.

Like tennis players or athletes, singers and dancers often keep their teachers with them throughout their working life. Once writers are pushed into the world, they are, like actors, left to fend for themselves. Writers must keep their hands in, as regularly as practitioners of other art forms must. Creative writing provides a period of 'constant schooling', and the space and time to practise in language and form, for writers also stand in danger of stopping halfway. Constant schooling is a habit of mind that the teaching of creative writing can inculcate. To come fresh at knowledge, despite our learning, and to go on our nerve occasionally, is to acknowledge that we are constantly beginners. It is what opens the mind to illuminations in research, and in the imaginative ability and growing fluency of the actor, the painter or even the surgeon. As writers, our actions are to take and make the parts of speech. In Chapter Nine, I will demonstrate some ways in which creative writing works with other art forms such as performance, music and the visual arts.

Writing Game

RESPONDING TO ART
As a group, visit a museum or art gallery, and spend at least half a day responding in writing to several paintings or photographs. Work these responses into stories and poems. OR hand out postcards of art and paintings in class, and respond directly to them in writing.

AIM: Responding to art in this way is called ecphrasis, and is a stimulating tradition in creative writing. You write something in homage to a piece of visual art, or use visual art, sculpture or film as stimuli for writing.

Reading and the individual writer

Reading is a kind of rewriting but by many hands and eyes. Writing is only a more exacting form of reading, individual in its action and exactions. To become, and to remain, an original creative writer you must first become, and be, as original a reader, and pursue your individual taste with restlessness, competitiveness and trust in your intuition. Most writers agree that the best way to write well creatively is to write for yourself. It follows that the best way to read as a writer is to read for yourself. In *How to Read and Why*, Harold Bloom claims, 'Ultimately we read . . . in order to strengthen the self, and to learn its authentic interests . . . The pleasures of reading indeed are selfish rather than social' (2000: 22). It is taken as read that you enjoy reading and that you are interested in language: in words, sentences and paragraphs, and by the sounds words make when they collude and collide. It is one of the greatest of human pleasures. If you are not interested in reading the work of other authors, ask yourself this hard question: Why should anybody be interested in reading you?

Why we read

Novels and poems are usually the first causes of wanting to be a writer, and you must start and stay with them. Reading poems, stories and novels is of the first importance to every individual writer at whatever stage they have reached, for it offers you models, helps you find a style, teaches you technique and builds your vocabulary. Reading nonfiction, creative and otherwise, is as vital. Nonfiction is a vault of information, opinion and experience. It is useful for research, obviously, but is not only about research, for nonfiction will supply you with ideas for the subject of poems, for characters and situations in stories and for the creation of further nonfictional writing on subjects that excite you. If you ever feel blocked as a writer, reading popular science, history and biography will be certain to force you out of the corner in which you have placed yourself. Nonfiction is also a good space to relax, or to hide from the gravitational pull of other creative writers' voices while you are working on your own stories and poems.

Reading literary criticism and theory is less likely to lend itself to creative writing, but can be a good way of lying fallow when, and if, you do not wish to write in the open. In all these ways, writers are perpetual students of their pursuit. What you need to do now is move outside the small playhouse of this book. If you want to be a writer, at least one hundred books of original creative writing for every book about writing seems a minimum ratio – and public libraries will be your havens.

Writing Game

ADVENTURES IN READING

Go to your nearest library, but make your way adventurously to a subject or genre area that you have never previously visited. Select two books, the titles of which, by their language alone, interest or intrigue you. (Many people find poetry is a good place to start.) Take these books home and read them through as quickly as you can, even if you find the process difficult. Make notes on parts of the book you continue to find interesting; these are your 'findings'. Then write a story or a poem that fuses both sets of findings, even if the poem or story feels somewhat forced or artificial. Repeat this process until the reading begins to become a habit, and/or the writing begins to feel easier or more natural.

AIM: Creative reading does not come easily to everybody; sometimes you have to compel yourself to read work that is not familiar or useful. Yet some of a writer's best ideas arise from serendipity, and you have to make space for that serendipity to happen! Reading widely, even randomly – picking books out for qualities that many non-writers find slightly wayward – is a way to surprise you into making creative connections that have not existed before. This is one path to creating originality of perception and of voice. As some birds weave their nests from objects that offer them visual stimulation, so a writer weaves ideas and books from many sources which are often unconnected but which excite them at the time. It is also vital to force yourself to read beyond what you know, to open up new ways of writing but also of perception; to begin to write *what you do not know*. This kind of reading strategy, coupled with reading the books you like, makes reading first a habit, then a hunger almost like an addiction. Writers are compulsive, even wayward, readers and *mis*readers. We are nest-weavers, pillaging other writers for material.

Language's music

Reading is also a form of listening; and the tunes of language trigger new writing. You may feel wordless, but your mind bristles with language; it is constantly alert to the tones and coloratura of speech. To translate itself from silence, and into your mind and voice, your wordlessness looks for a form, for shape. Habit, practice and receptivity all assist in this neural process. Nadezhda Mandelstam, writing in *Hope Against Hope*, describes the effect on her poet-husband:

> I imagine that for a poet auditory hallucinations are something in the nature of an occupational disease . . . a poem begins with a musical phrase ringing insistently in the ears; at first inchoate, it later takes on a precise form, though still without words. I sometimes saw Mandelstam trying to get rid of this kind of 'hum', to brush it off and escape from it.

He would toss his head as though it could be shaken out like a drop of water that gets into your ear while bathing. But it was always louder than any noise, radio or conversation in the same room.   (1971: 70)

It is not just a question of the mind's eye; it is also a question of the mind's ear. We learn to attend to the aural qualities of the language in which we write and speak, or – as Joseph Brodsky named it – to the sound of its tide. It is important to stay fresh as a reader, and keep your senses alert to the noise of language, whether on the page or off the page. Learning to attend to language's music will make for a more nuanced writer, as well as a more sensitive reader and critic. You can put most authors to the test by reading their work aloud, and some writers read their own work aloud as they are drafting it. The author Bruce Chatwin used to read aloud the entirety of his pre-final manuscripts to his publishing editor. Testing the music and precision of language on the ear is why you should always read your own work aloud, and why we do so in workshops. Reading, say, a poem aloud is probably *the* measure of its success as a self-standing entity, something with its own life. It returns the poem to its roots in speech, and in the sharing of that speech with others in your audience. You must apply this test to your work at whatever stage of your career.

As language is polymorphic, so the sound of language is polyphonic and – taken over a distance such as a novel or long poem – even symphonic. There is pace and timbre in the delivery of speech, as there is cadence and rhyme in poetry. And there is any permutation of these, with infinite cross-pollinations across genres, language's soundscapes, and the mutating languages in the dictionaries, in the idioms, slang, jargons and dialects of our world. There are many frequencies, and you learn to tune your ear to receive, replicate and combine as many of them as you can.

One of the best ways to train your ear is to memorise stories, as storytellers do, and learn poems by heart, not by rote. A complementary method is to listen to music more actively, and learn to appreciate and emulate the various colours mapped within a composer's sound as well as the counterpoints and the deviations from expectation. This training will become more natural, and you might begin to hear your own voice among all this noise. You may even begin to hear your own writing, the soundscapes of your own poems and prose as auditory hallucinations, or a musical phrase that then takes on a more clear-cut shape in your mind, even though it is lacking words. Later, it will begin to find the words and you can then help wrestle them into place while writing and drafting.

Writing Game

Listening and reading aloud

As a class, make a list of stories and poems that you value, and make an anthology of these pieces. Ask each student to read their choice out aloud to the rest of the class, with a preliminary statement about why they chose it. After each reading, the other students should tell the reader how they felt about the sound of the writing, and which qualities of sound they found attractive. In addition to this, each student should memorise either a short poem or part of a short story every week. If they do not wish to do this, they should try to memorise some work of their own or of a fellow student. Every few weeks, students might meet informally, say in a café, for a performance of memorised work. Another good game is to parody the sound of a writer's voice. This game, borrowed from musical composition, involves memorising a piece of work by yourself or somebody else, and performing it aloud in a style belonging to another writer. The audience has to guess the identity of the other writer from the aural parody of their language. It is the equivalent of playing Bach in the style of Duke Ellington.

Aim: Not only is reading aloud a good test of style; but it is also a good way to think aloud about writing and writers. Memorisation provides the new writer with a repertoire of voices on which the unconscious can work, searching for models and musical phrases. Memorising your own work is good training for later, should you take part in performances of literature or promote your own work on reading tours. It is also an impressive party trick. Playing the tune of your own work through the tunes of another writer allows one to test its originality to some degree. Does the association swamp the work or does it stand up for itself? All these games are highly effective ways of establishing a small community of new writers with shared interests, meeting outside the times of their formal workshop.

Creative reading

Creative reading is the kindest favour students can do for themselves if they aspire to be a creative writer. Serious writers allow themselves to be open to influence. Writing is a form of knowledge creation, and imitation is an honourable and ancient tradition in writing, and the arts, as it is in science and other forms of knowledge. As Socrates said, 'Employ your time in improving yourself by other men's writings so that you shall come easily by what others have laboured hard for.' Mary Kinzie describes an active reading process for poets, but her explanation holds for other genres:

> Reading is like writing in beginning in uncertainty and driving towards speculation and experiment. The reader follows . . . the many paths that were not taken by the author, but whose possibility leaves a shadow like a crosshatching on the paths that remain. To read this way keeps a poem

always provisional and still in the making, which is how the process of reading absorbs the act of writing to their mutual improvement in terms of skill and understanding. Eventually writer and reader see their present way more clearly than the paths not taken. (1999: 13)

For a writer, all reading is useful and dynamic. For the Russian poet, Osip Mandelstam reading was an 'activity', not osmosis. He checked his reading against his own experience, testing it in the light of his own ideas for writing, as you must learn to do. As his wife and biographer, Nadezhda Mandelstam said, 'reading of the passive type . . . has always made it possible to propagate pre-digested ideas, to instill into the popular mind slick, commonplace notions. Reading of this kind . . . has an effect similar to hypnosis' (1971: 226).

Writers use reading as a type of caffeine, rather than a lotus blossom. It is a form of waking up and paying attention. Writing is a type of unriddling and reading can help you solve local difficulties in your own writing *while* you are writing (it is a good idea to keep several books about you during your writing sessions). As the novelist Cynthia Ozick says, 'I read in order to write . . . to find out what I need to know: to illuminate the riddle' (Plimpton, 1989: 295). Bear in mind that no reading is ever wasted – nothing – even reading the signs as you speed through a city, although you do not stop there. The best way is to follow a curriculum of reading, a task to which the study and practice of creative writing lends itself constructively.

Reading across time

We learn by example. The problem is that contemporary examples prove imper-manent. They might not survive the next critical twist or sally. Even without those artificial eclipses, writing can wither on the bough. It can seem dated because its concerns, style, its references, are too redolent of a fixed time or a particular style of mind of that time. It cannot be helped also that fashion shadows our perception of writing (as it does with criticism or literary the-ory). Reappraisals rot into neglect; favouritisms deform into denunciations. More innocent, but as destructive to reputation or posterity, cultural amnesia consigns most writing to oblivion:

> The name of the author is the first to go
> followed obediently by the title, the plot,
> the heartbreaking conclusion, the entire novel
> which suddenly becomes one you have never read, never even heard of.
> Billy Collins, 'Forgetfulness' (NA2: 3030)

Style is eternal; fashion is temporal. One of the gracious aspects of the academic study of literature is that it can restore or refresh the reputation of neglected or forgotten authors. It also decolonises writing; it creates many countries of literature. In that sense, academia can be a very healthy place for writers and apprentice-writers. The writer-as-reader finds themselves in an orchard of all seasons. Unfortunately, fashion strips the leaves even there.

Literary quality outlasts cultural or academic fashion but, as Arthur Koestler said, 'A writer's ambition should be to trade one hundred contemporary readers for ten readers in ten years time and for one in one hundred years.' Posthumous luck is unreliable: a writer's work requires advocacy to endure, and this needs to happen within a writer's life also. Recognition in life is vital if a writer's heart is not to become stone, or voice to fall silent. Few of us possess the stamina for the solitude and shadow-life of Emily Dickinson:

> Publication – is the Auction
> Of the Mind of Man –
> Poverty – be justifying
> For so foul a thing
>
> Possibly – but We – would rather
> From Our Garret go
> White – unto the White Creator
> Than invest – Our snow –
>   (NP: 1123)

If you are writing against the current ideologies, mores or fashions of your time and place, then you must be prepared to resist pressures to conform to them if this is the artistically honest path for your work. To do otherwise would be to face creative death. The same goes for reading: do not fossick only in the present day, obeying the market's mood for what is deemed acceptable or applicable to the auction of your time. We have to live and work within the auction, but become aware that market forces are a suffocating and manipulative force on writers, almost as much as a government or society that does not value freedom of speech. That attrition applies to both the 'literary' text and bestseller. As Carlos Fuentes commented, 'The bestseller lists . . . are, with a few lively exceptions, a sombre graveyard of dead books.' Like an actor, the writer is only as good as their last performance.

Reading across taste

Reading is about your individual appetite and ability. Many students come to creative writing because they are genuinely excited by what they have experienced as readers. A powerful narrative, for example, a tale shot through with some moral dimension and fleshed out by strong characters, may shape not only the way a reader reads and reacts to that book in the quiet of their mind, but the messages and examples then leach into their own lives to the extent that it alters and guides them as individuals.

If you are going to read as a writer, you need to read competitively around the curriculum of your time, a dance for your mind – *around . . .* and backwards, sideways and in many languages or translations of those languages. Your choice of reading says a great deal about your individual character. You might begin to develop ideas about what might come next, what might go forwards. To choose otherwise is to write in a creative vacuum.

Follow the advice of Henry Thoreau: 'Read the best books first, or you may not have had a chance to read them all.' However, do not be such a snob that you imagine yourself *above* reading what is fashionable or popular. Read backwards in time, and slide your eye sideways across genres, across literatures in translation, and even across disciplines. Your hunger for reading marks you out as a writer. Feed it, but you will always find you wake hungrier.

Appetites and abilities

Who tells the best stories wins the crowd. There is a strong history, and mythology, of the weak defending their lives by their power to weave a story. Many children, if lonely at home or school, recognise implicitly the power of fantasy, and of projected narrative, and the power these exert over their family, teachers and peers. A lie can save you and others around you from harm. We, all of us, create narratives out of the particular that we then apply to the general. Storytelling is no different. If those narratives are honest in their precision and winningly paced, then new readers embrace those particulars as their own.

Scale that effect to a child lost in a book. A fantasy, for example, fitted to everyday reality, might lead a reader to play-act their lives through imagined roles, as a hero with destiny. Faced by their everyday, the reader not only rides through or above their own world's limits by borrowing the imagination of the original writer; they grow to aspire to create such worlds for themselves, no longer by play-acting and self-fantasy, but by the act of writing and making. Creative reading is the engine for influence and imitation – and for masking.

The appetite to become, and be, a great storyteller can arise simply from the wish to become, and be, admired; or even to protect oneself from mockery or harm. Students and new writers also come to creative writing out of an appetite to impress or pose creatively. They accept the received image of the writer as the enigmatic ingénue or even *flâneur*, but they reject the apprenticeship necessary to become, and remain, a writer-as-reader. Annie Dillard explains in *The Writing Life* how

> Hemingway studied Knut Hamsun and Ivan Turgenev . . . Ralph Ellison studied Hemingway and Gertrude Stein. Thoreau loved Homer; Eudora Welty loved Chekhov. Faulkner described his debt to Sherwood Anderson and Joyce; E. M. Forster, his debt to Jane Austen and Proust. By contrast, if you ask a twenty-one-year-old poet whose poetry he likes, he might say, unblushing, 'Nobody's' . . . he has not yet understood that poets like poetry, and novelists like novels; he himself likes only the role, the thought of himself in a hat.   (1989: 70)

How can you make claims to originality unless you know what is already out there? Ignorance will find you out as writer, hat or not. Thus, writers are competitive and ruthless readers.

Writers can often be profoundly motivated by feelings of competition with other authors, living or dead. It is not solely a question of contest; you need models from which to work. If you do not read, if you do not enjoy reading poetry and fiction, then your time might be better spent doing something more productive in another arena, for you will get nowhere in that competition if you do not read as competitively and as creatively as writers. You should allow yourself to be influenced, and you should use reading to imitate other writers in order to find your voice. 'If you don't have time to read, you don't have the time (or the tools) to write. Simple as that' – Stephen King.

It is a hard lesson that we do not know how to read. Were we not taught at school? Our alphabets are simply our first passports into knowledge. There is far more to language than verbal skills. We know enough to get by; we read books to please our favoured teachers; we might even equip ourselves with reading some authors in translation in order to impress. But when we decide to write, we feel our fingers freeze in the effort, as our minds are rinsed by our ignorance of language, form, structure, strategy. We have wasted time, and now time wastes us, for we find we know our alphabet but cannot speak, let alone play with, our language.

We have arrived at the place where we will make things, and we have neither the tools nor the materials even to begin the task. In fact, we feel we have not been to school. We have been carefully truanting from knowledge, and from our own potential, for many years out of the fear of being seen to be different. We have lost our individuality through a lack of interest. Or we might wish to prolong our childhood into adulthood by adopting inertia as a means for getting by – a kind of extended adolescence of the talents. Those of you who really wish to write might truant from your abilities out of the fear you might actually succeed, that you may have something to say.

Success, however minor, brings responsibility, even if it is only the responsibility of expectation. We must relearn *how* to read and write. Instead of accepting our position with humility, and turning instead to educative reading, we press forward to produce what we believe is original. What stirred us as young readers is something we recall episodically and impressionistically; we then replicate it as our own. 'We all take pleasure', says Aristotle, 'in any imitation or representation . . . because our knowledge is naturally agreeable to us.' Then we become frustrated and resentful on discovering that what we have produced is second-rate, or worse, second-hand.

A new maze

To make our way as readers – to begin to break at last through the snow of pages around us – we should set ourselves a distinctive reading list, which is itself a pathway, and is itself a new maze. However, at least it is our path, and our maze. Better still (and this is one of the best reasons for the discipline of creative writing in education), ask a teacher or mentor to create a reading list that fits the way you, as an individual, write at this time. Have them change and extend this reading list as your writing changes and extends its borders. Have them set work that begins, unhurriedly, to challenge your individual style and its precepts of composition. Then, request that they set you reading that opposes your way of writing entirely. You should watch carefully which choices are made; learn to do this for yourself, and later do this for others.

You will learn to read against yourself, and against your whim and tastes and, in that way, you will begin the slow escape from the hypnosis of passive reading, and from the apprentice's art of imitation. By having your reading tailored to your needs in this way, you can both plough the canon of literature and cultivate its margins. After all, you are not studying literature; you are turning it over, harvesting what you require and hopefully reseeding it.

In the same way that creative writing must teach you to write on your own, and beyond your own intelligence, so the lessons of creative reading must teach you how to read on your own, and to read against your nurture and nature. When we find our voice, when our voice exerts its gravitational pull on our reading, pulling to it everything that is of use, it stimulates our progress as a writer. Then, and only then, we must go about *un*learning how to read, and begin striving for simplicity not allusion; for clarity not echo; for finding ourselves in our writing, seeing that those others we wanted to be, whose voices we were echoing, were ourselves already.

Writing Game

WRITE WHAT YOU KNOW: YOU AS A PERSON

Look around you. Make a list of the things around you, all of which say something about your likes and dislikes, about your past and possible future, about your character – as you are, now. Now, look in a mirror, and try looking in your own eyes for no less than ten minutes. If you flinch, make sure you turn back to the mirror when you are comfortable again. Maintain as much direct focus as possible. After a while, you will begin to notice certain new things about your face and your whole appearance. The way you dress, the way you style your hair: these say something about you and the decisions you take about the way you conduct yourself. Make further notes on what you have discovered. After you have done this, look again into the mirror, but try to see yourself as another person, maybe another age even. Draft a poem, a story or a short prose biography, which is about somebody, who is recognisably you, but who has a different past and future. Situate your writing in the present day, using the first person ('I'), and use as many of the observed details about yourself as possible. Do not make anything up. At this point try placing the piece in the third person ('he' or 'she'), changing the verbs and possessive articles accordingly. Once you have finished, put the writing to one side for three weeks, returning to it to complete the project.

AIM: In Chapter Seven, we will write about what you *do*: what you know, for example, about work. The focus, here, is your self and selves. In the same way that a detective itemises objects found on a person or a crime scene, the things around you say a great deal about your character. Your thoughts often tell you not only what you know, but also what you *seem* to know. How you want to be seen by others is not always how you seem to yourself. This project helps you to get to know several dimensions of yourself, one of which is how others see you. Apply this rigorous perception to how you see not only yourself but also to the several dimensions of the people you meet. You will learn to read people, and their many layers.

Recommended reading

There are two particularly fascinating studies of the history and evolution of creative writing as a discipline: D. G. Myers' *The Elephants Teach: Creative Writing Since 1880* (Prentice Hall, 1995) and Paul Dawson's *Creative Writing and the New Humanities* (Routledge, 2005). Seminal introductions to the neuroscience underlying literary creativity and the nature of metaphor creation are George Lakoff and Mark Johnson's *Metaphors We Live By* (University of Chicago Press, 1980) and Mark Turner's *The Literary Mind* (Oxford University Press, 1996). There are hundreds of books on the nature of creativity, but Rob

Pope's *Creativity: Theory, History, Practice* (Routledge, 2005) is not only an innovatively written text in itself, but also provides a beguiling synthesis of thought and practice, crossing disciplinary boundaries and making fascinating links between the critical and creative. Although originally published in 1934, the reprint of Dorothea Brande's *Becoming a Writer* (Tarcher Penguin, 1981) presents some of the most realistic ideas still on teaching and learning creative writing. This new edition carries an excellently provocative foreword by John Gardner on some of the root problems of creative writing teaching and its teachers. John Gardner's own *The Art of Fiction* (Vintage Books, 1983) and Annie Dillard's *The Writing Life* (HarperCollins, 1989) bring illumination to the daily practice of writing and the purpose of reading as a writer. Frank Smith's beautifully concise *Writing and the Writer* (Heinemann, 1982) contains fascinating material on the writer–reader contract, and the ways writers control readers. A fine book on the value and method of memorisation and reading aloud is the poet Ted Hughes' *By Heart* (Faber and Faber, 1997).

Chapter 2

Creative writing in the world

Some form of compulsion seems to be far more important, in the making of a writer, than innate literary gifts. It is as if one grain of talent – in the right psychological climate – can become a great harvest, where a load of grains – in the wrong climate – simply goes off. The really unusual thing happens, no doubt, when the load of grains meets the right climate. Then, maybe, precocious abilities really do prove that they are convertible to real abilities. But the suspicion remains that we are talking about an unhappy not to say disastrous state of affairs, where this immense biological over-supply of precocious ability is almost totally annihilated, before it can mature.

TED HUGHES, *Winter Pollen* (1994: 31)

An act of criticism is, at best, also an act of creativity: they are hemispheres of the same world. Historically, in the West at least, criticism and creative writing are two phases of the same activity, and criticism illuminates most sharply when practical experience of writing is at the bottom of it. The best criticism creates new open spaces for creativity.

Creative writing and creative criticism

Many university creative writing courses place an equal emphasis on the study of literature and the practice of writing. Out of a belief that criticism must rest in balance with creativity (or motivated by an unvoiced qualm that too much creativity numbs or softens critical intelligence), many writing courses are asked to require that students submit for assessment a reflective essay, or a commentary, on the aims and processes involved in writing their portfolio of creative writing.

Reflective criticism

As a writer, you are a student of the world. You do not have to be taking a writing course to profit from writing critical, reflective self-interrogations, narcissistic as the process may appear at first. Despite protestations to the contrary, and the occasional gratuitous mystification, many writers in the real world like to explain themselves, as a form of setting up their stall, and for creating an audience that understands their approach and purpose. They often do so vicariously when writing about, or reviewing, the creative writing of other authors. They discuss their working processes; they advocate and opinionate; they make no secret of their influences, enthusiasms or motivations. You must practise at this mirror. You *reflect* on the aims of your writing and the process – for example, of drafting – by which it arrived at its final form. You also give *critical* attention to your own writing – for example, the affinities you may feel it has with the work of other authors – and by placing your work in any intellectual, aesthetic, social or other context you feel it should be seen in.

Reading lends you knowledge; knowledge offers you power; but self-knowledge helps you understand the shaping and fledging of your abilities. It may even help you realise them, and to fly alone. At the very least, it helps you to gauge where you are at, and where you want to get, and this process begins in your notebooks, as we will see in Chapter Four. Whether you are inside or outside an academy, critical self-reflection is a means to develop some self-understanding, and to create and evolve some sense of your poetics; of the aim and purpose of your personal practice. This task is also useful training should you later eke out your income by literary reviewing, teaching or by writing biography. What applied to your processes might apply to another writer's processes. It allows you to think your way inside of writing in the same way that writing a poem or story helps a non-creative writing student to better understand what they are studying. At best, these essays are personal examples of creative nonfiction (see Chapter Seven).

Writing Game

WHO ARE YOU?
Why do you write and how do you write? Are there pressures in your life that force you into a writing silence? Write a statement of no more than eight hundred words describing your current reasons and methods. This is your first statement of poetics, a personal credo. Be sure to write about those writers, living or dead, who have influenced your thinking and direction. What drives and what hinders you? How can you improve your writing conditions, how can 'you do it as you can'? Use these questions as headings from which to write quickly and without too much deliberation. Read it aloud to somebody who knows you well and will be able to tell you which parts of your statement are honest or phoney. Revise it accordingly, then put it to one side for a year.

AIM: We write for many reasons; sometimes those reasons converge into writerly purpose. They might include a desire to: play with language and/or form; share a part of yourself; describe an emotion; communicate with the world; bring a character to life; express your opinion; or simply tell a story. When you reach the final chapter of this book, I will ask you similar questions. I want you to use this first statement as a measure of how far your creative thinking and reading has progressed. It is a good idea to examine your progress in this way every year. Please be utterly honest with yourself. Do not pretend to achievements or ways of speaking which are not yet your own, or with which you feel uncomfortable. Writers must not fool themselves – except when they are writing.

Writing reflective essays

In Chapter One, I talked about how a novel or poem is the visible part of an iceberg, that the knowledge a writer brings to their creation is the invisible submerged section of that same iceberg. Reflective essays capsize it; they show that working knowledge, partially or completely. They let the world back in. There is personal judgement involved: you are assessed not by your ability to interpret literature and knowledge, but on how you 'translate' them into something else, preferably something recognisably of your own invention; and on your capacity to understand the process realistically, not idealistically. Your reading will form the basis for the literature that influences and excites you. The knowledge you are translating into new writing may be non-literary; it could be experiential or drawn from non-literary areas.

It is better to write about details than big, abstract ideas. As Samuel Beckett said, 'What do I know of man's destiny? I could tell you more about radishes.' When you write a reflective essay, bear in mind that creative writers seldom begin writing *from* a theory or *to* a big theme. John Gardner writes that 'Nothing . . . could be farther from the truth than the notion that theme is all' (1985: 40). Of course, some writers rationalise a theme, a theory, or even a credo of propositions, *after* the act.

In the case of theories, they are often acts of provocative creativity that say a great deal about the writer and their own practice, such as Ezra Pound's 'A Retrospect' in 1918 or Frank O'Hara's 'Personism: A Manifesto' in 1961 (both reprinted in Herbert and Hollis, 2000). However, in the same way that translation theory has little effect on the practice of translation, so literary theory generally has little impact on the way creative writers go about their business. It has to be said that some writers find it creatively disabling to read literary criticism; they find it stalls them in the act of making, or it alters their expectations of literature in ways which are simply false or destructive. Many writers simply write for themselves, and reading about writing can undo a writer's useful selfishness to an extent. The poet Elizabeth Bishop warned a would-be writer, 'you . . . are reading too much *about* poetry and not enough poetry . . . I always ask my writing classes NOT to read criticism' (Herbert and Hollis, 2000: 105).

Reading yourself as a writer

Reflective essays on the creative writing process tend towards being small, alert studies in critical realism, what we might term here creative critical realism. This is because they possess personal and interdisciplinary awareness; a demand for evidence, as well as argumentative coherence and consistency; and realism about the act and action of writing. While the creative work submitted alongside it may be affectedly postmodern (or not), the account of how and why it was written will be realist to the letter.

At the heart of such an essay is an attempted illumination of two dark questions about your aims and processes, questions that provoke and prick at writers from whatever time. Why do you write? How do you write? They are short questions. They are not small questions. Given how various we all are, they appear at first to require variations and permutations of thought beyond our grasp. Surely, you will say, *critics* should address these questions. No. You are your own critic. You may not be able to articulate it yet, but you know that when you are drafting your own writing (or even writing it) you must become, as it were, somebody else. You read yourself as a writer.

Reflective, critical writing of this type possesses at the very least: a sense of argument and development of argument; critical thinking and self-reflection; evidence of actual research for writing – for example, interviews with other writers; the critical context of your writing; the problems faced and overcome or not overcome; and, to round it off – to show you've read in order to write – a bibliography of creative reading. One of the best ways into your reflective essay is to set up a literary problem and explore it using your own work and influences.

Writing Game

REFLECTIVE THINKING

Here are ten titles with which to begin writing a self-reflective essay. Please adapt these suggestions as you wish, or use them as starting points to create your own title.

- How do I write what I know?
- Where does my knowledge take my writing?
- Is freedom from form a freedom from art?
- How does a writer ensure that their work is truly their own, instead of merely a replica of ideas absorbed and reissued from the world?
- Where and who is our audience?
- How have contemporary writers dealt with cultural hybridisation in the face of racial stereotyping?
- How do writers find and develop ideas?
- Finding a style
- An examination of truth in fiction and poetry
- Does the novelist depend upon a sense of place in order to create a good story?
  Does this sense of place have to be a physical landscape?

AIM: Titles like this set up small literary mazes you can explore with some end in view. They help you to plan the essay and focus your attention on only a few important issues. In answering, you reflect on the aims of your writing and the process by which it arrived at its final form; and you give critical attention to your own writing, for example the affinities you may feel it has with the work of other authors.

Notional subjectivity

Your experience counts, and the foreknowledge that you do not place yourself into the work you write, but that you discover yourself there. Yet, you say, if that is the case, then how can one rationalise an aim out of something that was not (apparently) deliberated? How can one be objective about processes that are subjective? First, I would suggest that notions of subjectivity and objectivity in art have long proved unhelpful, but also unattainable, and even science has a problem with them (which is why nothing is ever certain in science and why its practitioners rely on degrees of mathematical significance and on practical falsifiability). Second, I would argue that experience informs and inhabits the most honest and enriching statements of poetics, as it does the most successful essays on the aims and processes of creative writing.

It is vexing to trade with the labels of subjectivity and objectivity when dealing with a writer's experience. While such vexations have led to some remarkable developments in philosophy, they do not tend to influence creative writing directly. Indirectly, of course, creative writers and artists pillage, use and parody such ideas and their hermetic jargons at will. However, some writers find the kind of language used in these discourses at best diverting and at worst inhibiting.

Why do you write? How do you write? A creative writer's deepening knowledge of learning through practice frames their own answers to these questions. They also show an awareness that the answers that hold firm and clear now will no doubt change and grow more intricate as they progress in their art. The experience of other writers also informs truly effective arguments. Self-interrogation will become another part of your way of life, as necessary as your interrogation of the world around you.

We remain students: a writer is a student of their discipline all their lives, both in practice and in effect. Criticism, like creative writing, is another open space for engaging an audience, and engaging with the world. Leading critics and interpreters of literature have themselves had substantial experience of imaginative writing at the deepest level. Many of our best writers have also been among the more insightful critics, among others: Sir Philip Sidney, Ben Jonson, S. T. Coleridge, Percy Shelley, John Keats (from his letters), Matthew Arnold, T. S. Eliot, Ezra Pound, George Orwell, W. H. Auden, Randall Jarrell, Virginia Woolf, William Empson, Saul Bellow, V. S. Pritchett, Geoffrey Hill, Ted Hughes, Joseph Brodsky, Thom Gunn, Adrienne Rich, Seamus Heaney, Eavan Boland, Chinua Achebe, John Ashbery, Ngugi wa Thiong'o, Les Murray, Margaret Atwood and Paul Muldoon. Take comfort from Harold Bloom that 'criticism . . . is either part of literature or nothing at all' (1997: xix); and take heed of John Gardner that 'Nothing is harder on the true writer's sense of security than an age of bad criticism, and in one way or another, sad to say, almost every age qualifies' (1985: 36).

Classrooms on the world

Like speech, like the world's languages, all writing is creative. Sometimes it is imaginative writing and sometimes it is expository or critical writing, but usually there is overlap between them. Of course, *writing* can be taught and learned. What everybody is hunting for is the pedagogic key to creativity, the metamorphic knack to take teachable matters like metrics and syntax and recombine and transform them into something entirely innovative, producing writing in a style not yet seen or heard. As a creative writer (unlike, say, the writer of an aircraft design manual), what you write *about* is far less important than *how* you write it: 'All the fun is in how you say a thing' – Robert Frost.

There is no magic key to this as such, but, as any professional burglar knows, there are different ways to unlock doors, and writers are good thieves. Later in the book, we discuss the importance of concentration and practice to achieve fluency, and demonstrate how playfulness and cunning can be hugely rewarding in yielding the unpredicted in writing. As we shall see, the qualities of fluency, unpredictability and syntax are not far along the spectrum of writing from originality. It is a matter not of what you say, but how you say it. As Goethe wrote, 'The most original authors are not so because they advance what is new, but because they put what they have to say as if it had never been said before.'

Writing as teaching

You cannot play a musical instrument you do not know how to play. What we can all probably agree on is that talent, like taste or character, can be cultivated, creativity nurtured or protected, and the purpose of creative writing as a discipline is to develop the talent and technique of new writers. Most teachers of writing recognise this, which is why, when people sign up for a creative writing course, they are often required to submit a folio of work, and they are selected, and sometimes self-selected, on its strengths. Teachers of writing, who are usually practitioners, then build on this potential. They teach them how *not* to write and students learn how they *might* write. Whether a writer can teach creative writing is another matter, and it is worth your knowing why your teachers might be there, rather than at home, or on the road, scribbling and living the literary life.

'Those who can't, teach', the adage goes (it goes on divisively). It is a much more complex matter, and those famous writers 'who can' may also prove to be ideal teachers. What motivates writers to teach? Responsibility – as accomplished film directors feel responsibility for the refreshing of their medium by taking on apprentice directors and training them, so writers often wish to give something back to the medium by which they live. For writers such as poets, certain literary novelists and critics, whose work by its nature – if not by its quality – cannot support living costs, teaching their art form provides a crucial income.

The same goes for music or painting. Mozart taught; it subsidised composition. Leonardo da Vinci and Auguste Rodin taught, by taking apprentices and, in the case of painters and sculptors, students not only provided an extra pair of hands, but were trained to do some of the work by which their masters were known. Art does not pay enough, and never has, but most of the work that people do is like that. Teaching supplements life as a working artist. Artists may even want to use teaching to pass on their own artistic practices and philosophies. They want their aesthetic or ideology to survive, so they adopt protégés as ambassadors, as carriers of their message – a process vulnerable to backlash once the artist dies.

For some writers, teaching is part of the process of creating an audience and catching them young – in this case, unlike public readings, an already captive audience. A fusion of idealism and a sense for the communitarian draws some also into the teaching room. Some writers are natural educators by dint of their work or their character. For them, teaching is performance; their performance is their writing; they are performing themselves. In *Fires*, Raymond Carver writes of his experience of being taught the practice of fiction by the novelist John Gardner:

> One of the dangers . . . lies . . . in the overencouragement of young writers. But I learned from Gardner to take that risk rather than err on the other side. He gave and kept giving, even when the vital signs fluctuated wildly, as they do when someone is young and learning. (1986: 45)

In *The Point: Where Teaching and Writing Intersect* (Shapiro and Padgett, 1983), a number of writers present the view, based on experience, that teaching writing feeds into the making of writing, and certainly that is my experience. However, for some writers, teaching is an interruption, although sometimes that interlude is welcome owing to the solitude of their work. It offers them a scaled-down sense of community with other writers, and their apprentices, even though they might write out of a dislocation with community.

A marriage of heaven and hell

The worst thing that can happen to a writer is that their teaching begins to impact on their own artistic practice; their work 'begins to sound like a teacher writing – intended, crafted, lifeless, and too clever by half' (Freed, 2005). Writers may even view the classroom as intrinsically anti-creative. They may have had an alienating experience of taught literature, or they may favour study at the University of Life.

The world, of course, exists outside books. Engaging with the world is likely to yield material that is more genuine, funny, more exacting in integrity; and experience teaches lessons as necessary to a writer's development, as any primary texts, let alone criticism or literary theory. Some writers feel it is best to avoid any second job that involves either the study or making of literature. Better to be a grave-digger, a long-distance truck driver or wait at table, they feel, than to be a teacher of literature or writing.

Some writers perceive such work as having more innate moral integrity than teaching, because it connects with the real world, and is work for the hand not the mind. They see physical work as nobler than mental work, and holding more potential for material and writing. Such writers sometimes mimic physical activity through travel and the taking of part-time jobs as a form of research. Like lottery winners, many of these same writers, on becoming successful, flee the physical workplace. However, successful writers do not flee the classroom as a rule. It is possible that teaching is less vicarious of experience, and more rewarding, than some writers make it out to be: not heaven exactly, but certainly not hell either. As a writer who has held dozens of menial jobs, without knowing at the time that they were considered menial, I think you need to beware of hubris masquerading as experience. A well-paid executive or surgeon could consider teaching and writing relatively menial.

Experience of the world is vital, but our classrooms are part of that world. Our lives can be as closeted and narrow, as a university or library can be open and remarkable. Wherever we write, however we write, we must let in the world, let in people. It is why I argue later for universities to act as bridges to their communities. This is as important for the creative health of the writers brought in to teach the subject as it is for the students. It is less a problem *outside* higher education. Creative writing has always had a wide constituency of practice, thriving in schools, hospitals, adult education and wherever else writers seek to make their temporary homes or residencies. Downtown, purgatory is always more bustling. In these situations, the isolation of the writer becomes impossible, and their work as a writer becomes a functional part of those local real worlds.

Many of these incentives and reasons combine and recombine as a writer's career progresses, or regresses. There is a balance between teaching and writing; it teeters one way or the other, but generally the writing gains a slight or more numinous (often unspoken) preference. This is an intuitive procedure while also being pragmatic, since original research informs the best teaching, and writing is the writer's living version of research. 'Creative activity could be described as a type of learning process where teacher and pupil are located in the same individual' – Arthur Koestler. The energy of live creativity rubs off on students, a little like standing close to somebody lucky. It electrifies, it enlightens the way they approach teaching: those who can, teach, and they do not need to be in a seminar room to do so.

Experience

We are all creators of language, but to return to the prospectus offered by the University of Life, although creative writing has rediscovered its historical-rhetorical home within the academy, it is blindingly observable that you do not have to pass through an academy to be a writer. As I said, a writer is a student of their discipline all their lives. Being taught or being shown how to write; being taught technique; being given time to work – all these can help the right people at the right time. However, at some point the course ends and you are on your own, fledged, pushed out of the nest into your own voice. There is a world elsewhere in which you have to learn to teach yourself. It is best to start preparing for this now.

Capturing ideas for writing

William Faulkner said, 'A writer needs three things, experience, observation and imagination, any two of which, at times any one of which, can supply the lack of others.' Experience heads the list. Experience is not all about action and your physical reality, although it can be. It is also about your psychological reality; even your imagination and dreams. It is about your fears, uncertainties, failures, terrors, losses. Experience, for a writer, is an art of losing. Even in a triumph, there is cost. The cost of experience is currency for creative work.

Even dreams are part of experience, and you should start keeping an account of your dreams in a notebook. Dreams are a means for reflection, and a preparation for situations we might yet face, so the imagination can work as a teacher and maker. Many good writers create characters and situations without undergoing a real-life experience *as* that character or *of* that situation. They use a sympathetic imagination to reach and explore; they 'make it up'. Imagination and dreams are parts of your reality.

Choose to keep notes on anything that stimulates you in the news. Do not copy from life exactly, since its very reality tends not to make for an effective fiction. By questioning events and by thinking your way into them, you begin to tear at that reality and make it your own. Taking other people's stories has the same effect. Listen to older people – encourage them to talk about their lives, and practise listening to your friends and family. You might even choose to eavesdrop in public spaces, such as cafés.

What we know and what we do not know

Stories and poems are transformations of reality, but you are halfway to making them so by collecting examples *from* reality: your personal reality, other people's reality and the natural realities that surround you. Writers are often told to 'write what they know', but the problem is we do not usually know enough about what 'we know', because we do not know ourselves. Most of what we meditate upon is external to us, and we have probably all been taught at some time that we are not particularly important, and that self-knowledge can be only another word for narcissism or the public display of self-pity.

We need to get to know ourselves better and, in that way, reconnect with what we know: our selfless knowledge. Writing assists this self- and self*less* knowledge, to a point. However, writing 'what you do not know' contains possibilities too – those of the imagination. In an interview, Cynthia Ozick commented on this aspect of creative writing teaching:

> The point is that the self is limiting. The self – subjectivity – is narrow and bound to be repetitive. We are, after all, a species. When you write about what you don't know, this means you begin to think about the world at large. You begin to think beyond the home-thoughts. You enter dream and imagination.   (Plimpton, 1989: 305)

You might choose to explore this process by seizing stories, characters and ideas from myths, lore and old tales, and using them as templates for a 'reality' in your writing. The ultimate exercise in 'writing what you do not know' is to try to write a poem or story on the subject of *nothing*. For example, in 'Tailpiece', Beckett writes: 'who may tell the tale / of the old man? . . . // the sum assess / of the world's woes? / nothingness / in words enclose?' How might we 'enclose' nothingness in words?

The thing is that *fiction* (and by this I mean plays, poems *and* fictional prose) has the mysterious property of carrying the quality of truth more effectively than what we think of as our reality. This is a quality which creative nonfiction adopts and exploits, as you will read in Chapter Seven. In *Poetry in the Making*, the poet Ted Hughes delves into this mystery further. Writing on his poem 'The Thought Fox' (see NP: 1810), Hughes talks of capturing ideas for creative writing as being like capturing animals – a process of hunting and fishing for poems using language:

> If I had not caught the real fox there in the words I would never have saved the poem. I would have thrown it into the wastepaper basket as I have thrown so many other hunts that did not get what I was after. As it is, every time I read the poem the fox comes up again out of the darkness and steps into my head . . . all through imagining it clearly enough and finding the living words.   (1967: 20–21)

Our reality includes the world of work. Sometimes we see daily work as time wasted to writing, but it need not be if you *read* it as a writer. There are arguments in favour of learning outside the academy, not least the need to gain physical experience of other worlds, other people, and the work we do to get by in those worlds. These provide material in plenty. Some creative writing courses incorporate work experience, but this provides a temporary and possibly illusory experience. You need it to be personal. Daily life and work are unavoidable; become used to them and start using them and losing them. They will start to surprise you.

The personal work of life is another rich source for ideas. Pain will teach you lessons at first-hand that some books cannot. Love will astound you into thoughts you cannot understand until you have gained, lost it, betrayed or misplaced it. Loss can shape you into a clearer writer, by giving you the sharpest of human perspectives on grief. As Elizabeth Bishop wrote in 'One Art' (NP, 1528):

> the art of losing's not too hard to master
> though it may look like (*Write* it!) like disaster.

Writing against your experience

Let us focus on one world experience we all probably share: humiliation. Humiliation is a position from which many writers work; it is the private face of the art of losing. The demands of working and shaping language lend themselves to humiliation as well as humility. The world of work can be a great humiliator and destroyer of the soul. However, personal humiliations also provide energy, material and purpose. One example: writing is widely seen as not being a 'proper job', or inferior in value to other forms of study, or work. Whether inside or outside the academy, you risk being looked down upon. You can accept this as a challenge and, by your action, defy it.

Feelings of humiliation may already be familiar to you. We feel it, for example, when a boss or teacher puts us down for making a useful suggestion, or an intellectual corrects the pronunciation of a word back to us by including it in their reply, sneeringly *italicised*. The act of correction is a burst of contempt: they are showing us our place, for we have crossed some invisible border into a country whose language and ideas we should not be allowed to speak – let alone write.

At times like this, it is a good idea to remember that you have probably purchased your ability at a greater price, through your birth, hardships of background, and the lottery of education. A lot of successful people spring from inauspicious backgrounds. You are blighted by disadvantage but this makes you fight harder. Remind yourself, at such moments, that the dictionary of your experience is worth much more than any dictionary of privileged language, status and received ideas. Moments like this should fire you up for writing: for writing *back* and *against* those who have colonised your language. Humiliation, like humility, creates articulate energy; anger and a sense of injustice can help you find your voice and your subject.

Freedom, play and magic

Creative writers are not great 'joiners'; they sometimes kick against what is expected. They prefer to be seen to be outside the club or playhouse, even if they are life subscribers. As Groucho Marx would not join any club that would have him as a member, so the attitude of creative writers standing apart (even if it is a pose) rubs off on others, on all of us.

Creative writing and freedom of expression

One of the most striking aspects of a creative writing workshop is that opinions are voiced with freedom. Sometimes, students in those workshops find it hard to get used to this freedom because, in their past, those opinions have either not been sought, or they have been ignored, or they have been shamed as foolish. Yet inexperience can be inadvertently wiser at times than experience. It carries fewer preconceptions. Language belongs to every human. It lives by evolution, by being played with and by being hit at fresh angles.

However, creative writing's capacity for the creation of illusion-as-truth, and the precision of its language, makes it doubly dangerous to authorities whose power depends on the formulation of illusions, and the debasement and twisting of language. Standing apart makes you even more vulnerable to assault. 'Every compulsion is put upon writers to become safe, polite, obedient and sterile' – Sinclair Lewis. The word 'sterility' here is precise; it connives with the dead hand of authority.

One of the gut instincts of government is control: seize the language and you control not only speech but also its contexts, the terms on which discussion is based, and the permissions and prohibitions of speech. Look at the manner in which war is presented by politicians and the media. Observe the terms for atrocity and killing tamed to acronyms and newspeak. War takes place 'in theatre'; soldiers are 'taken out', 'dropped', as if killing a person was the action of ushers removing a theatregoer from the playhouse. Force-feeding illegal prisoners of war is 'introducing internal nutrition to detainees' as if they were wilful children. The poet C. D. Wright comments, 'If you do not use language you are used by it. If you do not recognize the terms *peacekeeper missile* and *preemptive strike* as oxymorons, your hole has already been dug' (2005: 40).

Such language places what is described at several removes; it does not change the intolerable actuality. It tampers quite deliberately with our reaction to it, attempts to neutralise it. It infantilises us in our complicity or passivity, and this is the intention and design: to deter or deflect our humane objections by dampening our emotional responses. Writers are the antennae for language, designers of speech, and you, as new writers, should similarly be alert to language's abuse and debasement.

Political regimes, even regimes whose ideologies oppose each other, have found cause to target creative writers and intellectuals, to bend them to the will of their ideologies, to use writers as apologists or celebrants of dogma. Should writers prove uncooperative, they are, at best, humiliated publicly, exiled, marginalised, and silenced, say, by banning publication. At worst, they are murdered. As PEN, the international writers union, reveals, there are many writers in prison, or under threat, throughout the world *because of their writing*. What George Orwell argued in 'Politics and the English Language' seems to replay for every generation:

> When one watches some tired hack on the platform mechanically repeating the familiar phrases – *bestial, atrocities, iron heel, bloodstained tyranny, free peoples of the world, stand shoulder to shoulder* – one often has a curious feeling that one is not watching a live human being but some kind of dummy . . . his brain is not involved as it would be if he were choosing his words for himself. . . . And this reduced state of consciousness . . . is at any rate favourable to political conformity. (NE2: 2468)

Writing Game

WORKING AGAINST LANGUAGE ON BEHALF OF LANGUAGE
Read some of the past week's newspapers and magazines in your library. Make detailed notes on, or photocopy, any articles about a current conflict or war in which politicians or military officers are interviewed. Note the terminology they use, and ensure you understand what they mean in basic English. Now read both sections of Henry Reed's 1946 poem 'Lessons of the War' (NP: 1564) set in an army training camp in World War II, or *Catch 22* by Joseph Heller. Write a poem or story that uses, and possibly subverts or parodies, the vocabulary for military conflict. Knowingly substitute everyday words with your own neutralising or far-fetched neologisms and acronyms. Do not be too earnest in tone; a light approach will gain greater effect.

AIM: We need to keep a check on where language is being led – by its nose. Make use of such language, subverting it into fiction, poetry or nonfiction. Use it for comic effect, parody, or as a form of witness, or turn the weapon on language's assailants. The best writing of this type does all of these things.

Serious play

The action of writing, as the poet and scientist Miroslav Holub put it, is an action of 'serious play', of wilful and sometimes wild experiment. The pleasure principle walks out in the world wearing serious clothes, set off by a clown's cap and bells. Boisseau and Wallace, speaking of poetry students, make a strong generic point when they argue for the play of experiment in a writing class:

> A course called 'Creative Writing' might better be called 'Experimental Writing'. Faced with the daunting specter of a blank page, the poet may feel intimidated by the injunction to *be creative; create.* But, being told to *experiment, to try something out* can be more attractive.   (2004: 2)

Play is still a challenge, even if less daunting than the frown of High Art. In Charles Dickens' *Great Expectations*, Miss Havisham instructs the child Pip: 'I have a sick fancy that I want to see some play. There, there!' with an impatient movement of the fingers of her right hand; 'play, play, play!' This is like a writing tutor who has shut out the world and experience as influences; and sometimes his or her Pips find it intimidating to 'play to order'. Yet, as writers, we must sometimes obey the Miss Havisham inside us. We challenge ourselves to reach a word count of fiction by a route defined by character or by *that* situation or by *this* point of view. We conduct investigations into nonfiction driven by the desire to poke fun, or out of a rage of injustice. We push ourselves to grasp a cracked crown of sonnets. What can we do but laugh (or else we cry) at the elegant (entirely useless) brick piles of language when we are finished?

Sometimes the play becomes irksome, the elbowroom reductive. Therefore, we push over those brick towers of form and language, and free-write, free-associate, make free verse or on-the-road prose. Then we realise that all this freedom gets us no nearer the truth, especially the truth of our abilities as writers. We turn back to playful restrictions and experiments and, by stealth, approach that place of balance between imagination and form where good art gets made. Play, however, can be deliciously dangerous.

Serious difficulty

We find we are on a tightrope; we recognise where the tipping-points are within ourselves, and try to stay on it for the rest of our lives, writing and balancing all the grand binaries: imagination and rationality, doubt and confidence, achievement and failure. We give a performance of ourselves along such spectra, within a small or invisible circus of our readers. Yet all our difficulty (and that includes both thinking and feeling) must seem – must be *made* to seem – inevitable. 'A good style should show no sign of effort. What is written should seem a happy accident' – Somerset Maugham. The difficulty and the opportunity lies in the word 'seem'.

"PLAY IS STILL A CHALLENGE, EVEN IF LESS DAUNTING THAN THE FROWN OF HIGH ART."

We labour to make art, and then we labour again to conceal it. The play never ends, however vulnerable it makes you to self-defeat. The reader must not know about the effort that went into any particular story, nor the toil made to overcome overwhelming forces of insecurity and inexperience. Difficulty must be invisible, yet forged thoroughly so that it looks unforced. A writer is a trickster: it must seem that their work came into being quite naturally, always inevitably, even as Keats puts it 'as leaves to a tree', even if you have flayed them to its branches. It must seem like a species of magic, but a natural magic. Language is a natural form; writing probes that form with difficulty, with trickery. It does not create life from it; it tricks its life from it. Play is the player; dance is the dancer.

Language's magic

Natural magic, like language or natural history, surrounds us: in the speed at which species nest and fledge; in the dynamic connections of chaos in subatomic and planet-sized physics. Mathematics and the arts are not poles apart, but the same pole reached by different routes. You can write a poem or story based on the order of Fibonacci numbers: sequences of numbers found in the patterns of leaves, grasses and flowers; in the branching of bushes and trees; or in the arrangements of tines on a pine cone.

These patterns seem distant from the machinery of politics and the media. Censors do not understand it. Natural magic does not just surround us: it *is* us, as much as we are part of the environment. It informs every function of our own bodies, plots our life span, and operates the way we perceive. In the same way that the natural and seemingly rational magic of the natural world simply gets on with things, so we as writers must simply get on with our work.

The way in which the best writing workshops are conducted is to supply the right environment for a kind of rapid learning; what I would call a stochastic evolution of talent, one that runs in phases and leaps of progressive learning. As environmental change forces species-evolution, so the environment of the workshop causes a natural response and a progression in expertise: new wirings in our brain's neural networks. As form gives body to language, so writing gives form to the brain. What works is given *a chance*; what does not work is laid aside as a useful lesson, a neutral selection, a phase from which we receive no harm. That *chance* can take the form of a story, a novel, a play or a poem. There is a natural history to language which takes place inside us – a matter of alternative forms, variation and mutation. Workshops premeditate and push such variation.

We push students over into the natural magic of the language of fiction, nonfiction and of poetry, almost to make them lean into books as the writer of that book must once have leaned, daily, in despair, curiosity, pleasure. We read books as readers, but we learn, by that leaning into language, to read books and worlds as if we were their writers. We learn to write and live as writers, in that risky position of near-topple and exposure.

There is a danger involved in such teaching and learning: the danger that students might fall so badly against their own inexperience that they are hurt to a degree that they turn away from writing, that they lose confidence in the long game. That is why it is important that we must learn to play at such moments. To play with our reading and writing, to play with language, even when in danger of falling into pretentiousness or opacity or simple mediocrity, is to take control of the situation. The more control we have, the less likely we are to be controlled. The more practice we have of this, the more playful we can become, and the more confident in our ability not only to control – but also to let go.

Why not be a Writer?

" The only way I can write narrative is to get right outside my body and experience it. This can be exhausting and at times dangerous. "

—Wm. S. Burroughs

"...In the course of [a] working day of eight hours I write three sentences which I erase before leaving the table in despair... Sometimes it takes all my resolution and power of self-control to refrain from butting my head against the wall. I want to howl and foam at the mouth but I daren't do it for fear of waking the baby and alarming my wife. ..." —Joseph Conrad

Freud, in The Problem of Anxiety describes writing as an act "which consists of making a liquid flow from a pen onto a sheet of white paper." "This act ... can be eroticised to the point of causing hysterical paralysis of the hands. The act of writing, in effect, brings into play all the libidinal impulses combined in the 'polymorphous perversity' of infancy..."

Sigmund Freud argued that 'the creative writer does the same thing as a child at play. He creates a world of phantasy which he takes very seriously while separating it sharply from reality . . . As people grow up, they cease to play, and they seem to give up the yield of pleasure which they gained from playing.' Ever the metaphysician first and the physician second, nevertheless Freud's reflection will be seized and understood by our own thoughts and self-experience. You will observe it, any of you who are mothers, fathers, brothers, sisters, teachers. Is creative writing's job to reintroduce us to play?

Rediscovering pleasure

In the afterword to his book on teaching children to write poetry, the American poet Kenneth Koch addresses the question of teaching teachers to play again with language and creative ideas: 'Such writing might begin with something as simple as writing a wish poem before they ask the children to . . . If an unprepared six-year-old can write a wish poem, probably a teacher can, too. It's a pleasure to . . . rediscover one's feeling for poetry, which life and (mainly) education may have scared out of one' (1999: 311). '(Mainly) education' springs a billion traps, but the damage is reversible. One can be released back into the continent of writing; there is no need to be scared of play.

There is no need to be scared because writing is ultimately pleasure. Of course, we must play, or rediscover play and pleasure. However, as creative writing keeps growing as a discipline – as it becomes more and more accepted, even respected – we must be careful it does not become part of a machine to produce more teachers of creative writing. Is it getting too respectable? Is it getting less playful? Whose rooms are we in? As Aristotle taught his students, so we must also remember that, historically, the impartiality of learning an art form is possible only because of the rapacious material interests that allow that process to take place. In that sense, creative writing already stands in a very interesting place in the world, and possesses some interesting allies.

Writing Game

WORKING WITH NEW LANGUAGE

Open a book of popular science, or a scientific textbook, and make notes on any aspects that catch your attention, especially the scientific language that is used for names of species, concepts or equipment. Your first task is to write a very short poem that 'tells' the story of what you have read using some of that language as accurately as possible. Now, rather than showing this work to another writer or teacher of writing, find a willing scientist or science student, and share your work with them. How did they view it? Your second task is to take your poem and, without changing a word, place it into the mouth of a character in a new story. That character could be modelled on the scientist you met. Write this story in such a way that the 'speech' is a natural progression of the narrative.

AIM: Using non-literary language accurately is exacting but essential, and can be fun. To write about an idea or concept using a poem teaches you to reframe that language in a genre not easily given to the transmission of information. Placing this piece in the mouth of a character will help you write in a way which is both expected (you know the poem must be deployed) and unexpected (the context must be played with to make it seem natural).

Publishing and editing

Many writers avow that the process of creation is intrinsically more personal and satisfying than publishing: its production routines, marketing and tours. They are right. Many writers, once they finish a project, undergo a psychological, even a physical, leave-taking. Their focus then swivels ruthlessly to the next project. The time lag between finishing a book and the book's publication is usually protracted. By the time of publication, the most important matter for its writer is the work on which they are *now* concentrating. Nevertheless, the demands of publication are themselves fascinating, and writers – like tulip farmers – must sell their products, however engrossing they are to plant and tend. Publishing is another open space, and an art form in itself, sometimes an art of politics.

A creative writing student and a creative writing department neglect the art and the business of publishing at their peril, for this is where we meet the world head-on. Most writers wish to publish for all sorts of reasons, not least recognition. Publishing is itself a literary purpose, a business that is also half art. Books about creative writing rightly investigate the process of writing but often ignore the fact that, although writing can be an end in itself, for most people the purpose of writing is to communicate to as many people as possible, while they can.

There are, of course, books that deal entirely with publishing (see 'Recommended reading'). However, they are always and necessarily of their time. The publishing industry, from the small presses to the international conglomerates, is a dynamic business. Publishers come and go; there is no stasis. Not only that, but the favoured tastes for one generation are the oblivion of the next as societies change and literary expectations and fashions mutate; and this varies from country to country. Any advice, any list of presses, especially in an age of globalism, will date fast. Therefore, what we offer here can be no more than generic points, which are non-specific to their time and nation, but which may hold some resilient information.

Circles for survival

Before you submit your writing to a literary magazine, or a book to a publisher, be sure you are completely satisfied that your writing has reached a steady, if not a final, state. This brings us to the importance of developing an association of honest friends who are writers: they will be your first real readers. In Chapter Four, we examine how such networks develop through workshops; how they mesh under the pressure of shared learning, shared experience, or even a shared literary prejudice or agenda.

This is what I term a circle for survival, a half-visible network that nudges the writing industry in one of its directions occasionally. Such circles are as old as writing. This circle is your cadre, 'your side'. It sounds surreal, but all these writers eventually become aspects of each other's writing selves. You should show your finished work to these writer-allies before you submit it for possible publication. They know your mind and your working practices. They also know what you can take, in terms of criticism, and how to communicate that criticism without misreading you, or upsetting you.

Group criticism

You should regard this process as a symbiosis, and be as willing to read and criticise their work as thoroughly and as sympathetically. This is not like the relationship you have with your creative writing teacher or mentor. Instead, it is a balance of individual ambitions and communal aims. You are pulled together by the desire to publish the best work that you can in order not to let yourself, or your side, down. Moreover, your group will recognise when you have done well (or poorly) because it will reflect on them also to a degree: all for one, and one for all. You will find these friends very willing to put your writing through some very tough, and often meticulous, critical reading, because it is in their interest also, and because they like you. However, the motivations of liking and of self-interest are often coterminous.

'Writing is like getting married. One should never commit oneself until one is amazed at one's luck' – Iris Murdoch. In the same way that marriage is culturally larger than the two people bound within that contract, so the group is bigger than you, and has its own life. It can give you luck; can make you increase your chances for luck in writing and publishing. Therefore, do not be a parasite on such a grouping by exploiting the expertise too often, or too obviously. Do use this process to satisfy and extend your competitive drives, by submitting your very best work.

Displays of skill need not necessarily create resentment among your peers. If the group is close, and there is sufficient trust, it will have the effect of making everybody in the group feel, or want to be, a better writer. By occasionally being dazzling, you 'up the game' of your side, making everybody in it desirous of improvement, of wanting to be the centre of attention. You will find you will take that role in turns, and learn to bask in shared accomplishment while also feeling jealous as hell.

Clearly, most of the revising will go on face to face in workshops and meetings, and this is an efficient use of the writers' time. However, the prospect of reading, say, a friend's entire book can be daunting, because it is not being read for pleasure or instruction, but for criticism and reinvention. It is being read from *within*, from the writer's point of view, and that requires not only considerable skills of reading but also considerable gifts of imagination, of thinking yourself into the writer's fingertips. Restrict your use of the group in this way; submit to them only what you expect you would be submitting to a publisher. In that way, you set yourself before two high fences rather than one: the need to revise in the light of your fellow-writers' comments, and the need to revise in the light of your editor's views. A better, leaner book, however, will be the result.

Etiquette for writers

Five practical points about publishing: always send your best work; know the kind of work that a magazine or publishing house prefers and submit writing that suits that taste; do not send the same work to different magazines or publishers at the same time; enclose a stamped addressed envelope with sufficient postage to allow the return of your submission; and always send out several pieces of work, and keep these circulating, adding new work when you can and correcting old work when it gets returned, so that when one of them returns with a rejection note you can still retain some hope of acceptance. Remember that when a piece of work is rejected, it is the work that is being rejected and not you. Do not take it too personally; it happens to every writer. If an editor has given a reason for rejection, then follow up this advice and rewrite it.

You will come across as a tyro if you write to an editor, agent or publisher with a new version of a poem, or story, or book, which has not yet been accepted or rejected. You will provoke both the editor and yourself by revising work after it has been taken for publication, although again this depends on the nature of the relationship you have with your editor, and it depends on the nature and sympathies of your editor. Many poets revise their poems ceaselessly; good poetry editors recognise this, since many of them began as poets themselves. However, that does not mean they have to put up with it when time is so valuable. Many editors of literary fiction and nonfiction are themselves men and women who not only have a store of experience gained from editing many books, but also from editing in other fields such as the media. Some of them are writers, or people who are on the way to becoming writers.

Some have emerged from years of hard, thankless work editing within the small presses and small magazine scene. The graduates of that small press scene are graduates of one of the Universities of Life, of poetry usually. They bring a hard nose to writing and editing gained at cost, where money is tight or invisible. They will be impatient with negligence, and constant revising can look indecisive and negligent. The 'nose' they acquire for choosing good writing is coupled with a knack for knowing when a work is complete, and when a writer is bankable – do not reduce your value by hubris. You must learn not to be naive, or at least to master the pretence of experience. Demonstrate a writerly presence in the way you deal with the world as a person, as a serious writer-in-waiting.

The editor

A good editor is the angel of artistic conclusion and closure. At some point, all that discontinuous, necessarily messy, work on an artistic piece must finish, and the world must be let in. A good literary editor knows, probably as much by professional familiarity as by instinct, when your book is final, something you may never know without a great deal of experience. At some point a book reaches a place beyond which it can be spoiled by further revision, say by over-exacting retrenchment – cutting it too savagely so that its interior logic begins to stutter, or paring the language over-beautifully so that it becomes falsified and etiolated. The editor is the hand on your shoulder, and they have been there before. Although all writing is rewriting, there is a station reached in the writing process when you must be unburdened. Better that it is done to you at first than for you to drop the work too soon or too late. Become friends with an editor and watch their craft carefully and gainfully.

Creative writing and the publishing industry

Without the author, the literary industry would implode; its bustling world – publishers, agents, accountants, libel lawyers, departments of literature, reviewers – would suffer the equivalent of nuclear winter. Doris Lessing wrote, 'all this vast and proliferating edifice is because of this small, patronized, put-down and underpaid person': the writer. Most major publishing houses take literary decisions in the marketing and finance departments, making the editor a rare and marginal hero and the author a super-pliant creature. The work of editors falls largely now to the creative writing departments. You might argue that the literary industry has made itself even more dependent on authors. What has happened is that we now perform three jobs – writing, teaching, editing – where once we did one or, at most, two.

This is why some publishers and literary agencies help fund creative writing programmes. It offers them access to some of the best, new writers for a small investment. The proffered talk to students on how the industry works is well intentioned and generally useful, but it is also a camouflage under which talent scouts can move. They know that many of these students will have had their work expertly edited by serious writers, which means that much of the labour-intensive work is in the bag. Some of those writer-teachers may belong to the literary agency, or publish with that sponsoring publishing house, and will be able to make close comment on the talent and resilience of the student, and whether their character – watched and nurtured throughout the course of teaching – is that of a real writer who will produce further volumes of work from which the agent and publisher might profit.

Creative writing programmes tend to produce novelists and poets whose work can feel self-consciously *literary*. Some of them do very well for them-selves but, for many, it is unlikely their work will sell, however superb their writing. Publishers know that well-written creative nonfiction sells far better than literary fiction or poems (see Chapter Seven). The foremost magazines and journals publish vastly more creative nonfiction than they do fiction or poems. Even newspapers carry it. Creative nonfiction creates an audience through their curiosity about a subject, and then (so writers hope) carries that audience into other genres through their interest in the writer. Publishers track a commercial scent. They sign up new poets and novelists, capture their promise in one genre, turning it to other more lucrative ends by encouraging them to write creative nonfiction. All this may seem Machiavellian, but it is simply business. It is another circle for survival in a small world.

The saints of the small press

One of the ways you can learn the skill of what to choose to submit, and when to cease a book is, obviously, by active reading. However, this is probably too long a lesson, despite it being one of the central exhortations of this book.

A more active and rapid method is to become an editor: to choose and to improve the work of other writers. You do not need to apply for an editorship. In fact, such opportunities are few. Instead, many new writers gain pleasure and literary discrimination from setting up their own small presses and magazines, or becoming literary editors. You create a physical or virtual open space for new writing, using print or the internet.

Small presses are small worlds, but they are the lifeblood of new literature, and most major writers have participated in them, or even created them. They also create circles for survival, for not only does the instigating writer become their own publisher, they become the publisher of their allies and friends. One of the purposes is to create your audience, and to create the taste by which your own work is recognised, or that of your circle.

Virginia and Leonard Woolf ran the Hogarth Press from their home, publishing many of their friends and associates. T. S. Eliot edited the journal *Criterion* to bring the work of fellow Modernists, such as James Joyce and Wyndham Lewis, to an audience. Eliot published his own poetry and criticism there, and was acute enough to leaven the avant-garde with mainstream contributors whose work pleased the middlebrow aesthetic of his patron. In the previous decade, his friend the poet Ezra Pound had produced the magazine *Blast* as a rendezvous-in-print for modern writers; shock tactics and reputation blasting were part of its performance. Such magazines are flares sent up before a literary coup d'état. There is nothing vain or venal about this process. Publishing does not give much space to the new or difficult. Those ignored must make their own luck. If that requires fireworks and shock tactics, then so be it. Such enterprises become literary movements. With luck, they turn over the literary world. However, writers need not delude themselves. Small presses are necessary, but they are a rite of passage; and few writers choose to stay with them if they can gain a larger audience or higher profile by publishing elsewhere. Small presses are literature's virtuous poorhouses. When they become well funded, they risk making their writers complacent or insular – no readers: no distribution: no problem! Art for art's sake; at least my book exists. A world reduced to a perfect indivisibility: one writer, one reader; both the same person.

Running such a small press requires talent, willpower, judgement and a determination to perform thankless work. As Michael Schmidt, the editor of Carcanet Press in the United Kingdom, says in *Lives of the Poets*, 'Those [publishers] who specialize are poor and have been poor for centuries. Why? So that poets – a few of them – can prosper. Publishers get written out of the story . . . we are dogsbodies of the art: we edit, correct, scribe, typeset or key, print, bind, tout. Are we remembered?' (1999: 5). Half the trouble is that authors will abandon a press if they become commercially successful, even though commercial success is no measure, historically, of literary quality. However, editing can develop into a passion. Improving the work of others is a far more rapid form of 'writing' than writing: 'No passion in the world is equal to the passion to alter someone else's draft' – H. G. Wells. That process will teach you more in a year about writing and writers than staying outside the arena, and hoping against hope that your talent will be recognised and rewarded by those inside it.

Writing Game

SETTING UP A PUBLISHING HOUSE
Become the editor for your community of writers or class. Request contributions from anybody in any genre; offer amendments and constructive criticism; and then, using the simplest means possible, for example a website or a photocopier, produce their work as a book or magazine. Choose a title that means something to you and the group. Do not neglect to use some of your own work and write an editorial describing the aims of the book or magazine. Be sure to publicise the new enterprise as widely as you can, and invite known writers to contribute.

AIM: You will be surprised how this enterprise takes off, and contributions pour in. In the process, you will learn just how much bad writing is produced, not only by unknowns but also by known writers. Choosing, then casting, these various materials into shape will also teach you a great deal about editing and shaping your own work over the long distance of your first novel or collection of poems. Finding the finance to keep this enterprise going and maintaining a list of subscribers or advertisers will offer you a rapid apprenticeship in the business end of writing and publishing. It would also have the effect of making your own name better known in the literary field. However, your enterprise must aim for high quality if a good reputation is the desired outcome.

Recommended reading

The balance between the critical and creative is returning to the humanities slowly and surely, and interdisciplinarity assists this recalibration. Elaine Showalter's *Teaching Literature* (Blackwell, 2003) contains fascinating studies of the creative teaching of literature, and is positive about the role of creative writing in universities. When writing reflective critical essays, it is essential to offer critical context; to say what other writers think about the issues you have faced in creative writing. Literary biographies and autobiographies provide good material, as do some authors' websites and weblogs. The *Paris Review*

Interviews, downloadable at the journal's website, is the best resource for testimonies by writers, especially fiction and literary nonfiction writers, about their working practice and philosophy. There are other rich sources. Walter Allen's *Writers on Writing* (Dent, 1948) and Sean Burke's *Authorship: From Plato to the Postmodern* (Edinburgh University Press, 1995) are thematically organised anthologies of statements on writing made by mainly canonical authors. For statements of poetics as well as insightful accounts of the practice of poetry, read Clare Brown and Don Paterson's *Don't Ask Me What I Mean: Poets in their Own Words* (Picador, 2003) and W. N. Herbert and Matthew Hollis's *Strong Words: Modern Poets on Modern Poetry* (Bloodaxe Books, 2000). William Harmon's edition *Classic Writings on Poetry* (Columbia University Press, 2003) ranges in sources from Plato to Laura (Riding) Jackson. James Scully's *Modern Poets on Modern Poetry* (Fontana, 1966) collects statements about poetry 'as a "making" or strategy'. John Haffenden's *Viewpoints: Poets in Conversation* (Faber and Faber, 1981) offers useful interviews on praxis with poets such as Paul Muldoon, Geoffrey Hill and Seamus Heaney. The contributors to Anna Leahy's *Power and Identity in the Creative Writing Classroom* (Multilingual Matters, 2005) explore with academic vigour the pedagogical debates and challenges in teaching creative writing on both sides of the Atlantic. Lynn Freed's article 'Doing Time: My Years in the Creative Writing Gulag' in *Harper's Magazine* (July 2005) is a short but essential field-guide to the hazards of teaching writing. Two essays from Raymond Carver's *Fires* (Picador, 1986), 'On Writing' and 'John Gardner: The Writer as Teacher', are a generous corrective to those dangers, and a testimony to how creative writing lets in the world. That charity of spirit informs, once more, Frank Smith's analyses in *Writing and the Writer* (Heinemann, 1982) in which he offers a wonderful synthesis of the natural histories of language and writing in the world. *The Point: Where Teaching and Writing Intersect* (Teachers and Writers, collaborative 1983), edited by Nancy Shapiro and Ron Padgett, presents small and extremely persuasive essays about how a writer's teaching feeds the making of new work. Creative writing is often stimulated by going outside your experience and outside the arts. Read about the magic of the natural world in Nigel Calder's *Magic Universe* (Oxford University Press, 2003) and use some of the concepts as starting points for stories, poems or articles of nonfiction. Creative writing and freedom of expression finds its focus and champion in International PEN (www.internationalpen.org), the worldwide association of writers, with 141 centres in 99 countries. PEN exists to promote friendship and intellectual cooperation among writers everywhere, to fight for freedom of expression and represent the conscience of world literature. The situation in publishing is dynamic, but clear guidance can be found in *The Writer's Handbook*, which is published in national editions for many countries and updated annually. Another annual, *Writer's Market*, will help you decide where and how to submit your writing to appropriate markets in the United States and Canada. For writers of fiction, Carole Blake's *From Pitch to Publication* (Macmillan, 1999) is a bible on the subject of novel publishing and literary agencies, used as much by literary agents as it is by aspiring authors.

Chapter 3

Challenges of creative writing

> But for women, I thought, looking at the empty shelves, these difficulties were infinitely more formidable. In the first place, to have a room of her own, let alone a quiet room or a sound-proof room, was out of the question . . . The indifference of the world which Keats and Flaubert and other men of genius have found so hard to bear was in her case not indifference, but hostility. The world did not say to her as it said to them, Write if you choose; it makes no difference to me. The world said with a guffaw, Write? What's the good of writing?
>
> VIRGINIA WOOLF, 'A Room of One's Own' (NE2: 2181)

The major challenge to any writer is the work itself: getting the book written; making characters believable; allowing subject and form to work together; and creating verisimilitude. In this chapter, we look at some significant challenges – and opportunities – that we might be able to bend to the purpose of our writing, including cultural and social pressures, quality, translation, experiment, design and your own mind's workings.

Challenges to writers

The phrase 'enemies of promise' entered the language as the title of Cyril Connolly's (1961) compendium of circumstances that inhibit writing, and is very much of its time: self-centred, brimming with masculine concerns, and obeisant to elite literature. However, the book is thoughtful, even cunning: a white, upper-class forerunner of *Silences* (2003), Tillie Olsen's feminist study of the frozen opportunities for women writers, working-class and black authors. Although we can now give notice to Connolly's aversion to 'the pram in the hall' as an enemy to the sensitive male novelist, there are moments of illumination concerning the impacts on writers and writing of politics, conversation, drink, journalism and worldly success. Those moments have more to do with Connolly's real purpose: his precision and style rather than the subjects he assays. *Enemies of Promise* is biography in disguise – creative nonfiction. Olsen's *Silences* possesses similar self-purpose and resonance. Writing these books allowed their authors to send plumb lines into their own posterity and those of their friends and allies. Olsen's aim is to articulate liberation; Connolly trades in articulate desperation. In a sense, both works are reflective dissertations. As we discussed in Chapter Two, writing such prose might seem self-regarding, but it is often necessary as a means to define one's self-purpose and practice: to think yourself forwards into the kind of writer you want to become (or to cease to be the writer you have come to dislike). Like creative reading, this is one way to find allies to your own promise in yourself. You then find other allies, such as mentors, teachers of writing who are practising authors, your fellow student writers in workshops, and the circles for survival that grow around you as you edit and publish.

Indifference

The world's indifference to your writing is remedied by the corrective action of producing and publishing only your best writing, and even then nothing is guaranteed. Change the scale of what you expect; it is self-corrosive to play to such a big (unknowable) audience. Think locally in the hope of being prized so: small worlds link, making greater worlds. Your creative class is world enough to begin with. Try to answer *their* indifference for new writing. Trust to the notion that life is short and art is long, and then just keep practising.

Rival media

Some of the social and cultural constraints described by Virginia Woolf (see epigraph) may have loosened, but others have arisen to take their place, not least a popular view of literary writing as an art form that offers far less than film or digital media, in social and political terms, and even in imaginative experience and technical daring. To what extent do you, as a new writer, accept this as a challenge rather than a threat? Make an ally of film and digital media, by either creating fiction that becomes (but challenges) film, or writing that exploits and expands new technologies for its transmission. See the section 'Electronic performance' in Chapter Nine.

Sentimentality, or kitsch

The poet and critic Mary Kinzie has pointed out that it is difficult for new writers to recognise clichés of feeling in their writing such as:

the idea that spontaneous reactions are the most trustworthy; that problems should be shared; that trying is more important than succeeding; that everyone is a winner; that the old regret not being young; that the outward reflects the inward; that beauty is somehow 'correct'; that appetite is finally natural or healthy, and so forth.

(1999: 376–377)

Kinzie labels these lame notions as kitsch: 'suffused with sentimentality and linked to moral corruption'. She cites Nabokov's suggestion that such clichés of feeling are the basis for advertising. We could argue that they are also the bread and butter of Hollywood and Bollywood: that sentimentality is a risk worth taking sometimes. However, many writers pull against sentimentality and clichés of emotion, knowing that they lead to platitudinous expression.

Displacement activity

You provide the chief alibi for inaction: displacement activity. You do a thousand things to avoid writing: tidying up, rearranging the files on your computer. Think of it this way: only you can write your novels, poems and creative nonfiction. Hemingway believed, tough-mindedly, 'there are no alibis . . . You have to make it good and a man is a fool if he adds or takes hindrance after hindrance after hindrance to being a writer when that is what he cares about' (quoted in Phillips, 1984: 59). Even the gentle-minded Thoreau advocated focus: 'Write while the heat is in you. The writer who postpones the recording of his thoughts uses an iron which has cooled to burn a hole with. He cannot inflame the minds of his audience.' An annual literary prize in North America is given to a nominated writer to make them *stop* writing; to say, *for God's sake – enough*. If you have distractions, they are usually of your making. By allowing and even encouraging distraction, you award yourself your own prize for quitting.

Talking it away

New writers prevaricate when they should act and, worse, new writers develop a bad habit of 'talking away' their work, instead of writing it down. The creative reservoir inside you will dip as you talk about your ideas for stories, poems and articles. 'I have lost stories and many starts of novels . . . Telling, you see, is the same as a hiatus. It means you're not *doing* it' – Cynthia Ozick (Plimpton, 1989: 296). Writers can fail on the rocks of their own volubility and sociability. Conversation is expensive oxygen. Do not talk about your work beforehand; write it, do it. You will find you have many opportunities to talk about it afterwards; say, with your tutor during the revising process or should it become successful.

Criticism and journalism

There are dozens of displacement activities; talking and self-distraction are simply the most obvious. More insidious are those activities that simulate the act of creative writing but are actually its surrogates, such as writing criticism and reviews. These are fine for when you are fallow, or between projects, but they are disastrous forms of displacement when you are writing at full pitch. On the other hand, maintaining a daily weblog or diary are excellent exercises in concision and discipline, and provide a more enduring means for warming up your writing mind for the day. Take the craft and precision of creative writing to criticism and journalism and remake them as creative nonfiction.

Fantasy and perfectionism

Some writers do not fulfil their promise for a number of reasons, such as their addiction to a fantasy idea of themselves, spinning daydreams of success, while not comprehending that creative life involves exceptional levels of attention. A parallel enemy is perfectionism. Many creative writers strive for perfection in their work and working practice, but not enough of them achieve it. That is because they are *striving* rather than practising, and because *perfect* writing does not exist, only provisional versions that you revise until they have their own life. If your writing reached perfection, it would read as if it were dead. 'The essence of being human is that one does not seek perfection' – George Orwell.

Politics

'Politics is the enemy of the imagination' – Ian McEwan. Or is it? Politicians campaign in bad poetry and govern in worse prose. Writing is a campaign with no election and an invisible constituency. Party politics may traduce a writer's judgement, and clarity of language, although they make good material. Many writers are aspirant but unengaged politicians, whose political views are held together by a defensive solidarity and sentiment, uncomfortable with authority, power or management. Politics *outside* of an official party is a different animal: writing engages with politics by default. A writer's imaginative freedom can be a cause of envy or marginalisation (commercial success relieves them of that freedom). However, as Auden said, 'poetry makes nothing happen', and naive politics generally make for etiolated writing, or writing that has, as Keats said, 'a palpable design on the reader'. Literary politics, however, are like academic politics. They generate heat because the stakes are low and opportunities few. They also make for good copy.

Pagefright and word-blindedness

There are moments when new writers think they have writer's block. Part of this is a kind of pagefright, aversion to the empty stage of the page, incomprehension of their role in filling it and performing to an invisible audience. Try to overcome pagefright using some of the techniques in Chapters Four and Five; use the translation ideas in this chapter; or try the Writing Games in this book. Your allies are experience, practice, levity and bluff. Take the enterprise less seriously, or take the mask of a fluent author. A writer may also become word-blind. This happens when a fluent apprentice has produced a great deal of work in a short time and cannot read themselves as a writer; they are blind to that perspective. The way to recover is to stop writing, to print the manuscript and not look at it again for at least three weeks. After this period, it will seem sufficiently distant from your creative mental processes, as if it were the work of somebody else.

Out of depth

Feeling out of your depth is a common state of mind for many writers while writing, one of the reasons many of them find apparent certainties intolerable. Writing beyond your skill or experience is frightening and can make the creative process slow or even static. Either you may feel that you do not know enough about what you are writing, or the means for expression seem beyond your grasp. Research and playful invention will cure the first of these, while familiarity with difficulty is something to which you will gravitate. Working within the level of your skill or experience is a frictionless option, and you will end up riding in circles. Writing out of your depth allows you to locate and occupy further levels in your own character and your writing, making you keen for further advances into that abyss. The graphic novelist Alan Moore argues that you should risk everything by setting the level of every story higher than your last, throwing your talent, as it were, off a cliff with your stories: 'Apparent recklessness . . . will lend them an energy and unpredictability inaccessible by other means.' He likens the challenge of writing yourself out of the inevitable *Splat* to knitting oneself a helicopter while in freefall (Moore, 2005: 46).

Self-doubt

As Stephen King puts it, 'Writing fiction, especially a long work of fiction, can be a difficult, lonely job; it's like crossing the Atlantic Ocean in a bathtub. There's plenty of opportunity for self-doubt' (2000: 249). Self-doubt functions like self-censorship. What the poet Ted Hughes termed as our 'mental secret policemen' sometimes get the upper hand; they prevent us from proceeding or even believing in our ability. Writers who do not feel self-doubt occasionally are lying to themselves. It comes with the job, like perpetual dissatisfaction. You grow used to the sensation of freezing up when writing, of proceeding in fits of stops, starts, ease and block. You find times when it is not only the words that will not come; the arc of the *entire* piece disappears in your mind. When self-doubt strikes, you must proceed by nerve alone, and by stealth. This is a moment that is defined in action and boldness *by* your character, not only as a writer but as a person. No guts; no glory. Your only response, if you wish to continue, is to get used to its distress signal. You are not being held hostage by your work; this is *your* work; you command the situation. Choose to write with a colder eye, as if the task did not matter. The feelings of self-doubt will pass: it is an intense but small wave of panic, and does little harm if you do not let it. Self-Doubt's fiendish opposite, Overconfidence, should also be shown the door. As Annie Dillard says in *The Writing Life*, 'The feeling that the work is magnificent, and the feeling that it is abominable, are both mosquitoes to be repelled, ignored, or killed, but not indulged' (1989: 15).

Work–life balance

Perfection of the life or the art is not possible because, as E. M. Forster put it, life is a muddle. Writing out of the muddle may supply us with material – for autobiographical creative nonfiction, for example. Blaming life for shortfalls in our work is like blaming everybody we know for shortfalls in ourselves: irresponsible, morally indefensible. Yet many failed writers comfort themselves this way. What you do and what you say are your responsibility. Only you can write your poems and stories. Discipline in your working practice has to be reflected in discipline in your life, but without being autocratic about this with other people. Make the work–life balance work *and* live. One way is to be honest with yourself and those around you about what you want to do. Explain the demands on your time and your hopes for writing, then discuss and decide what is possible and achievable rather than what is impossible or idealistic. By setting yourself realistic (and even short-haul) objectives in writing, you stand a chance of carrying out many of them, without carving yourself a double disappointment of life and literature. You may even achieve some impossibility without knowing it. However, you must do what you have said, even if you do not succeed; otherwise you are not only letting yourself down but also tarnishing the goodwill of those around you.

Youth-envy

Too many new writers are transfixed by the matter of age versus achievement in literature, even to the point where it freezes their progress because they feel they have fallen behind their peers, or writers whom they revere. Publishers exploit youth as a selling point, but this has little connection with quality or achievement. This disabling condition arises partly from a cliché of feeling that writing is a young person's game and the brilliant among us perish early. It also arises partly from competitiveness. Sometimes, creative writing students study the birth date of their favourite authors, calculate their age at first publication, and then vie to match them. This is destructive, not least because you open yet another route to failure, and one that has nothing to do with finding your natural rhythms for writing. Naturally, you should tap your creative energy as early as you can, but this might be during your forties or fifties. It is never too late to begin writing seriously, and there is no virtue in being published young, or before you or (more importantly) your work are ready.

Age

As it is, some writers grow freer as they get older. No pagefright for them; no time for it. Edward Said believes the 'late style' of creative artists 'is what happens if art does not abdicate its rights in favour of reality' (2006: 9). Writing of the final poems of Cavafy, Said commends 'the artist's mature subjectivity, stripped of hubris and pomposity, unashamed either of its fallibility or of the modest assurance it has gained as a result of age and exile' (2006: 148). Mellowing – even literary mellowing – is thought of by some as virtuous, as is the damnation of 'geniality'. Both are manipulative legislations foisted by new writers on their elders to seize the game off them. For some writers, in fact, the incubation and gestation times for writing speed up with age, several books running through the cognitive assembly lines simultaneously. The apprenticeship is long over, yet they write with the ease of beginners. As Beckett wrote, 'Death has not required us to keep a day free.' Like form, awareness of mortality is no prison to creation. You write against it: *its* restriction.

Children

Nurturing your children is one of the deepest, toughest joys in life, but can feel at odds with writerly discipline – both are justifiably needy. While some of the workplaces of the real world have begun to look more closely and compassionately at the work–life balance, a writer is often constrained by the vagaries of being freelance. Women writers suffer in this respect particularly. There is only one way around this, and that is to evolve a routine of writing around child-care, exhausting though this will be at first; and to ensure that you take up, or demand, as much support for your writing time as is reasonable. Be meticulous and structured in creating a schedule. Ensure and assert that everybody understands that writing is your job, and that it is to be treated with the same respect as any other form of work. With this pressure, it is not the amount of time, but the *kind* of time: *how* you use it. As Seamus Heaney once said, 'The thing about writing is that, if you have the impulse, you will find the time.' Remember, too, that writers who choose not to be parents often find child-surrogates to explode their schedules – all things can tempt them. They may even view their *books* as if they were children, without realising the exactions of shelf life. Many writers with children write *for* them, and make them the first audience for linguistic play or stories. As children get older, be sure to help them to understand that writing is your work; and that it might be fun (and even educational) for them to try some of your tricks, too. Some writers, when they grow older, miss the regime of discipline created by their presence, questions and needs.

Writing Game

ENEMIES AND ALLIES

Make a list in your notebook of the factors that stop you writing: 'enemies of promise'. Make a second list of factors, such as circumstances, that help your writing: 'allies to promise'. Be ruthlessly honest. For example, you may hate deadlines, but if deadlines help you to write, then they should be in your second list. On a large sheet of paper, make a timetable of a typical week in your life, giving as much detail as possible. Using the first list, go through your weekly timetable and identify all the moments when any of your enemies of promise are active. Try to weigh the degree to which *you* control these moments, or these moments are controlled by external agencies (such as the kind of work you do). However, having identified the moments over which you have control, think of ways to remove these enemies from your weekly schedule. For example, if one of your enemies of promise is *time*, then think of ways in which you can increase the amount of time available to writing. Some writers, for example, rise early and attempt to get as much writing done before they go to work, or before their family wakes. Do you watch a lot of television? Cut down. Do you spend a lot of time talking about your work? Try silence. Do you suffer from pagefright? Try Writing Games. If one of your enemies is prevarication, cheat yourself into writing by resolving to carry out a Writing Game, some freewriting, writing in a set form, imitating or translating.

AIM: You will be astonished at how much time we waste through displacement activities and distraction. Create a new schedule that excludes self-made enemies of promise. Keep to this schedule. It will become natural and less of a pose (for pose is also an enemy of promise).

Challenges of translation

Many writers use translation as a means for taking an internal vacation from their own processes; to collect ideas and borrow verbal energy from other writers; and to pay homage to writers in other languages whom they admire. It is also an effective medicine for fallow periods in writing, say when you are between major projects. If you believe in writer's block, then translation is a part-cure, in that one writer leans on another to walk a line of words across a blank space of paper. All these reasons depend on the otherness of the process. This is *not* translation strictly; it is about taking the work of others and possessing it for yourself: otherness-translation.

What is lost in translation

For creative writers, translation shares the continent of writing. For a growing number of professional literary translators, it is another form of creative writing; after all, they own the process. Yet 'Poetry is what is lost in translation. It is also what is lost in interpretation' – Robert Frost. Writers have often seen interpretation as an enemy of creativity. However, Frost's famous remark says more about the nature of poetry than it does about the process of translation. As we have discussed, language is a shifting and evolving system. Some words are charged with particular meanings in their host language, but that does not entail their carrying those associations into another tongue.

Stealing across a spectrum

Meaning is one thing, but we cannot ignore the importance of sound in language; of cadence and voice; and, in poetry, of rhyme or a line's inner music.

Is there a perfect or perfecting way to carry such cargo from one country to another? – No. What is it that gets lost in translation? – Everything a writer values: the poetry of the author's inner ear, its intentions and intuitions. Are we even more ruthless than that? – Yes, even given our respect for the original, and for the host-writer we are parasitising.

That 'respect' glitters greenly across a spectrum of approaches. Some creative writers practise the adaptation of an original work by a dead author. However, some writers mix the colours in the palette of otherness-translation: adaptation → equivalence → version → imitation → variation → artistic theft → plagiarism. As creative writers, you work across this spectrum by exploring it, even exploiting it by going around it, although poetry lends itself more easily to this process than fictional prose. Some adopt the modes of parody or pastiche.

For some writers, the challenge can be one of possession, not fidelity. Some writers steal, without quoting their source. When done well, critics and readers consider it an act of homage; when done badly, they cry plagiarism. As Lion Feuchtwanger stated playfully in *Adaptations* (1924), some creative writers acknowledge the debt to the host-writer by putting the little word 'after' before the name of the host-writer. If the host is dead, you can be sure that all the flaws of the work will be attributed to the living writer and all its worth to the dead writer. To paraphrase Ngugi wa Thiong'o, translation moves beyond and around language. Many creative writers argue that all writing is translated in that it is 'translated' from silence, but it is also translated through a writer's prism of influences and artistic sympathies.

Variation's mirror

A writer may well be fluent in the language they are translating. More likely, they may acquire only enough of the language to translate the pieces to which they are drawn, or they may use a gloss – for example, the prose gloss of a poem, such as John D. Sinclair's exemplary 1939 translation and commentary of Dante's *The Divine Comedy*. Instead of faithfully translating the other language, the writer imitates the original to produce a version of it; plays variations upon it; or uses it to create starting points for a wholly independent piece of work. The final aim is to *own* it, and this is a writing exercise you should try for yourself. Your own writing gains by this use of translation. If artistic creation is a mirror to nature, then variation is a mirror on a mirror.

The work becomes that of a translated other, a melding of the two writers' creative minds. Important and controversial examples include Robert Lowell's *Imitations* (1961), energetic versions of European poets, a process of working that Lowell likened to moving 'into a new air' (Hamilton, 1982:

289); Ezra Pound's 'equivalences' of the Troubadour poets; and Don Paterson's fascinating spiritual portraits of Antonio Machado in *The Eyes*, a process of otherness-translation he writes of as having 'many dead friends you can talk to' (1999: 60). For an inventive creative writer, 'translation' must seem a type of literary super-oxygen, reviving as it does the dead from the cells of their words.

Some writers fake this process entirely, fabricating an original work and author and 'translating' them into their own tongue (an effective creative writing exercise). Sometimes the process is consciously fraudulent, although the result often possesses considerable compositional panache. Historically, the most famous and tragic illustration is the poet Thomas Chatterton, who committed suicide at the age of eighteen. He published a pseudo-archaic travelogue, a version of an 'original' which he claimed to have discovered in a chest in the church St Mary Redcliffe, Bristol. Chatterton then released poems that purported to be the work of an imaginary fifteenth-century monk and poet, Thomas Rowley. The shame is that Chatterton is remembered more as a figure of youthful misfortune than as an inventive imitative poet, a maker of 'translations from silence'. As Antonio Machado stated, 'In order to write poetry, you must first invent a poet who will write it.' Chatterton's inventiveness effaced itself completely. Be careful.

Writing Game

NOT TRANSLATION

Go to a library that holds some books of fiction or poetry in a language you do not know. Take out at least three books and choose poems or excerpts from stories. Read these aloud. 'Translate' one of them into your own tongue without any regard for the literal meaning of the original language at all.

AIM: This is translation's opposite, a deliberate raid on another writer's material in order to generate new work that otherwise would not come about but which might offer some interesting possibilities as you revise it. It is a raid on language. There will be more distance between the original text and your own than there would be were you imitating the voice of an author in your own tongue.

Challenges of experiment

Sometimes, the challenge to creative writing is not to make something final or assessable, but to make something *potential*, a kind of audition with language, or even a playful confection of words and letters – art for art's sake; play for play's sake. On the continent of writing, no citizens have as much fun as in the country where the OuLiPo live.

The OuLiPo

100,000,000,000,000 Poems consists of a sequence of ten fourteen-line sonnets by the French writer and former Surrealist Raymond Queneau (1961). Each sonnet has an identical rhyme scheme. In the original edition, the sonnets are printed on the recto (right) side of each page, and the lines cut into fourteen strips. If a reader lifts one strip of line on any of the pages, except the last, a completely new sonnet is revealed. If a reader lifts more strips (more lines!) then different sonnets continue to be revealed, and so on in many millions of permutations. Thus the title: *1,00,000,000,000,000 Poems*. The author calculated that someone reading the book twenty-four hours a day would require 190,258,751 years to complete it. They would also need to keep a careful note of the combinations along the way, and obviously be enthusiastic about the book. Queneau's poem gave birth to an idea.

As war is the continuation of diplomacy by other means, so the OuLiPo is the continuation – by *other means* – of literature. Writers, mathematicians and academics founded the OuLiPo or Ouvroir de littérature potentielle (Workshop for Potential Literature) in 1960. Subsequent membership is by election, but that need not stop you from trying out their techniques, or inventing some of your own.

Their purpose was to find out how abstract restrictions combine with imaginative writing. They advocated the use of severe, self-imposed limitations during the act of creation. As Queneau put it, they are as 'rats who construct the labyrinth from which they propose to escape'. Two of its most famous members are Italo Calvino and Georges Perec (who wrote an entire novel without using the letter 'e'). Still formidably active, the OuLiPo is now recognised as one of the most original, productive and provocative literary enterprises to appear in the past century.

They spawned related groups such as the OuLiPopo (potential detective fiction), with their array of methods for inventing and solving crimes; the Oupeinpo (potential painting); and the Oubapo (potential comic strips), devoted to finding new ways to combine drawing with text. All these groups have their rites: annual dinners, outrageous minutes of meetings, bizarre rules and manifestos and mind-bending techniques. However, their purposes are generous, despite closed membership. They seek to expand the variety of what literature *might* do, rather than dictate what it cannot do or should do. They are a positive, enlivening presence in the discipline of creative writing, and students and new writers are urged towards The *OuLiPo Compendium* (1998), edited by Harry Matthews and Alastair Brotchie.

Exercises in style

One of the best places for new fiction writers to start is Queneau's tale *Exercises in Style* (1947). On a crowded bus at midday, the author observes one man accusing another of jostling him deliberately. When a seat is vacated, the first man appropriates it. Later, in another part of town, the author sees the man being advised by a friend to sew another button on his coat. That is all there is to it – except that Queneau retells this unexceptional tale ninety-nine times, employing the sonnet and the Alexandrine, 'Ze Ffrench' and 'Cockney'. An 'Abusive' chapter heartily deplores the events; 'Opera English' lends them grandeur. It is a tour de force in stylistic demonstration, and teaches even as it pleases.

The playfulness of OuLiPo behaviour and ideas can be liberating, especially in a generative fiction or poetry workshop. There is nothing especially new about the practice of 'restriction being liberation'. Certainly, in ancient poetry, as in mathematics, the art of numbers was the art of everything. It is a reformalisation of a practice whose roots lie in rhetorical and compositional challenges that medieval teachers set for themselves and for their students, as we saw in Chapter One. It echoes the tight technical work of the troubadours, as well as the games with form played by Elizabethan Court poets, and even highly popular Victorian parlour 'word games' enjoyed in the world before television and cinema.

An Oulipean Sunday school exercise

One of the more straightforward exercises for you to try (to gain an idea of what OuLiPo can offer you) is 'N + 7' or 'NOUN + 7'. Take a pre-existing creative work, or one of your own. Read through the piece (it can be fiction, creative nonfiction or poetry) and note the position of all the nouns. Look up these nouns in a dictionary one by one, and then count forwards in the dictionary by seven nouns (not seven words) for every one. For example, taking the first stanza of John Keats' famous ode (NE2: 872):

> **To Autumn**
> Season of mists and mellow fruitfulness!
>   Close bosom friend of the maturing sun;
> Conspiring with him how to load and bless
>   With fruit the vines that round the thatch-eves run;

To bend with apples the moss'd cottage trees,
And fill all fruit with ripeness to the core;
To swell the gourd, and plump the hazel shells
    With a sweet kernel; to set budding more,
And still more, later flowers for the bees,
Until they think warm days will never cease,
    For Summer has o'er-brimm'd their clammy cells.

Using a school dictionary, I counted forward seven nouns from the word 'season' and reached the word 'sea-wall'. Every single noun is swapped by the serendipitous new word; a quite different 'potential poem' develops:

To Aviation
Sea-wall of mistresses and mellow fruitfulness!
    Close bother fringe of the maturing Sunday-school;
Conspiring with him how to load and bless
    With frustration the vintners that round the theatres run;
To bend with appointments the moss'd cotton trench,
And fill all frustration with rip-tide to the cork;
To swell the governess, and plump the headache shelters
    With a sweet ketchup; to set budding more,
And still more, later fluids for the beggars,
Until they think warm deaconesses will never cease,
    For summons has o'er-brimm'd their clammy cellulite.

The point is not to produce a new and great work of literature, nor is the purpose to subject existing work to ridicule. The point is *to play*, and to yield fresh ideas and connections. The approach is clever and charming, but it is not an ideology as some followers think; it is the opposite. The OuLiPo create thought-experiments out of a scrabble of letters and language. Nothing might come of it, but the potential is there, as in scientific and thought-experiment. One might do worse, for example, than write a poem that takes as its starting point 'headache shelters'; or to write a short story that unfolds the reasons why the vintners are frustrated and why they might be running around a theatre, who is bent with appointments and why the governess is pregnant.

Writing Game

EXERCISES IN STYLE
Write a short story of no more than a hundred words. It must be as mundane as possible. Rewrite this story ten times over using different styles or points of view. Here is a selection of styles from which to choose:

opera libretto	vehicle manual
soap opera	insincere self-therapy book
bullet-point list	political broadcast
passive tense	nihilist suicide note
phrasebook translation	end-of-dinner speech
news report	post-modern novel
comedy	a series of haiku
abstract language	confessional TV chat show
concrete poem	scientific paper
minutes of meeting	memo
romantic novel	impenetrable critical prose
sonnet	free verse
erotic novel	sensationalist
permutations by groups of 1, 2, 3 and 4 words	enigmatic

AIM: All writing is rewriting to some degree and this game is a humorous means for student writers to do the equivalent of practising the scales of their voice, as well as fitting a body of words within a 'form' of style or a form of poetry.

The challenge of design

The composer Igor Stravinsky claimed, 'Whatever diminishes constraint diminishes strength. The more constraints one imposes, the more one frees one's self of the chains that shackle the spirit.' We design our writing by the use of form, of formal patterns and devices, and by various patterning, shaping and restrictive devices. For brevity, we subsume all these designing and restricting acts under the heading of form. The challenge to new creative writers is that form is there to be used by you with imagination and wit; you should not be used by form.

Restrictive liberation

Form is a powerful tool insofar as it can teach you how to break with it, or bend it, once you have mastered it, but you master it first. Form in fiction, for example, may be used interchangeably with genre, and novelists use many formal devices to shape a narrative, or allow a narrative to be shaped. Any repeated element lends prose fiction a sense of pattern that is itself an aspect of form. Do not forget that form itself *is* fiction.

A paragraph's design, or the design of a poetic line, should suggest possibility, not cast-iron certainty – even though the structure may be as involuted as the genetic design of a rose, or eye. Form provides a pattern or shape for prose fiction or poems, but is usually most effective when it is the least obvious. So: form must seem inevitable. In stories and poems, form must also be near-invisible, a presence in dialogue with the writing. A work of fiction or a poem must not be completely driven into being by its desired form. A self-conscious creative writer can sometimes over-emphasise their formal ability so that what the reader sees and hears is 'all pattern'. If you follow this path, you risk becoming a skilful technician whose work suffers through efficiency or technical exhibitionism.

Using form to design fiction or poems is often emancipating for new writers who find it hard to *surprise* themselves in their writing, but, when faced by the mathematical scaffolding of an exercise in style, or a sestina or pantoum, find themselves in the mental position of problem-solvers rather than what they consider a special mind-set that artists possess. They begin to understand that problem-solving and 'designing language' has much more in common with artistic creation than the popular image of the artist suggests. Form is a useful tool of itself, since restriction lends itself to liberating new ways of saying. Form liberates imagination in fiction as much as poetry.

Restriction in poetry and fiction: two examples

The Welsh poet Dylan Thomas's public image in the twentieth century was that of a mage of inspired art, a bardic image fostered by his admirers and reinforced by the highly rhetorical manner in which he performed his poems. Yet, when Thomas sat down to write in his boathouse in Laugharne, he soberly lined up a list of rhyming words (with alternatives) along the right-hand side of a page and, having created the exoskeleton of his poem, he filled the gaps in this design and revised them until they came right. He designed and calculated poems until they sounded like natural songs of the earth, possessing inevitability. The rhymes were usually separated from each other by several intervening lines, so seldom appeared obvious or forced.

Similarly, in the novel *X20* by Richard Beard (1996), the writer has the protagonist smoke twenty cigarettes in the first chapter; nineteen in the next; and so on until we reach the twentieth and final chapter in which one cigarette is smoked (part of the narrative concerns giving up smoking). Each cigarette is a vertebra making up the spine of the novel. However, like Thomas's rhyme schemes, the reader does not notice these subtractions and additions, since so much shaped language stands between the mathematics and the reader's alert eye. The restrictions are woven *into* the narrative or poem, even though they acted as orders, props and pistons to move the writer forward and upwards while they shaped the superstructure. Inspiration does not exist; calculation and design bring more reward. Like scaffolding, these restrictions can even be removed at the end once the superstructure of the novel or poem has been built. It is why form has been sweetly termed 'the necessary nothing' (Boisseau and Wallace, 2004: 27).

Form's game

Robert Frost remarked, 'Making little poems encourages a man to see there is shapeliness in the world. A poem is an arrest of disorder.' The same goes for stories. He also famously wrote that writing free verse was like 'playing tennis with the net down'. Form can be seen as a game of shaping. John Redmond suggests that 'the position is analogous to that of someone who is designing a game, while the reader's position is analogous to that of someone who is playing or watching the game' (2006: 9). Not so long ago, people used to play poetic forms while harvesting. To this day, serious and lively competitions of performance based on the command of traditional Welsh metres take place at annual eisteddfods around Wales.

Form provides a creative writer with simulation exercises, giving them a series of objectives and rules, such as rhyme scheme, metre and repetition. Such game-play can offer practice, but it also readies you for the times when you might write something more apparently immediate. Writing to a restriction coerces you to create ways of saying things that would have not have occurred to you if you were left to your own netless game-plan. It can make you write better than you think you can, make you a better player at the art, and you will end up by astonishing yourself when you are *driven* to write something unexpected. Novelists use similar devices, and the Oulipeans provide them with rich resources to plunder.

Form is also elemental; it is a wholly human and social invention. For example, poetry's origin is oral; its presence today is still partly oral. Storytelling as an oral form is at the root of fiction. Form came into being in order to make the conduction of a poem or story easier by making it more memorable to the ear. It is easier to memorise sentences that use repetitive devices and reprises as in storytelling; or sentences that are in metre, that have a certain step and dance to them, and rhyme is a means to jog the memory for what line comes next. Rhyme and rhythm are mnemonic devices. Form has therefore performed a strong function in helping literature's survival and adaptation within cultural natural selection.

Form is fundamental to the way we grow to perceive the world of language. The baby in the cot may learn new words by listening to a nursery rhyme, but the real delight lies in the way it is said: the pattern, the repetition, the rhythm, the rhymes, the metre – the form. It creates language's music in their head, a dance of language. Writers are composers: many begin writing a poem or story because the music of it occurs to them first, and demands that words be written to fit that noise. This is a wholly natural process, as straightforward as making up songs or even jokes. Jokes, too, have form and music: the setup, the punch line, its taut rhythm pulling you in.

Against design

Form has its detractors. Some creative writers, especially those new to writing, view form as artificial rather than elemental, human and organic. They view the arts of poetry and fiction as fields for uncontrolled expression. They have forgotten their childhood pleasure in the naturalness of rhythm and repetition, and overlooked the fact that language is a plastic material to be played with. For example, such writers are drawn like wasps to sugar to the word 'free' in the term 'free verse' without understanding its origin, or that the best free verse gains power from its dialogue with form.

They create poems and stories that are as disordered as they are egotistical, and think this free spirited behaviour. The idea that such low-wattage prose and poetry might work better were it 'designed' better does not occur to them, or if it did they might find such a notion both traditional and boring. Their work is on the far end of a spectrum from those highly competent versifiers whose work is all patterns. However, their extreme positions and practices have more in common than they might wish to acknowledge. The discipline of creative writing takes this challenge head-on.

Those who reject form sometimes label its advocates as reactionary. However, the rejectionists' approach privileges the individualistic and indolent over technique and work. It also tends to promote overbearing emotion (the insistent sobriety of which evinces its insincerity) above human playfulness and inventiveness. A creative writing student's reaction against formal writing might simply result from an allergy to the word 'formal', in favour of the affirmative antonym 'informal'.

In the end, the decision to use form is down to you. Think about it carefully: we tend, as people, to prefer the work of craftspeople and strong designers when we are choosing our furniture, music, cars, films, paintings, clothes, buildings or computers. The challenge to creative writing is no different: it needs to be well made to be desirable, even when it is *apparently* without form.

The challenge of quality

Perception and reception

Some creative writing students find it difficult to know how 'good' or 'bad' their writing is. The dynamics of workshops, whether in the academy or community, are more used to lending themselves to enablement than discouragement. As I have argued, there is no easy answer to this apart from rigour, and making the right kind of structures so that positive versions of creativity can grow, while also being examined through a critical lens. No doubt, the learning process in any discipline is a pathway littered with good intentions. However, there are times when the writing that is produced in these situations is *exceptional* in quality, but the fact that it has been achieved through the discipline of workshops means that it is not treated, critically, in the same way as it would be had it arisen *ex nihilo*. This is a challenge to our prejudice as much as it is a challenge to our critical generosity.

The media often denigrate fiction that has come about through studying for an MFA or MA degree. Partly, this is because the media promulgate a romanticised view of writing and writers, but also partly because they distrust academia. Journalists prefer writers to be born not made, to be versions of the noble savage rather than the savant. The terms of critical reception are therefore twisted within a double bind of preconceived expectations. The public are asked to share these prejudices, despite the very high quality of some graduates of creative writing. As a result, some writers learn to conceal their qualifications and training, pretending to a different, more streetwise, apprenticeship.

Literary reputations glow and fade under public light. Sometimes it is a matter of waiting for your writing to find its time. Your audience will not wait for that time; you must create the audience first, and then wait. Some reputations are gained honestly through attentive apprenticeship, and some by ingenious or mendacious marketing. It is difficult for some students of creative writing to read the work by certain critically acclaimed authors through the lens of apprenticeship or time. Often what is praised to the sky seems to them pedestrian, stale or clumsy. This is not because these students are arrogant or too clever by half; it is because they have become critically alert by reading *as* writers. Literary quality, for them, has become the goal of their life, and they are naturally astonished when they find that this goal is not shared by everybody in the profession, and certainly not by the publishing industry, for whom the bottom line is profit.

An exercise in perspective is to take the works of renowned contemporary writers, and have the students type some of their works word for word: whole stories, poems and creative nonfiction. Typing another writer's published works is like reading it aloud: it is a sure-fire test of its qualities or lack of them. As John Ruskin said, 'All books are divisible into two classes: the books of the hour, and the books of all time.' The wonderland worlds of literary reception and perception are important to understand. There are fogs and false lights. A poem or story written in a workshop, and sent to a distinguished literary journal, is more likely to be accepted, however good or clumsy it might be, if it bears the name of a well-known practitioner. Thus it is, thus it has always been. The magazine will sell more copies with a famous name than a nobody from nowhere.

One of the ways to lift quality within a creative writing course is to lift the level of expectation in reception. Writing a poem, story or investigative article, and knowing it is being written to be marked as part of a course, is not an *intense* inducement for writing out of your skin. However, if you attach publication to such a course, the level of expectation increases. If you, in fact, were to offer a new, young writer a contract with a major publishing house, it is possible that they would find themselves writing *up* to that higher level out of the sheer desire to impress, or a fear to fail at that one shot at fame. Therefore, the creation of publishing opportunities around such courses should be encouraged, so long as they do not subsequently develop into closed shops, whose output is limited solely to creative writing students and their teachers.

Writing Game

RAISING YOUR GAME, AND RAISING THE DEAD

This is a group game, requiring role play. The workshop leader becomes Time personified: a maker and breaker of writers. 'Deaths of the author' occur. All students must forego copyright on their work during the game. (1) Everybody in the group carries out free-writing over a strict period of ten minutes. Each piece of writing is then 'damaged' in some way: ripped, burned, stamped upon or spattered with stage blood. It must be barely legible. The workshop leader as Time should be responsible for most of this damage, for this is what Time does to most creative writing. (2) Write the letter 'A' on the back of this burned or damaged page. Each piece of writing is passed to the person on their right. (3) The workshop leader must convince the group of two things: first, it is twenty years ago; and second, they are somebody else. Everybody in the group assumes the persona of *an archival scholar*, whose task is to reconstruct the piece of writing (piece 'A'). All that the scholar knows is that an author in another language who is now dead, and who died in tragic circumstances, wrote it sixty years ago. With this information, each student rewrites the piece as completely as they can, and using that information to flesh out any missing or damaged detail.

(4) Write the letter 'B' on the back of this new page. Pages A and B are passed to the person on their right. (5) Time disposes of the archival scholars, and replaces them with the personae of *minor writers*, working in the present day. Members of the group take on this persona, and have in front of them a piece of writing they have discovered within the archives of their local library. The minor writer decides to take this interesting artefact and write an imitation of it in his or her own contemporary tongue. (6) With this information, each student rewrites the piece completely, adding and subtracting at will, even reversing the piece. Please try any trick in this book to make this piece of writing your own. (7) Write the letter 'C' on the back of this new work. Each piece of writing (A, B and C) is passed to the person on their right. (8) The workshop leader receives a phone call from a major newspaper, and passes the following news to the group. They have all been awarded the Nobel Prize for Literature and must travel to Stockholm to receive it tomorrow. The newspaper wishes to print a new short piece of writing. They want to print what they are writing today. (9) Time disposes of the minor writers, and replaces them with the personae of Nobel Laureates, working in twenty years' time. Members of the group take on this persona, and have in front of them a piece of writing, by a minor writer, which they are going to pass off as their own for the sake of the newspaper's deadline. Obviously, it must be rewritten skilfully in order to cover the Laureate's tracks. (10) The students rewrite the piece to the best of their powers, writing up to the expectation of a Nobel Prize and a major newspaper publication. (11) Write 'D' on the reverse of this sheet. (12) Time disposes of the Laureates, and you are now *yourselves* again, whoever they are. This piece of writing is the final product, and is your own.

AIM: This game works on three levels simultaneously: raising the quality of writing because of an increase in expectations; altering the terms of reception so that writing is seen as a cultural object sliding through the dynamics of time; and getting to grips with the spectrum that includes translation, imitation, variation and literary theft. (1) If you raise the level of self-expectation and audience-expectation, it is possible that new writers find themselves writing *up* to a new higher level of quality. The psychological confidence this playacting brings is often enough to help you make breakthroughs, and locate more voices in yourself. (2) Look at the whole process in terms of the perception and reception of literary work. The way in which we view somebody's writing can be affected by our view of the author, and this viewpoint may include all manner of matters, such as the circumstances in which they wrote, how old they were, and any details we know about their lives. (3) All writing is an act of translation, between authors, across time, and between author and readers. You might use the lessons embedded in this game to carry out exercises in imitation, the aim of which is to produce new work of your own. I have carried out another version of this game that has a twist at the end: the original author is discovered alive and well, and visits the Nobel Laureate. The students rewrite the piece better to reflect its origin as an adaptation, and script a short story describing the fictional meeting.

Assessing creative writing

Creative writing students as well as academic staff often ask the question as to how to assess creative writing, and how assessors arrive at a grade. After all, what grade would one give to *The Divine Comedy* or *Middlemarch*? Most teachers of writing would attest that it is a matter of experience and wide reading, and that we – as students, readers, writers and critics – 'grade' creative writing every day in the act of reading and the acts of criticism or writing reviews. Even as we talk about books and authors in our classes and in our daily lives, we place a metaphorical 'score' against our experience of reading, comparing it with the writer's previous work or with the works of other authors.

Grades are metaphors for the progress a writer has made both of them-selves, and in comparison to the others *in the class*. Usually, two or three tutors, who look at the work independently, carry out this grading. Context is important, and the context of a classroom is the people inside it, a group of student writers – not a group of student writers plus, say, the ghost of Goethe. As we discussed in the section 'Reflective criticism' in Chapter Two, many writing courses are assessed by a portfolio of creative writing and an essay or commen-tary on the aims and processes involved in writing. Some modules also carry examination. Essays and examination materials tend to be assessed using the same criteria as for an expository essay. When designing a course, the tutor usually starts with the parameters of assessment, and then works backwards to the syllabus of the course: the exercises that will be set and the texts that will be read. Assessment is so important that it takes first place in the process of course-creation. If a course does not carry formal assessment, you can be sure there will be an eagerness in the group to find some other way of measuring progress, and validating effort, such as publications or readings.

The writer Celia Hunt argues thoughtfully that if students work through difficult, emotionally sensitive matters in their writing, then assessment should consider this personal dimension. She contends that creative writing is judged mostly by literary criteria, and these criteria may fit the critical mind but are not always sympathetic to emotional and personal matters (Hunt, 2001). She opts, in the early stages of the programme of study, to assess only reflective papers and learning diaries, and not the creative work. It is true that creative writing has traditionally been seen as individual and subjective. The academic world has been happy to teach methods of critical approach to established works and to assess the student's critical responses. The trained critic has been reluctant to judge creative works 'in process' and reluctant to define the criteria by which student performance in learning to write may be judged. However, wide varieties of assessment methods are used now within creative writing modules.

These include the setting and assessment of creative writing exercises, reflective critiques, logbooks, diaries, journals, community and work placements and performances. More emphasis is placed on the importance of drafting original writing, and student logbooks and records of how and why they have changed their creative work are regarded as important aspects of the learning process. In the end, the answer to how creative writing is graded is: it is graded out of a hundred, but how that grade is arrived at may also depend on the context in which it was written.

Recommended reading

Tillie Olsen's *Silences* (The Feminist Press, 2003) was first published in 1978, and revolutionised literary studies. It inspired an explosion of new creative voices, especially women, black authors and working-class writers. Her book identified many of the social and cultural challenges to the writing process and, like Virginia Woolf's 'A Room of One's Own' (NE2: 2153–2214), is invaluable reading about the circumstances that make writing possible (or impossible). Cyril Connolly's *Enemies of Promise* (Penguin, 1961) is delightfully of its time in its analysis of the 'characteristics of the Clever Young Men and their Dirty Deeds', but it offers a fascinating historical picture of the pressures on some of the major writers of the early twentieth century. All three of the above will prove useful in thinking critically about your own writing. They are also interesting for thinking about standards and quality of writing. How free is a creative writer to make something new out of another writer's work in another language? Issues of translation and imitation are a minefield, but one you should be brave about exploring. Reuben Brower's *Mirror on Mirror: Translation Imitation Parody* (Harvard University Press, 1975) is a starting point for some of the theoretical and philosophical issues involved. A further crucible for many creative writers has been John D. Sinclair's English prose renderings of Dante's *The Divine Comedy* (Oxford University Press, 1961), with its Italian text and Sinclair's commentary. Think about ways you might use such a prose gloss as a means to create a formal poetic version of excerpts from the poem, or new poetry or even fiction that imitates or takes the language of the gloss as a starting point. Although out of print, an exemplary text for poetry in translation (with prose gloss and original) is *The Poem Itself* edited by Stanley Burnshaw (Penguin, 1960). If this area of creative writing interests you, then consider learning another language. For those of you beguiled by the possibilities of potential literature and the OuLiPo, read and exploit *The OuLiPo Compendium* (Atlas, 1998), edited by Harry Matthews and Alastair Brotchie. To gain a bigger picture of the issues and debates concerning literary design and writerly calculation, fiction writers should turn to the excellent *Narrative Design: A Writer's Guide to Structure* (Norton, 1997), which has the benefit of being written from a novelist's insider point of view by Madison Smartt Bell. Bell uses examples of student writing from his creative writing classes to illustrate key points of narrative design. H. Porter Abbott's *The Cambridge Introduction to Narrative* (Cambridge University Press, 2002) artfully examines designs of narrative in literature (and usefully in film and drama).

Chapter 4

Composition and creative writing

Whether it is right or advisable to create beings like Heathcliff, I do not
know: I scarcely think it is. But this I know: the writer who possesses the
creative gift owns something of which he is not always master –
something that, at times, strangely wills and works for itself. He may lay
down rules and devise principles, and to rules and principles it will
perhaps for years lie in subjection; and then, haply without any warning
of revolt, there comes a time when it will no longer consent to 'harrow
the valleys, or be bound with a band in the furrow' – when it 'laughs at
the multitude of the city, and regards not the crying of the driver' –
when, refusing absolutely to make ropes out of sea-sand any longer, it
sets to work on statue-hewing . . . As for you – the nominal artist – your
share in it has been to work passively under dictates you neither
delivered nor could question – that would not be uttered at your prayer,
nor suppressed nor changed at your caprice. If the result be attractive,
the World will praise you; if it be repulsive, the same World will blame
you, who almost as little deserve blame.

CHARLOTTE BRONTË, editorial preface to *Emily Brontë,*
Wuthering Heights (1847)

We have seen how the composition of fiction, poetry and creative nonfiction
is mostly a matter of reading and practice. However, there are many ways of
building on the open space of writing and working beyond your intelligence.

Habits of mind, principles of practice

I said at the beginning of this book that you must learn to trust your own
judgement. There are few true rules for a writer, except the rules that writers
set for themselves but, for new writers, there is a responsibility to give them some
guidance, even if they reject it. I suggest here broad brush strokes of practical
judgement that unite not only many teachers of writing but also many writers.

Most of these notions emerge through their everyday practice, through feeling and instinct, and by failure.

Parallels of practice

Despite the fact that writers, as a mark of their office, tend to be determinedly *not* of the same mind, it is surprising that so many of them agree on a few principles when they are writing *about* the act of writing, or when they are engaged in criticism of fellow authors. There is an intriguing side to this: an artist who writes criticism, about their own practice or someone else's, ends up telling you more about what they themselves are up to, or what they aspire to achieve in their own art form. It is further intriguing that when we then look for parallels of artistic intention and practice we find them in some quantity.

Practicalities that hold in part for poetry often hold in part for fiction, and poets can learn much from writers of nonfiction as they can from makers of fiction, and vice versa. Of course, those genres make their own precise, creative and technical demands. However, it is important to know the overlaps, not least so you do not typecast yourself prematurely as the practitioner of one genre. All genres flow into each other – water and water, not oil on water. A luminous poem and a short story share concisions and economies of scale. Many poets go on to write novels and creative nonfiction, and bring precisions to prose. Some novelists write nonfiction, and bring narrative to fact. There are creative writers who practise several genres.

Writers may espouse legislations on artistic practice only to have the mischievous pleasure of debunking them later through the action of antithetical writing; through the creation of anti-narrative; or the making of their own species of anti-literature. The world of painting passes similar laws only to expose them. The rationalism and humanism of Dürer's age cultivated detailed rules for the geometry of human proportion. Michelangelo unravelled them with his dictum that an artist must possess 'compasses in his eyes rather than in his hands'. Felicity of execution, not rule, became the *new* rule. Every age devises its own sheet of law, and has it torn by the next, for writers can be very anxious about the influence of their forebears.

Life makes lawmakers of us all, but invention and reinvention require lawbreakers and law-remakers. For every so-called tenet selected below, I can think of an equally robust anti-tenet. We could name remarkable passages of fiction, nonfiction and poetry within which economy is *not* all; for which clarity is a *secondary* consideration; and where adjectives, clichés, adverbs, archaisms, abstractions and inversions achieve harmonic virtue. My point would be that such writers were not guilty of malpractice. They knew what they were choosing to ignore, and they composed with such panache of style that they defied their own inherited legislations, evaded their own mental secret police and censors. However, you have to know what you are doing first. You earn panache; you learn style. You can only break laws by knowing them. As John Gardner argues, 'Every true work of art . . . must be judged primarily, though not exclusively, by its own laws. If it has no laws, or its laws are incoherent, it fails – usually – on that basis' (1983: 3). An artistic legislation is to some degree an oxymoron. They are very much of their time, as was the poet Shelley's legislative reliance on inspiration in his *A Defence of Poetry*.

So, my hand is not on my heart in gathering, nor should your heart be in your mouth, since there are few surprises. Ezra Pound said of literary rules in his *ABC of Reading* (1960), 'the ignorant of one generation set out to make laws, and gullible children next try to obey them'. By repeating this, I am not shooting down these flags before raising them. I am asking you to keep an open mind. You will begin to see quickly, however, just how many of these statements are about how *not* to write, or they concern habits of mind or of practice that you might wish to acquire in order to accelerate your apprenticeship.

- In the Writing Game, we are all beginners.
- For new writers, making it work might be more revolutionary an objective than making it new.
- Clarity is hard-won, and of first importance.
- Economy is all.
- Style, above all else, is your aim, and it should show no sign of effort.
- Energy, in language, is eternal delight.
- All writing is rewriting.
- The best writing is honest.
- The best writing conveys truth, although it may not be the truth.
- Like a second chance at life, a writer writes to improve on the truth, or upon *their* truth.
- Defamiliarise the world, to make us see things afresh, as if for the first time.
- Only by writing for yourself can you hope to please an audience beyond yourself.
- Inspiration does not exist; calculation and design bring more reward.
- An early interest in language is a mark that a person might have a talent for writing.
- Writing must appear inevitable, 'as easily as leaves to a tree'. Even if those leaves took years to grow or to make, art conceals Art.
- Reading will make you a better writer, but reading-as-a-writer will make you even more fluent in style, teaching you technique and building your vocabulary.

- Imitation and influence are not anxieties; they are your early allies. Be open to influence and ready even to steal from other writers.
- The more you practise writing, the more likely you are to improve and find new possibilities.
- Write often; write when you can by any means necessary; and conduct this practice with as much ruthlessness and tenacity as your circumstances and character will permit.
- Writers are born and made.
- Natural talents, and your ability to learn, play a strong role, but your own character and stamina will determine whether you endure as a writer.
- Showing is more effective than telling, certainly among newer writers.
- 'Writing what you know' is a necessary step.
- 'Writing what you don't know' might later hold as much potential as 'writing what you know'.
- 'Finding your voice' might be only one stage on the way to finding your voices, or finding your style.
- Your writing voice must be distinctive; it must be differentiated from its precursors or your reader will stop listening.
- Form is a useful tool of itself, since restriction lends itself to liberating new ways of saying.
- Form is a useful tool in so far as it can teach you how to break with it, or bend it, once you have mastered it, but you must master it first.
- Striking phrases contaminate with their beauty; you should excise them.
- Adjectives and adverbs are the first to feel the spotlight of redrafting.
- Clichés, archaisms and inversions must earn their place or be burned off the page.
- Any word or phrase that distracts the attention of the reader from the book is redundant.
- Concrete language usually has more resonance for the general reader than abstract language.
- Audiences do not wait; you must create them.
- Know your audience; bore an audience and you will lose it.
- Whom you know, can help you – but not forever.
- Writing is one of the most joyful and playful activities for the human mind and body. It is as physical as it is psychological, and the real rewards of writing lie within the process of writing, not in publishing.
- You will learn more about writing if you give yourself the permission – sometimes – to write badly.
- There are no rules, except those you set for yourself, and they will be many and complex.

As Stravinsky said of music, 'Academism results when the reasons for the rule change, but not the rule.' For any writer, rules are for testing and for challenging; rarely are they for obeying. There are no magic formulae or secret tricks. A passion, an enthusiasm, for writing provides some early motivation. Obsessiveness helps, but endurance works even more effectively, in the same way that genius is identified as a combination of talent, concentrated focus and years of hard work, and wrongly self-identified as the exhibition of apparently intense passion. This book is testing these principles in permutation, and so will you through your writing, rewriting and the Writing Games within each chapter.

Your job is eventually to create your own principles, and to test yourself against accepted ones. Your job, if you like, is to turn the earth of language over and create a fresh approach to making literature. That is literary tradition: it is read and reread. And it is red in tooth and claw. It is always open space. It changes as each generation surprises itself into defining itself by the action *of* reaction. This is the moment when there is 'no longer consent', as Charlotte Brontë writes of her sister's practice in her editorial preface to *Wuthering Heights* (see the epigraph to this chapter).

You will surprise yourself and, in your turn, you will be turned over and replaced, because your 'surprise' has become the orthodoxy, the standard by which others measure, and are measured. Or you may choose to give your place, and share the territories, rather like a teacher does. Like King Lear, how gracefully you allow yourself to be overturned will say a lot about your character and quality. Think of it this way: knowing some of the principles we have listed might save you some time, although writing *against* such principles could teach you something. Mistakes are worth making, and are even a necessary part of a process (as they are in scientific research), and writing clumsily is a necessary stepping stone to writing well.

Writing Game

RULES OF ENGAGEMENT
What are the rules by which you write? Make a list of at least fifteen of *your own*, and be utterly honest with yourself, even if those rules include throwing aside rules and relying on what some call inspiration. Now, take each of those rules and write a short statement of no more than twenty words justifying each rule. Use examples from your own reading and your own practice. At this stage, aim for clarity rather than wish-fulfilment or mystification. Write a story or poem, the literary qualities of which meet at least five of those rules. Put this list of rules aside for the next six months and do not read it, but put your creative piece aside

for only two weeks, and return to it once you have read the rest of the book. Rewrite the piece without recourse to your original rules of engagement. In six months, I would like you to repeat this entire exercise again, again without reading your original set of rules.

AIM: Rewriting is as important as writing, but our frames of reference alter with time and practice. As original writers, we are as hampered by what we know, or think we know, and what we do not know. We must do a lot of learning, but most of all we have to do a lot of *un*learning, for our preconceptions of writing are usually based on received opinion, our experience of teaching, or on what Nadezhda Mandelstam called the 'hypnosis' induced by passive reading. As we write and read more actively, not only does our writing mutate and become newer to ourselves (and so easier to revise), but our frames of reference become more complex and dynamic. We grow less inhibited by our own experience, or the mores of others. We have clicked our fingers and woken up.

Writing badly and over-writing

It is important to give yourself the permission to write badly, and learn through rewriting. 'Far better to write twaddle or anything, anything, than nothing at all' – Katherine Mansfield. Bad is the road to good. It is imperative to recognise what works and what does not work, and teach yourself to appreciate when you are being a writer, and when you are being a poseur or fake. 'Many are called; few are chosen' – Anon. This has the same quality of sneer as 'poets are born, not made' and 'those who can't, teach'. Who calls? Who chooses? Defy such expectations. Instead, try calling on yourself; try choosing yourself. In the end, you must simply do it yourself: 'you must do it as you can'.

As somebody at the beginning of a writing career, you need to give yourself other permissions, too. You are sometimes asked to 'write to order'. Workshop games and Writing Games ask this of you and, in the professional world, such 'commission' is commonplace. Clear writing can be made in this conscious way, but good style is tricky to write to order. Style is more of an unconscious process. It needs to be worked into your piece after the first draft. Therefore, do not seek to create astounding sentences the first time round; otherwise, you will spend an hour on one sentence rather than producing one hundred, and that one sentence may end up being self-consciously 'literary', or over-written. Better to cover pages with words, then later to cut them back to their essence, than to write one sentence only to cut it back to one word.

Over-writing, too, is a cardinal symptom, not a sin, of creative writing classes. We are trying to impress our audience, but we are also trying to impress ourselves, by *elaborating*, rather than making, sentences. This style evinces insecurity and insincerity, an absence of style actually, or one heavily borrowed from a few favourite authors, rather than absorbed from reading so many authors that the reader is secure and natural in their relative anonymity of voice. Overwriting does not feel or sound natural. Read aloud, it will strike listeners as artificial or dense with allusion. The new writer is trying very hard: leaning into what they consider an accepted mode of expression. They should lean back *into* themselves and write plainly and quickly. Slap the plaster on the page's walls; planing and rococo can come later.

Forces of language

Creative writing is a craft that requires continual learning; it is a long game. You may feel, as a student of creative writing, that at some point you will 'graduate' into being a writer. Be clear from the outset: there is, there will be, no metaphorical graduation, although publication will at first feel like an award of sorts. But the feeling is temporary. As I have said, in writing we participate as beginners. Every new piece of work has to begin again from nothing. Every time a poet sits down to write a new poem, as Paul Muldoon is on record as saying, they must relearn how to write a poem. Novelists, if they want their work to resist oblivion, must force themselves towards tougher targets and keep shifting their perspectives; there is no break time. As the novelist V. S. Pritchett noted,

> The fewer novels or poems you write, the fewer you will have the ability to write. The law ruling the arts is that they must be pursued to excess. Excess is not favoured by our conditions: a book which has taken two years to write dies in a few weeks.   (Treglown, 2004: 211)

The world slows for no one. Dissatisfaction with what has been written, and what has been published, is the common and perpetual state of mind of many creative writers. I would go as far as saying that this is one of the marks of being a real writer. 'You must learn to overcome your very natural and appropriate revulsion for your own work' – William Gibson. We all write badly, even when we write well (unless our vanity is unrestrained). The fact that you understand this already may prove two things. Either you are disillusioned to the point of cynicism, or you possess a vocation, and should make a friend of stoicism, the best friend of the rewriter.

Some guidebooks on writing offer various writing strategies and games; writers write the best of these. These guidebooks are, with very few exceptions, genuinely helpful, as stepping stones are helpful: as a means to avoid, but also to evade, the difficulty of certain realities, and the nature of vocation. The experience of making your own way through the river is likely to teach you more about endeavour; about error; about language's nature; about your own character; how to understand and balance all of these; and how to reconcile the difficulty of moving within the flow, the entirely natural forces, of language.

No maps

Certain how-to-write books (which I have not listed or cited, but have read) offer a series of ABC methods that, if practised, have the effect of taking the writer on an excursion of technique. The effect is highly useful; it is uninterrupted and unidirectional, like a course in learning the basics of inorganic chemistry in order to be a pharmacist. However, what writers actually do when they write, and how they keep re-forming themselves as writers, is not unidirectional or systematic at all. Language is not a series of symptoms shouting for prescriptions.

The process of writing is far more chaotic, a mapless place, a zone for experiments, and for the constant interruption of failures. Schaefer and Diamond in *The Creative Writing Guide* acknowledge, 'As any writer knows – or will discover – writing is often a confusing, organic, unorganized process of exploration' (1998: x). Writing is a more unforgiving experience than it can be made out to be. I have tried to reflect this unaffected aspect of the writing apprenticeship throughout this book. However much this troubled me, I had to reflect what writers say about their experience.

Consider, for example, the importance writers place on developing their own distinctive habits of composition; of discipline; and even a personal philosophy which, messy and provisional though this will be, at least throws a little light on why they are writing in the first place. Another example concerns the romanticising of the writing process, and how anybody who wishes to be a writer must learn to live within the disparity between how writers and the writing process are perceived – say, by readers, filmmakers and, surprisingly, academics – and the unglamorous, serendipitous life creative writing actually offers.

Discipline

Part of all of us does not like writing, or rather does not like effort. We displace that dislike on to our circumstances or on to other people in an effort to throw responsibility elsewhere. Some writers make this a lifestyle, but it is hell for those around them, and their teachers. There are other choices, and effort becomes a lot easier and routine with practice. It ceases to feel like effort, and this allows you to go beyond yourself as a writer. You escape the banal traps of personality, and write beyond your intelligence.

How to be good

Being good simply comes down to having routine and little rituals, and getting on with believing in your work. Begin by finding the place that best suits your writing, and make this your territory: 'a room of your own'. It could be a garage, café, library, outhouse or the traditional study if you can afford such luxury. Work in that space, and reward yourself in doing so, in small ways. After a while, the mere act of going to that place will begin to trigger the routine of writing.

Find the times of day that best suit your writing process, but bear in mind that you will find this time changes as you get older: young night owls end up as middle-aged nine-to-fivers. Stick to this time, though, while it works. Again, find some small way of rewarding yourself for beginning work, and for putting in the time at the end. Practise this daily, until it becomes ingrained, and you'll miss it when you do not follow it.

Having worked in your space for a fixed amount of time, it will be tempting to start taking breaks – ten-minute vacations from concentration (smokers are especially culpable) – but such breaks disturb and corrupt creative momentum. The novelist Ron Carlson puts it strikingly, 'If you want to be a writer, stay in the room!' I take it that you want a life, as well as a life as a writer. If you are not a stay-in-the-room writer, then your work will take very much longer, and you then have less time for life. One old trick of politicians and businesspeople is to snap the working day into two sections, separated by lunch and a catnap, allowing one to continue the second session with as heightened a concentration as the first. It yields two days from one. The enforced discipline (rather than a self-enforced one) is a strong attraction of creative writing courses in universities. They offer you a strict timetable for reading, writing and rewriting; weekly support and criticism; and they force you to stay in the metaphorical 'room' of the course. You then take these enforcements into your own life.

Being good can mean simply reaching a word count chosen beforehand. It is not the amount of time, but the kind of time and how you use it. Journalists pick up this habit as part of their job. Both Joseph Conrad and Graham Greene allowed themselves a relatively low daily word limit of writing. It is a pattern to imitate; it frees the rest of the day for experience and incubation. Many novelists and nonfiction writers set themselves targets. Writing *The Origin of Species*, Charles Darwin suffered a lack of discipline, so he set up stones in a small cairn on the sandwalk outside his study, the path Darwin paced as he worked out his ideas. Each stone represented a point Darwin wanted to make within a daily quota of writing. Each time he made a point, he knocked a stone from the cairn. Some writers find easy composition unnatural, but still force themselves forward. For the Irish poet W. B. Yeats, two *lines* of poetry a day represented a good effort. Gustave Flaubert often wrote thirty-five words. Given this constant daily accretion, you will find that books make themselves slowly and surely, like cairns, before your eyes.

Being good also means completing your task for the day, which you set the day before. Within your working day, try to complete a section of a novel or a piece of creative nonfiction, or take a poem through to its pre-final draft. Do not ask too much of yourself, but make practical targets and stick with them, and quit while you are ahead. Do not leave something uncompleted; it will call for you psychologically, goading you to finish. It is a good tip to complete some aspect of work, then think about what you aim to achieve the following day, even beginning the first lines or sentences of that new work. Go no further into it than as if you were unlocking the cage around it, but leaving the door still closed. You may now leave the next day's work to escape by itself; and it will do so unconsciously. You will find it waiting at the end of your fingertips the next morning, having nudged the cage door open. Writers often find it useful to warm up their minds at the beginning of a writing session by revising and rewriting the work they have completed the day previously. This form of self-reading reminds you of what you were doing, and where you might want to get to next.

Your regime need not be puritanical and punishing, for this would have the opposite effect in the end. As you get more experienced, you should increase your word count, and include a substantial amount of rewriting time to begin your working day. You should build in time for reading, for daydreaming, and for creating moments of receptive idleness. Dorothea Brande believed that reading immediately before writing was a bad idea, and that you should build in time for what she called 'wordless recreation' (1981: 133). She does not mean that you stop reading as a writer. She means you should stop prevaricating, and leave yourself open for your own language to emerge.

How to be bad

Being good requires a certain degree of ruthlessness, but the ruthlessness is directed at your own character, not at others. The error made by some writers is to exact silence and servility from those around them in order to affect routine and order. What they create may prove in the end to be good writing, but no writing is good enough to require other people to suffer for its creation.

"...BOOKS MAKE THEMSELVES SLOWLY AND SURELY, LIKE CAIRNS, BEFORE YOUR EYES."

Also, any conniving of circumstances to bring about your downfall is your own creation, a kind of anti-creation and self-destructiveness.

Do not whine about self-inflicted wounds in your time and work. Write about them, if you must. The corollaries of any inertia on your part are that no writing will get finished, and what writing there is will suffer in quality because it has received insufficient time and attention. Without a routine, the times when writing seems 'given' will decrease or become erratic as your fluency stutters from lack of practice, and submerged guilt.

As any such creative moment arrives, should your discipline have been lax, anxiety can lead to panic. Literary panic is an estranging emotion. Like literary envy, it has physiological effects on the body and mind, leading sometimes to immediate action or, more often, to a disabled sense of skill, hopelessness and helplessness. The self-made wound becomes septic. Leave it and it will fester, and bring disappointment down on you, as you grow older, blaming everybody else except yourself for your lack of progress (or even success).

This is what psychologists term a kind of 'learned helplessness', and it needs to be confronted and understood as an insidious self-enemy, as you would if it were an addiction (for in some ways, for some writers, failure, like acclaim, *is* addictive). You must fight yourself by staying in practice, and knowing that you have only yourself to blame if you do not succeed. At least you and those around you will know how hard you tried. At least you might write from that experience.

Notebooks and rituals

One thing an 'ABC of Writing a Book' does very well is talk of markets, audiences and that chimera for creative writing: money. However, since writing creatively does not always bring much financial comfort, one of its underrated merits for the beginner is that it is relatively inexpensive compared to other art forms. Later stages of a writer's career are more demanding, especially if research is necessary. The beginner's equipment is a notebook and a pen or pencil, and access to a computer.

A familiar question asked of writers at public readings concerns their choice of pen, pencil or keyboard. This is a disguised inquiry. It has more to do with whether the writer possesses some key to the writing process, and whether the thing with which you choose to write has some talismanic power. The secret knowledge they may find problematical to hear is that the difference between becoming a writer and not becoming a writer usually comes down to whether you carry a notebook; are prepared to work in it actively and regularly; and are willing to sit for hours typing and rewriting. However, as you shall see, the talismanic power of objects is psychologically real for some writers.

Recording and practice

If you have not done so already, buy yourself a notebook. Date it, and replace it when it is completed, but ensure you keep all of them safely. The notebook is a movable workplace. It may be paper-bound, or a hand-held computer. Whatever form, it must be practical, comfortable and portable. It must suit the way you conduct yourself as a writer. As the poet James Schuyler said, 'The first use of drawings for a painter is the same as that of notebooks, diaries and letters for a writer: keeping your hand in.' The pressure, the responsibility, to make a record of life instigates much writing and, if you ignore this primal mnemonic need, you must either possess a sponge-like memory or be content with a passive reading of your world. If you are carrying a notebook and do not use it, then you are not even taking part; you become background. A notebook will make the difference between a book being born and one that never achieves conception. A notebook is an active tool; but it is an error to believe that by carrying this spear on to the stage of writing you become a player.

You use it for writing regularly, but the main uses will be to record ideas for sentences while you are actively thinking about one hundred other matters; to take down interesting material while travelling; or to record sentences and dialogue you hear, or overhear. You will also use it as a scrapbook of sorts. A writer's notebook functions as what used to be called a 'commonplace book', in which you record sentences, lines of poetry, images and paragraphs by other writers that you find especially intriguing for one reason or another. In this way, you create a personal anthology, one that you can reread for ideas, encouragement and illumination of problems in your own writing.

Dreams

A notebook travels with you, even to your bedside. One of the most common times for ideas and images to arrive (gallingly) is during the period between trying to sleep and sleep itself. You may experience fascinating reveries when the conscious mind shuts down and dream or fantasy surprise you back into waking.

These are forms of active dreaming. If that happens, however tired you are, make note of any images that have arisen, or the phrases that have come to you. Do not fool yourself into thinking you will remember it next day, even though not everything is going to be of use to you, and some of it will seem asinine. Like giving yourself the permission to write badly, you need to give yourself consent to record freely and without self-censor. Buy yourself a hand-held voice-recording device and make your notes orally.

This period before sleep is an especially receptive one when you are engaged in a book, poem or article whose process absorbs your daylight hours. You have seemingly finished your day's work, but your mental processes will still be flickering on their reel. The reservoir of your creative thinking needs time to fill up – let your unconscious mind do all that filling and working. So, rather than holding a night-long vigil over your notebook, write enough to be satisfied that you have netted what is most important. It is like making a list of tasks ready for the next day. The point is not to get lost in them, or to lose them, but to put them on ice, while also keeping them breathing.

Fieldwork for writers

Your notebook is a fine-meshed net in constant trawl, collecting far more detritus than it does material you may later find useful. And, one of the tricks of being able to read any net is to know what that detritus might yield. Pretty well anything has some possibility and some beauty for a writer, given enough scrutiny. That which appears at first to be obsolescent, boring or ugly may prove to be ideal. Everything is quarry, everyone is material, and everywhere is fieldwork.

One of the most fascinating places to collect the noise of speech, and the speech of human behaviour, is anywhere in which a large number of people gather, usually to make a journey. Such places – airports, bus and train stations – have the effect of making everyday human concerns provisional, unstable and transitory. The heart is not here, far from home. Heightened emotions such as fear, suspicion and anticipation not only underlie how many people speak but how they then behave to each other. People try to hide, or group. The transitory passage of people can also challenge inhibitions: people often speak more freely about themselves on the understanding that they are unlikely to see this person again, or they go into role pretending they are something they are not. It is not so much that you are observing what people are saying, but *how* they say it and *why* they say it that way. It is a parade of styles. You are an ethologist – you study behaviour.

I am not saying you stake out such places, making notes parasitically or with a sociologist's eye for mass observation. I am saying you should view wide, indiscriminate human contact as a form of research for writing, and make this your ritual. If you are shy of contact, then you must work undercover, and you should then write up what you remember as soon as you can, in a quiet spot such as a café. In such open situations, the notebook is far less obvious, affected or threatening than an audio-recording device or a camera. It does not invite questions.

You should take your notebook everywhere and have it with you all the time. You should not, as some apprentice-writers do, limit your notebook work to places and times you think inherently 'inspirational and beautiful'.

To do so is merely to experience second-hand or custom-bound notions of aesthetic experience. Notebooks are rougher and readier than a Claude glass. How you organize your notebook is important, but do not use the organization of notebooks and files as a displacement activity for not writing. It is the equivalent of tidying your home before settling to work. A simple form of organisation is to possess two notebooks: one for recording and collecting, and one for writing and drafting.

Writing Game

FIELDWORK
Go for a walk with your notebook and collect the following 'data': two real overheard conversations; three species of birds; two brand names for food; the words from six signs; the name of one planet or star; the name of a lipstick; one time of day; the title of a book of fiction; the title of a painting; the name of a dead politician; two types of onion and one type of potato; the names of three items in a hardware store; a make of gun; and the speech of a child. Now, open a newspaper at random and write down one short phrase in it. This phrase is the title of your new piece of writing. Write a short story of no more than 500 words or a poem of no more than 40 lines that incorporates all the data you have collected. Revise this writing until the use of this data seems completely inevitable, and neither random nor forced.

AIM: Force yourself to make connections between disparate things, and your brain answers that pressure by making synaptic connections to make sense of them. This pressure, if applied constantly, will improve your facility with ideas, language and imagery. Force becomes habit; ability becomes facility and fluency.

Fetishes of composition

Writers can be ritualistic about *when* they work, and *where* they work, and this also goes for writing materials. Bruce Chatwin famously used a particular brand of moleskin notebook. The choice of what you write with is personal, but it is not inane. As with notebooks, writers can be fetishistic about the right kind of pen, pencil or keyboard. Thomas Hardy wrote each of his novels using a pen that he then had inscribed with the name of the novel (you can view them in a neat row in The Museum, Dorchester, England). Choose the tool for the job and stick with it, but try not to burden it with talismanic powers. What happens if you lose it, or it ceases to be manufactured? Another excuse for the circular helplessness of writer's block.

Composition's action

Movement

Some of our best ideas come when we are otherwise distracted, as when we are going to sleep or driving. Audio-record your thoughts on these occasions, but recognise that there is a good reason why good ideas come at such inconvenient moments: your unconscious and dreaming mind is communicating with your conscious quotidian mind. There are other ways to bring this state of open-mindedness into play. The classic pose of a writer at work is a person sitting still at their desk in silence. There are obviously times when this is essential. However, both exercise and music have the capacity to elicit creative thinking, by blocking conscious thought and inviting contributions from the unconscious: 'flashes of insight' we call them, or 'inspiration', or 'the given', when they are no more than the synaptic impulses of dreamers. You need to trial these practices to test if they work for you (and to make sure you do not use them as excuses to stop writing). Music and movement are as totemic to some writers as the place or pen. William Wordsworth composed poems while pacing the metres of his garden's gravel path. Ted Hughes used the concentrations of fishing. Try different forms of exercise before writing. If you begin to dry up while writing, then take a walk. *Solvitur ambulando* – it is solved by walking. Try playing different sorts of music until something begins to answer and propel the rhythm of your work.

Props and prompts for action

Aside from notebooks, pens and computers, a new creative writer needs the support of a Word Hoard, such as the *Oxford English* or *Chambers Dictionary*, to locate words and to use them precisely. Dictionaries are richly seamed places to spend time looking for prompts to making creative language. The etymologies of words are anecdotes told by language across time. Words bristle with meanings; they are prickly with their histories and usages. Precision of language is important in developing good personal style. Your style will be judged not only by the way you order and play with words, but also by your choice of words. Therefore, you also need an excellent thesaurus, such as *Roget's Thesaurus*, in order to find alternative words to keep your language lively, surprising and varied.

The dictionaries and thesauri that come packaged with word-processing programs are digitally tongue-tied when applied to creative writing (although they are generally fine for academic writing or reports). Strunk and White's *The*

Elements of Style (2000) and *Fowler's Modern English Usage* (various editions) are useful props while you are drafting and editing. They can be enemies to fluency *while* you are writing. Writers find it useful to have books by other authors around you, so that you can borrow or steal from their verbal energy if you find yourself floundering in the middle of a piece of dialogue, or have forgotten the order of lines in a pantoum or sestina. Exploit anything that prompts your processes, be they coffee or the Middle Dutch origin for the word 'prop'.

Writing Game

MUSIC, MOVEMENT AND BRAIN BLOCKING

This game has three parts. (1) Play some music while you are writing, and change the musical style entirely every half an hour, but keep writing the same piece. (2) Take a walk right now, taking with you your notebook, and return to writing immediately after one hour. (3) Pick up a pen and begin writing anything. Now begin counting aloud from one hundred to zero, but keep writing all the time.

AIM: Writing is as physical as it is psychological. (1) Music alters the manner in which your brain creates language; it affects the rhythm obviously, but it also acts as a stimulus to memory and association. Use music as an informal prompt for the unconscious, but use it less when you need to concentrate. (2) Exercise assists creativity in many ways, not least because it encourages creative dialogue between unconscious and conscious states of mind. One of the cures for writer's block is exercise. (3) This exercise can produce some surprising writing. Its purpose is to make different parts of your mind grind, metaphorically, against each other, and to block your conscious self-censor.

A mental switch

There is writing and there is not writing, and writing is a 'zone'. At some point, the readings and rehearsals are complete, and the stage is set. Action defines a writer, not the pose for action or the possession of the means by which to perform. We will look at the various processes of this action in Chapter Five. What most writers agree is that 'getting on with it', just placing down words, is the best advice for most new writers. How does one transmute the *desire* to write into the *will* to write? Many people talk about 'having books in themselves'. Martin Amis believes that 'much of the time you are writing the fiction that other people have in them' (2001: 6). The chance of people writing these 'books inside them' is slender. Margaret Atwood says that it is not just the nature of the activity, it is also because writing carries a symbolic role:

everyone can dig a hole in a cemetery, but not everyone is a grave-digger. The latter takes a good deal more stamina and persistence . . . You represent mortality . . . And so it is with any public role, including that of the Writer, capital W.   (2002: 23)

Writing is also an act of abnormal concentration and we tend to dislike such high-intensity action. There are a thousand other forms of action just as available to us, only more pleasant and more immediately rewarding. However, you have to learn to throw the mental switch to writing. As with the highest levels in sport or carrying out surgery, for example, the *switch* requires highly intense concentration coupled with action. In these counter-examples, society grants their practitioners status and financial gain. Initially, writing does not offer such rewards. There is even uncertainty that they may materialise at all. To take action in such a vacuum is challenging. We looked at some of these challenges to writers in Chapter Three. We need to assume that we are capable of meeting these challenges, and can answer the silence around us with action.

Freewriting

Try to focus on your writing as often as possible. The quickest and least frictional method for *beginning* to know the zone of writing is to practise freewriting every day. It is less useful for full-time writers for whom a deadline is incentive enough (see Chapter Five). Freewriting requires that you write fast; you do not even stop to think. We shall try a version of this now.

Do you recall when you were a child and you first realised that you could *think*? Often this moment occurs when you were having difficulty going to sleep. You comprehended that you were thinking, and this kept you awake. So, you tried to cheat your thought by *not* thinking. '*I* shall think white', you thought, or '*I* shall think "grey".' And you thought 'white' and you thought 'grey', but then you realised that both 'white' and 'grey' were still types of thinking. You can never stop thinking, but you can stop *thinking* you are thinking, and freewriting helps you do this.

Open a book – any book – at random. Place the fingers of one hand on a page. Write down the phrase covered by the width of your fingers. Close the book; forget about it. Pick another book; do the same thing again. Collect thirty phrases in one session. Place each of these phrases on separate strips of paper into a cup or hat, and leave them for a day. The following morning, pick one of these phrases at random, and write it down and immediately begin writing anything that comes into your mind. Throw the strip of paper away, then write as though you were flying. You are not producing a work of art, nor will you be asked to read this out to others. You can write what you like, but you must continue writing without stopping writing and without thinking. You will do this for five minutes every day. Each day of every month, you will select a new strip of paper from your cache of little phrases. You will renew this cache every calendar month.

Freewriting can produce some very interesting phrases and directions, and has been known to lead to some very fine work. However, it is most important in getting you used to the habit and action of writing. It helps you mimic fluency. Even though it may feel strange or artificial at first, this action can produce dramatic results. Recovering in a clinic from opium addiction, Jean Cocteau wrote his novel *Les Enfants terribles* in an act of extremely fast writing, about which he commented to André Gide: 'The real benefit of my treatment: work has laid hands on me. Les Enfants Terribles is *emerging without a struggle*. It *gives me its orders* . . . I'll have done *several months work in nineteen days*' (Steegmuller, 1970: 396; my italics).

Negative capability

Many writers find that, if they follow a routine of writing, or if they practice freewriting often enough, they achieve various degrees of fluency in their expression (even though the words will need chopping and planing later during rewriting). This makes the creative writing process sound conscious and deliberate. In fact, when you have an idea for writing, it asks very little of your conscious attention. You do not *know* it. It is an aspect of your mind John Keats called 'negative capability':

> several things dovetailed in my mind and at once it struck me, what quality went to form . . . Achievement especially in Literature & which Shakespeare possessed so enormously – I mean *Negative Capability*, that is when man is capable of being in uncertainties, Mysteries, doubts, without any irritable reaching after fact and reason.   (NE2: 889)

Here is another quotation about composition by Keats: 'If it does not come as easily as leaves to a tree, it had better not come at all.' The point is delectable, but too strongly spiced. It represents a false ideal. At *best*, that is what writing feels like. The creative process can be rather like going into a trance, in which the unconscious and unconscious minds talk to each fluidly if not eloquently, and much writing is achieved in a short time:

> It's wonderful, there's nothing else like it, you write in a trance. And the trance is completely addictive, you love it, you want more of it . . . It's an

FESTINA LENTE— HURRY SLOWLY

integration of the body-mind and the dreaming-mind and the
daylight-conscious-mind. All three are firing at once, they're all in
concert. You can be sitting there but inwardly dancing, and the breath
and the weight and everything else are involved, you're fully alive. It
takes a while to get into it. You have to have some key, like say a phrase
or a few phrases or a subject matter or maybe even a tune to get you
started going towards it, and it starts to accumulate. Sometimes it starts
without your knowing that you're getting there, and it builds in your
mind like a pressure. I once described it as being like a painless
headache, and you know there's a poem in there, but you have to wait
until the words form.   (Les Murray in interview, BBC Radio 4, 1998)

Writing produced in this state will often surprise because it seems better than you know; that is, it is *beyond* your conscious intelligence. You could not have written it had you sat down with that end in mind. Read back what Les Murray says above and, by freewriting, try to induce the painless headache in yourselves.

Writing Game

INDUCING THE PAINLESS HEADACHE
Light a candle, and focus your entire attention on the point at which the flame meets the air. Shut your eyes and hold that image in your head. Open your eyes and refocus on the flame's edge. Close your eyes again and hold on to that image. Keep doing this until you feel comfortable and relaxed. Begin writing a story or a poem while in this state of relaxation, and repeat this exercise regularly if it induces writing with which you are content.

AIM: Active dreaming of this type, like freewriting, is one of the more rapid ways to access creative ideas and associations, and to induce a state of trance.

Inspiration and duende

New writers mistake the state of trance with inspiration. When a writer or writing student says that they have missed a deadline because they were not feeling inspired enough to write, they make a simple error. 'Inspiration is the act of drawing up a chair to the writing desk' – Anon. The angel of inspiration tends to sail on the slow and steady tortoise, obeying the cherished Renaissance maxim to make haste slowly. Write something now and, having written, ask yourself what lies *beneath* what you have written. What is the nature of your iceberg beneath the visible tip? Finding what lies below your words is a way to find the physical and psychological drives of what we used to call inspiration.

Sometimes writers (in the main, poets) claim that they *avoid* writing in order to precipitate inspiration, as if apparently 'conscious writing' were something as forbidden to them as sex to a priest. They argue that the power of writing then grows through abstention, so, when its moment arrives, it strikes with greater force in shorter time. This seems precious and repressive. It leads to a writer getting out of practice, allowing the construction of excuses and blocks. This book contains many ways around writer's block, although writer's block, like a lack of inspiration, tends to be a metaphor for deliberated inaction or a kind of panicky inertia. Sometimes calculation works better than inspiration, and even humdrum daily practice can make a more conductive rod for creative

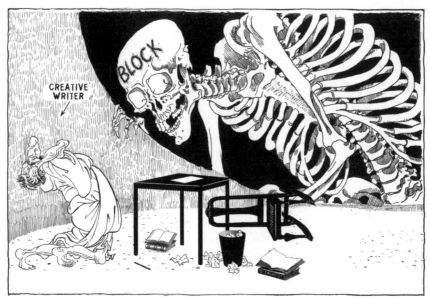

"WRITING WILL SEEM PHYSICAL IN ITS INSISTENCE, LIKE SOMEONE DEMANDING HIS OR HER OWN BIRTH."

lightning. The calculated uses of literary design and form were discussed in Chapter Three.

Writing proceeds forwards slowly, like a sand dune moving through night and day, simultaneously accreting and eroding. Much is lost or invisible, millions of grains of sand, millions of grains of language. Workshops formalise this natural process, this need to move against something solid, against and with somebody. Our writing requires not only analysis, intelligence as well as intuition – it requires discussion; evaluations and feedback from our peers and mentors. All these acts are parallels of inspiration. Keats looks to Shakespeare as a father figure, a mentor. Shakespeare sometimes collaborated too, and consulted his peers, and actors, as he drafted and wrought. Writing plays is, after all, one of the most collaborative of the written art forms.

If you are not used to writing regularly, you are unlikely to be attracted to your desk by the sheer habit of writing, a habit that gives pleasure even when difficult. Sometimes a new writer finds that planning and practice finally come together, and they write at speed, as if their mind were flying. This feels like inspiration, but it is really the symptom of developing a habit of mind. It has nothing to do with a divine wind blowing through you, or the Muse using you as a medium. At times like this, as Emily Dickinson wrote, your life feels like 'a Loaded Gun' waiting for someone to fire it (Eshleman, 2001: 29).

Writing is addictive and that is inspiration enough! In hospital with tuberculosis, George Orwell could not stop writing. His doctors took his typewriter away. He wrote freehand. His doctors put his arm in plaster to stop him. If you do not write, the result is restlessness and unhappiness. When you are driven to write in this way, your work will seem to take on its own life and momentum, as we see with Emily Brontë in the epigraph to this chapter. Writing will seem physical in its insistence, like someone demanding his or her own birth. This colours the language in your work, as though it had its own life and inspired its own breath. Lorca called this quality *duende*, a term borrowed from flamenco, and more useful than a notion of inspiration because it represents your own blood and metabolic rhythms. *Duende* is rooted in your own metabolism: your power of expression changes the metabolism of your own writing on the page, making it more alive and urgent to a reader. *Wuthering Heights* exemplifies the *duende* of its author and enacts the *duende* of the characters of Heathcliff and Catherine.

Language's mercury

Language evolves by use, but what language do you choose, what parts of speech work best for your voice? Writers favour whatever comes most naturally, and so you should begin with what you possess and imitating authors you admire. The order of words to achieve meaning – syntax – is where the springs of surprise come in a writer's voice. It would not be out of order to spend an entire week on phrase making. Although the order that words take arises from many pressures on language, including sound and sense, how a writer *makes* a phrase (and makes it seem inevitable) is one of the keys to their voiceprint.

Words are language at the cellular level. A novelist feels forward word by word, knowing that every sentence must advance the body of the plot, knowing also that any word or phrase that distracts the attention of the reader from the book is redundant. Every word of a poem is a tiny but essential part of the body and metabolism of that poem. Every choice of word ramifies the potential directions of a piece, and simultaneously shuts down other possibilities. Overwriting or pompous abstraction spreads cancer in the cells of language. Writers even weigh punctuation on the same scales as words – for a writer, punctuation is part of speech. A misplaced comma, hobbles a paragraph.

A writer thinks forward in their language and the permutations of possibility thrown up with every decision and the mercury-movement of language. The process becomes an elaborate series of gambles. All sorts of different stories or

CHASTITY GLOVE FOR WRITERS

" IN HOSPITAL WITH TUBERCULOSIS, GEORGE ORWELL COULD NOT STOP WRITING... HIS DOCTORS PUT HIS ARM IN PLASTER TO STOP HIM."

poems open up as well as the one that must be written: the inevitable final piece. How do you keep the lid on language? Sometimes you can and sometimes you cannot, and it is a good idea to let it blow or unravel. Students should try this. It is not about writing badly; it is about unravelling possibility.

It is even about making apparent mistakes in language. You might yield two or three lines or sentences that, by sheer chance, are part of the poem or story you were seeking to write (but did not consciously know), or some entirely uninvited poem or story that, by its sudden presence, raises your game. Even a misspelling or a misreading on rewriting can yield surprisingly fresh possibilities. Later on, those chances – like the chances created by a rhyme scheme in poetry – look like choices, and seem inevitable. The novelist William Burroughs allowed this chance-process full rein with his cut-up technique, pulling paragraphs together out of random readings – something you can try for yourself.

Have in the back of your mind that concrete language usually has more resonance for the general reader than abstract language, and editing usually takes care of this. As George Orwell writes in his essay 'Politics and the English Language' (NE2: 2470),

> When you think of a concrete object, you think wordlessly, and then, if you want to describe the thing you have been visualizing you probably hunt about until you find the exact words that seem to fit it. When you think of something abstract you are more inclined to use words from the start, and unless you make a conscious effort to prevent it, the existing dialect will come rushing in and do the job for you, at the expense of blurring or even changing your meaning.

One of the main purposes of writing workshops is to clear away verbiage and false language. George Orwell offered six rules for nonfiction, the purpose of which was to keep your language alive for the reader, and which are useful for self-editing or editing in poetry and fiction workshops:

- Never use a metaphor, simile or other figure of speech which you are used to seeing in print.
- Never use a long word where a short one will do.
- If it is possible to cut a word out, always cut it out.
- Never use the passive where you can use the active.
- Never use a foreign phrase, a scientific word or a jargon word if you can think of an everyday English equivalent.
- Break any of these rules sooner than say anything outright barbarous.

Writing Game

LANGUAGE WANTED DEAD OR ALIVE
One of the most audacious moments in Orwell's 'Politics and the English Language' happens when he translates a passage of *Ecclesiastes* into 'modern English of the worst sort'. This is the original:

> I returned and saw under the sun, that the race is not to the swift, nor the battle to the strong, neither yet bread to the wise, nor yet riches to men of understanding, nor yet favour to men of skill; but time and chance happeneth to them all.

This is Orwell's translation:

> Objective considerations of contemporary phenomena compel the conclusion that success or failure in competitive activities exhibits no tendency to be commensurate with innate capacity, but that a considerable element of the unpredictable must invariably be taken into account.

Your task is to parody this second type of language. First, take a short excerpt of creative nonfiction from one of the Norton anthologies (see Preface) and translate it into modern abstract or pompous language. Second, write a story in which one of the characters talks in pompous abstract speech. Third, take an example of abstract language from modern life (literary theory and particle physics are excellent sources) and translate it into a short poem, the language of which is concrete to its core.

AIM: Concrete language has more resonance than abstract language. One of the main purposes of writing workshops is to clear away verbiage. Practise both forms of writing and you will find it easier to identify and eliminate verbiage in your own work and that of others.

Influence and imitation

The writers who influence us are like heroic teachers. For a time, they are everything to our writing, a passion. Developed out of an acute, and sometimes touching, trust in a previous writer's workings, this process is a series of severe, short one-sided marriages, but one where the newer writer keeps the house as it were. The novice grows beyond one influence only to be captured by another, and weathered into a further knowledge of artistic practice, and even prejudice. Imitation as sheer emulation pushes them to see the original, and their own work, more clearly, sometimes beating the original at its game, an assimilation, of one writer becoming another or another person passing for another.

Writers pass through one another, cannibalising, synthesising, metabolising – making everything their own (see 'Challenges of translation' in Chapter Three). This is imitation as appropriation, dispossession of our elders as one part of the law, but it is also homage from follower to leader. Imitation is always in mutation. It is in mutation between both the generations of writers as they work within their time, and in mutation within the writing as it travels through time and before their readers.

It is often a good idea to choose models of writing that are plain in style, that have few nervous tics; they allow you to play variations upon a fairly open space before moving on. If you imitate a writer with a denser or extreme style, it can close down possibility if you do not possess the articulate energy to move on from their force-field. For imitation can be limitation: imitation that disables invention. This is when we mimic a writer's voiceprint slavishly, an error of the writing process that derives often from the character of the apprentice: afraid of challenging beyond an existing writer's linguistic territory, or unaware that they have remade a perfectly designed wheel.

One point of creative writing, as Derek Walcott has said, is to find out what we mean; and to find out what we mean, we must first find out who we are. When writers imitate too cosily, they risk yielding their identity; their work becomes anti-matter to the matter of the original. The stories and poems do not even have their own metabolism; they require the oxygen tent of the original to get by. Imitation is a literary tradition. It is as natural as natural selection, and as ruthless about what works and what does not. Most good writers move out of the shadow of their forerunner, and in that moving have imitated the lead-writer's behaviour. In Paul Muldoon's phrase, they have found new weather.

Writing Game

IMITATION

Ask each member of your writing class about the writers who have influenced them most, and also the writers against whom they have reacted. Bring copies of stories and poems by these writers, and ask the students to read examples to class, with illustrations of influence or imitation from their own writing. At the next session, each student brings an example of a writer whose style or voice is disliked. The game is to write a story or poem in imitation or parody of that writer.

AIM: It is important to develop taste. It is equally important to have the opportunity to say when we like something and when we do not, and why. New writers should try different styles as often as they can, in order to develop their facility and find a voice, and early taste can be a fickle guide to quality. At the beginning of workshops, students might write together in imitation of a writer's use of point of view, plot, style, character development or diction. It is often a good idea to use models that are not extreme or dense in style. However, extreme or affected literary styles are useful for exercises in parody or pastiche; try them as an icebreaker.

Workshops as open spaces

One of the jobs of a creative writing programme is to give new writers the time to develop themselves and their work. One of the ways to accelerate that process and save their time is through the writing workshop, although there are other approaches that simply require the writer to be alone in a room, remain there and get on with it. In industry and craft, workshops are places for innovation, creation and production. In creative writing, the function of the workshop depends upon the intents and character of the tutor, and upon the context of the event, such as it being a scheduled part of a university degree. There are of course workshops in other contexts. I have witnessed writing workshops in bars, parks, zoos, galleries, medical schools, hospitals, trains, nature reserves, museums, mountain tops and, of course, schools and arts festivals.

Purposes

Workshops serve many purposes, one of which is less visible but very important: the creation of a community of writers. Obviously, you do not need a workshop to start such a community – and workshops are recent phenomena – but they do act as a model that complements and even subverts previous models, such as the salon, the art school, the coffee-house reading and the soirée. The meetings of the Lake Poets, of the Bloomsbury Group, of the Beats, of the Dadaists, of the Surrealists, and so on, were, essentially, workshops by a different name.

Writing programmes mimic the phenomenon known as a literary movement. Their movements are united by their place and time, sometimes by a philosophy of teaching, sometimes by a philosophy of artistic practice. A workshop, like a literary assemblage or movement, serves as a catalyst for the careers of several writers, some of whom will become close friends, some of whom will become the pre-eminent and the most unswervingly severe critics of each other's work.

Literary friendships of this type have enormous cultural muscle and historical significance. The workshop is one basis for such a fresh literary network. It creates a peer group, members of which support each other long after the formal meetings are completed. Whom a new writer meets in a writing workshop may well be their professional and personal friends for life. That nexus can also help them later on in their literary career, when they are either too bigheaded for their own good and need bringing down to earth, or they are burned out on failure or benighted by experiment, and require an honest, helping hand, such as a new agent, a publisher, a reading, or even a job. What are required are connections. Workshops create connections. They can even become cults.

Some would call these networks friendships. They are, but many friendships tend to be fellowships founded on self-interest, mutual curiosity and cultural symbiosis. The fellowships of writers are almost like cults or clubs: fiercely competitive yet strenuously generous to those inside them, rebarbative to those outside the magic circle, or to those writers who have strayed or grown beyond the pale. The bonds between writers in these fellowships are powerful because they have shared the same experience of apprenticeship: they were tested together. They have witnessed a common vulnerability become a shared purpose; they have understood the way in which apprentices grow into experts.

These invisible networks exist in a kind of counterculture, in a world that parallels and mocks the more serious social and political networks that lend themselves as the subject of many novels. In some countries, there are overlaps between these cultural and political networks; what began in youth as pleasure and application later yields friends in high or right places. Never believe anybody who tells you that literary networks are not important to a writer's work, profile and audience. They are circles for survival.

The visible purpose of workshops is improvement of work. The essential aspiration for all workshop leaders is to help students discover not only what works but also what succeeds. The stratagem for exploring that concern is shared experience. Writing is a lonely business; workshops help you access other people's experience and strategies for writing. Workshops also palliate the loneliness of the writer, although one must be wary about getting too used to this palliation, since a great deal of honest writing emerges from the lack of it. The crucial but unvoiced aim of the lead-writer is to help new writers write better than they think they know, and to learn to appreciate that process collectively. The best workshops have simple, rather than subtle, purposes.

Origins

Writing workshops were born out of theatre writing which, like any performance-based medium, is necessarily more collaborative than writing. Their origin lies in the teaching of dramatic technique. The playwright George Baker (1866–1935) ran his '47 Workshop' at Harvard from 1906 to 1925, the purpose of which was to show 'the inexperienced dramatist how experienced dramatists have solved problems similar to his own, to shorten a little the time of his apprenticeship' (Myers, 1995: 69). They were open spaces; the emphasis of these workshops was not theoretical but practical, and that remains the case with writing workshops.

Writing workshops emphasise the practical: in technique, in the methods and devices for getting the desired ends, and in reading what best can exemplify those methods and devices. Writing workshops often use writing, good and even bad, as starting points for discussion of technique, or for imitation, or for redrafting. There is no particular category of workshop; every workshop runs to its own rhythm. In the same way that the audience in a theatre creates the atmosphere for an actor, so the characters and enthusiasm of the student-writers create the working weather of a workshop. Every workshop is like a first night.

Dynamics

The more engaged and responsive the students are, the more engaged and eventful the performance of a tutor. It is usually a good idea, therefore, to approach a workshop with a combination of an open mind and enthusiasm, and with a sense of communal purpose rather than self-interest. Communal self-interest, however, is a different animal. You will find that if you work hard for another person's writing, they will work as hard or harder for yours. Workshops are places of cultural symbiosis, even for the tutor who will test out their own ideas, and pick up one or two new ideas.

Bear this in mind, for when you first encounter a workshop the feeling can be more akin to terror. There is no escaping this fear, and there is no point downplaying it: anxiety about new situations is human. Presenting your work to a group of strangers is terrifying, even mortifying: one forgets that it is about the work and not the writer. At the time of initiation, the process feels extremely personal, especially if the writer is presenting a completely new work, or has no previous experience of working within a group. Like a new school, you will get used to it, or learn to live with it. Eventually, you will value it or even learn to love it.

Some new writers grow addicted to the process, to the point where they almost seem to stop thinking critically for themselves, relying instead on the collective critical mind of a group. They then move from group to group like migrant artists, not allowing sufficient time for artistic growth in one space, and sometimes presenting the same work to these different audiences. Their development tends to be static and their achievement sketchy: they try to please everybody. It is best to stick with one hard audience until you have outgrown it, at which point a writer must move on to where it is even tougher. The best workshop groups ought to have a strict life span, lest their participants grow too familiar with each other's critical and creative practice. It is one reason why workshops in university courses often achieve a healthy dynamic: the population of their workshops changes every year. They represent a compacted version of reality: time wipes out a generation of writers and replenishes from the next.

Generally a workshop takes one of two tracks or, if there is time, both tracks. There is the generative workshop, the purpose of which is to catalyse and create new writing, sometimes by creative writing exercises, and often by reading examples for imitation or rewriting. There is the responsive workshop, the purpose of which is to assist with a critical understanding of new writing. In these latter workshops, scripts of writing are distributed, read aloud and discussed. Student-writers collectively assist their peers in redrafting their work so that it reaches some kind of optimum state. This optimum state might not be exactly what the writer originally intended! It might not even be the state that most in the group can agree upon, for that would lead to homogeneous writing.

Homogeneity

One of the wintry criticisms of writing workshops is that they produce such homogeneity within a false democracy of tender critical standards, notions of worthiness of subject and tone in writing, and back-slapping. As poetry is what gets lost in translation, there is an argument that variety, ingenuity, individuality and originality are what get lost in workshops. That need not be the case. As with our discussion of teaching in Chapter One, rigour is again the answer. To foster variation and originality, the workshop leader must set the temperature of the event very carefully and maintain a close watch on proceedings like the director of a play. And, like an impartial referee, one of the tasks is to keep play flowing within the workshop, to ensure that everyone is involved and that nobody monopolises the time too greedily. The communal aim of a responsive or generative workshop is to make sure that every writer knows what every individual in that group must do to their own work to improve it or finish it. In that way, we learn for ourselves, and we learn from other models in the group. This is the most generous aspect of communal self-interest. You become many writers while remaining true to your individual aims.

The generative workshop

Within a generative workshop, another cure for homogeneity is for a rich variety of writing tasks to be set. The basic premise is to trigger a new piece of work, and that can be fiction, creative nonfiction, poetry, performance or drama. This is usually an act of simulation, although it can end up producing 'the real thing'. Actors use improvisation to feel their way into role, and generative workshops do the same. Improvising writing on the spot is an exercise in discipline but also in practising a certain degree of *wildness*. You learn to apply the improvisatory and wilder modes to your own writing when you are alone.

The trigger for generating new writing is often a sample of exemplary writing by a published author, whose style or subject you imitate. It may also be a thought-experiment: your tutor or fellow student talks you through a scenario out of which you write. Physical objects or actual incidents may be used to stimulate a response, as in an art or film school. Sometimes tutors use items of visual art, or samples of music, to prompt writing. Restrictions on your writing may be introduced, such as a form, or a verbal or mathematical pattern in which certain words or patterns are imposed or excluded (Chapter Three introduced restrictive writing and form).

The simplest, and often very fruitful, trigger is the challenge to write a story, article or poem on a subject or theme; and to compete to write the one that provokes most reaction. One of the most famous generative workshops (although its participants would be aghast to hear it called such) was that between the poets Byron and Shelley, the eighteen-year-old Mary Shelley, and Dr Polidori in the Villa Diodati, Geneva, in mid-June 1816. Their evening entertainment was reading ghost stories aloud from the *Fantasmagoriana*, reading which prompted Byron to challenge everybody and himself to produce a ghost story. Fiona Mac-Carthy describes how:

> The tale that Mary . . . published two years later as *Frankenstein, or The Modern Prometheus*, was the fruit of that competitive gathering . . . she had lain awake at night . . . evolving a narrative 'which would speak to the mysterious fears of our nature, and awaken thrilling horror'.
>
> (2002: 292)

Many fine stories begin by such happy accident and healthy rivalry. Many generative workshops benefit by beginning with freewriting, the very practice of which helps create as much 'happy accident' as it does gobbledegook. There are thousands of generative workshop exercises, enough to fill this book many times over. In the list of 'Recommended reading', I list other books containing the most interesting or intriguing writing exercises I have read, or seen used in class. Their accent on play is at first quite inhibiting for some writers, but is ultimately liberating.

Tutor and students should not repeat the same exercise incessantly. Some creative writing teachers devise a series of 'recipes' for writing which have worked for them, and they stick with those. The problem arises if the students of their workshops send their work to publishers or journals. The subjects, and the strategy for unfolding the subject, are identical. The weather within their writing reads as if it was the same, and not of their making. In effect, the lead-writer has written a new piece of work, or rewritten an old piece of work, through an act of mass ventriloquism.

Some workshops fuse the two approaches of generation and criticism, and some workshops also engage in collaborative writing, in which students work towards a piece that has been written and devised by the whole group or by smaller groups within the class. Fiction writers work on different parts of a novel together, or poets work on collective forms that accrete from their individual contributions, such as the Japanese form the *Renga*, or a crown of sonnets.

The responsive workshop

What makes the responsive workshop work? Students must receive enough self-responsibility so that the tutor could feel that they are almost not needed, except possibly as a guide, an initiator and then a timekeeper. Every student must contribute, either as a writer or critic, or both. That does not mean that everybody needs to *speak*: everybody simply has to show up with their minds open and critical reflexes on standby. When a student-writer reads from a work, there must be sufficient copies of that work in the room so that everybody can read it. If one or more students are blind, then the work is scanned on to computer beforehand, or given to them in electronic form, so that the student can have heard it, or read it in Braille, before the workshop.

It is vital that all work is read aloud to the group. There is no better way to test the honesty and inevitability of writing, the precision of language or the naturalness of voice. Errors and distortions are palpable in sound. Reading aloud helps situate a story in the mind of a reader. If a student suffers from a speech inhibition (they may have a stammer or be simply shy), then they can elect to have their work read aloud by one of their friends or by the tutor without comment or introduction. All writing should be read plainly and undramatically, lest it elevate the quality of substandard work through a persuasive performance.

When a student reads, they are encouraged not to open their reading with a qualification about the quality of their writing, nor should they offer an anecdote about its creation. The writer must leave their ego at the door. The writer should not talk about the knowledge that went into the creation of the writing, at least not at first; the subject of the workshop is like the visible part of the iceberg, the work that is above water level, the knowledge of creation below. The writing must stand alone, without prejudgement or rehearsed response. The writer elects one or two members of the group to lead the response to the work. After they have finished reading, the tutor allows a few minutes of reading time, during which participants make notes directly on the piece of work.

Hazards

There are whirlpools to negotiate. The first is covered above: the writer down-playing the work and, in that way, premeditating and guiding the criticism – a strategy to evade criticism. A second snare has the same end in view: to seduce the group with easy comedy. One of the least lines of resistance in writing, as far as criticism is concerned, is middlebrow humour: not extreme black humour nor tragicomedy, but an engaging, disarming and gentle writing that resists critical scrutiny. Laughter is one of the most wonderful sounds of the human world. It is wholly understandable that we are drawn to it; few experiences are more rewarding than causing it deliberately, and few experiences more excruciating than causing it without intention.

In a workshop, it is very tempting for a writer to play for laughs, and to bring writing that performs and pleases. The same desire to please leaps up when giving a live reading from work to a public audience: many readings open with poems or stories that are either funny or familiar, rather than dark or challenging. The crowd is pleased, but crowds are fickle. Easy comedy makes for easy gains but, critically, it does not create much forward momentum in a workshop, although it does make it fun, if temporarily, for workshops are fickle also.

Comedy is essential. In fact, the best and blackest comedy is the hardest to write, as Hemingway said: 'A man's got to take a lot of punishment to write a really funny book' (Phillips, 1984: 20). However, *easy* comedy etiolates a group, starving it of serious purpose, allowing a writer to manipulate an audience or group and get away with murder or, at least, mediocre writing. Leave the easy comedy for after the meeting, when the stakes are lower, and laughter and self-mockery are cathartic.

A third hazard, allied to the second, is for members of the group to fall into role play. You may act sanguine so long as your act is genuine. In the same way that members of any group or class tend to sit in the same seats in a room, so the role we play on first meeting somebody new tends to be the role we adopt and develop on subsequent occasions. If the writing group reinforces these roles, because they make for a frictionless social ride, then those roles can ossify. From an ethnologist's point of view, the most dangerous role play arises when a member of the group, a new writer, exceeds in talent the group leader. Everybody knows it, and the Salieri knows its Mozart. However, Salieri's duty is always to help Mozart (as historically he did), not to destroy him (as the myth has it).

We become what we seem, for it is far easier to play a character than to be our open selves – and we have spent considerable time creating fictions by which to live our lives – and to populate our writing with created people. Members of the writing group tend to play out caricatures: the clown or the cold fish; the ingénue or the iceman; the intellectual snob or the noble savage; the therapist or the perfectionist; the silent genius or the iron critic; the wallflower or the flirt; the artiste or an etcetera. Role play displaces responsibility; it is a defence device. Criticism at this level is not an attack – it is not an attack on you; it is not even an attack on your writing. Your writing is not important enough to warrant attack, and therefore it is not necessary to require defence. The writer should remain silent and attentive, not only to gain valuable criticism but also to signal their acceptance of criticism's necessity.

Critical not personal investment

At the level of a workshop, criticism is like business: do not take it personally. A constructed argument from an investigation of a piece of writing is useful to your progress as a writer. It is generous and functional, a rare human combination. What sort of things are we looking for to construct an argument? George Orwell claimed in 'Politics and the English Language' (speaking really of nonfiction):

> A scrupulous writer, in every sentence that he writes, will ask himself at least four questions, thus: What am I trying to say? What words will express it? What image or idiom will make it clearer? Is this image fresh enough to have an effect? And he will probably ask himself two more: Could I put it more shortly? Have I said anything that is avoidably ugly?   (NE2: 2468)

Have these principles in mind when formulating your responses to new work. For complete beginners, you may wish to use a slightly different recipe for critical thinking by making notes under the following headings while the writer is reading the piece aloud to the group: (a) specify what works for you about this piece of writing; (b) specify what does not work; (c) make one specific suggestion that will improve the work; (d) contribute one suggestion as to what reading might help the work or move the writer on from it. Specific and informed criticism is always more useful than general criticism or a personal, emotional, 'supportive' response. Invest in it strongly, and it will be returned to you with interest.

In my experience, to get things moving, the tutor should select two 'lead-critics': one to go first, the other to speak if the first one dries up. The lead-critics comment, initially, on three aspects of the piece. Firstly, what did they feel worked best? Secondly, what did they feel did not work? Thirdly, what changes might be made to remedy those parts that did not work for them? Finally, it is often useful to formulate a question or questions for the writer. Following this specific examination, the discussion broadens out to the bigger picture of the piece as a whole, and this is where other members of the workshop join in. A close eye must be kept on the time of these comments if everybody is to have their turn as the writer or as the critic.

Writing Game

THE ICEMAN COMETH

Think about how you and members of your workshop portray yourselves to each other when you are reading and commenting on work. Who plays the clown or the iceman? Who is the intellectual snob or noble savage? Who is the artiste or wallflower? Make a list of as many archetypes as you can, and decide to swap some of these roles around at subsequent meetings.

AIM: We relax into self-defined roles and our ability to think defaults from the character chosen. Changing roles will shake up a workshop's dynamics; it will lead to its participants 'finding a voice' for their critical minds.

Recommended reading

Rulebooks for writers risk being dull or disingenuous, but Ezra Pound's didactic *ABC of Reading* (New Directions, 1960) remains lively, controversial and self-mocking, and strikes home on choices of language. There are dozens of books containing workshop exercises, as well as guides to using and enjoying writing workshops. The most helpful of these are by writers who are also teachers of writing. Candace Schaefer and Rick Diamond offer inventive guidance for writing poetry, literary creative nonfiction, fiction and drama in their *Creative Writing Guide* (Addison-Wesley 1998), as does Paul Mills in *The Routledge Creative Writing Coursebook* (Routledge, 2006) and Janet Burroway in *Imaginative Writing* (Longman, 2006). Highly innovative class and solo exercises can be found in *Metro: Journeys in Writing Creatively* (Addison-Wesley,

2001) by Hans Ostrom et al. For fiction specialists, I recommend *What If? Writing Exercises for Fiction Writers* (Quill, 1991) by Anne Bernays and Pamela Painter. A thorough introduction to workshop culture and practice can be found in Josip Novakovich's *Fiction Writer's Workshop* (Story Press, 1995) and Carol Bly's *Beyond the Writers' Workshop* (Anchor, 2001). Poets seeking first-rate poetry workshop games should consult *The Practice of Poetry: Writing Exercises from Poets who Teach* (HarperResource, 1992), edited by Robin Behn and Chase Twichell, and *Writing Poems* (Longman Pearson, 2004) by Michelle Boisseau and Robert Wallace. Taken together, these volumes contain thousands of inventive generative workshop exercises *by* experienced writers *for* new writers.

Chapter 5

Processes of creative writing

> As to the poetical character . . . it is not itself – it has no self – it is every thing and nothing – It has no character – it enjoys light and shade; it lives in gusto, be it foul or fair, high or low, rich or poor, mean or elevated – It has as much delight in conceiving an Iago as an Imogen . . . A poet is the most unpoetical of any thing in existence, because he has no Identity – he is continually in for and filling some other Body – The Sun, the Moon, the Sea and Men and Women, who are creatures of impulse, are poetical, and have about them an unchangeable attribute; the poet has none . . . If then he has no self, and if I am a Poet, where is the Wonder that I should say I would write no more?
>
> JOHN KEATS, Letter to Richard Woodhouse (Allen, 1948: 44)

Focus a clear eye on yourself to ensure you plant the natural stages of the writing process into your daily discipline. Creative writing courses mimic these stages, especially long-term or residential courses where the focus is solely on writing, and you are not studying other subjects. If you are not on such a course formally, then you must try to make your life imitate one, but one of your own devising. Your life is a course to which writing lends cause.

Seven processes

Preparing

The creative process begins in preparation, which includes active reading, imitation, research, play and reflection: all conscious actions. This is also the time when you are settling your project, deciding exactly what you are going to do, and researching ways to help you achieve it, including researching history and other factual data for fiction and creative nonfiction. At this stage, motivation helps, and discipline and habit will keep striking that light inside you every day.

Ask yourself two questions: What am I preparing for? and How shall I do this? Then, instead of answering them immediately, stare back along the sightlines of the work you have already completed in your life, and think about ways you might push your next project well beyond anything you have ever reached. Some writers and teachers feel that preparation is a setting of attainable objectives and the acquiring of little methods. It is, but it is also the setting of your own character's switch for the next few months.

You are going to become this project, and live within it for some time. You may as well make the experience as intriguing as possible, and sometimes to make something intriguing means to make it exacting or even impossible. If you embrace the possibility of tipping yourself into a new world, then set yourself targets that appear to be well beyond the sweep and scope of your current intelligence or ability.

The processes by which you reach them will be much more intuitive and less reasoned, and you are more likely to write out of your skin, from your heart, and within your own open space. If you choose this path, you must allow more time for incubation of the project, and for rewriting afterwards. However, thinking and working this way actually alters your character; it improves your capacity for endurance as a writer; and it throws open the door to artistic breakthroughs and evolution of talent.

Another question: Which genres do you want to adopt for your project? It might be the genre that you think suits you best; that you have practised already; or a genre that openly challenges you to change your style, voice or over-familiar frameworks for thinking. When fiction writers take a course in poetry, they do not necessarily wish to become poets. Some novelists regard poetry as a kind of calculus to their own long divisions in prose of character and scene. Drafting poems is a kind of training for their inner ear and for writing without verbal padding. They enter those lit cages of form, metrics and patterns, in order to hone the language of prose, or to invite new ways of saying, or of approaching their subject.

On the other hand, some poets turn to prose fiction and creative nonfiction, not only for the money (a chimerical objective), but also because their poetic voice may inhibit choice and exploration of subject in verse. Indeed, for some, prose offers a holiday from poetry's exactions, and they find they write prose rapidly. In addition, a poet or short story writer may elect to write creative nonfiction to take the concisions of expression into a genre that more people read: these miniaturists of style seek a larger audience out of a desire, say, to share some important issue. All of them begin their preparation through reading, and some degree of conscious planning.

Planning

Planning of this type can include research, but can also include other factors, especially acts of premeditation. For example, a poet may choose to produce a collection of poems that possesses a governing architecture, mentally structuring a whole book of, say, connected confessions; or a book with one or two leitmotifs running through every poem; or a poetic sequence. A creative non-fiction writer usually begins with subject, not structure, and makes a choice; they research the subject, and carry out interviews and archive and internet searches. They may also use brainstorming games to cluster ideas and images for later use.

With fiction writers, it is almost as if its practitioners were groups of twins divided at birth, and whose upbringings were quite different. On the one hand, there are short story writers and novelists who forge ahead with their work with little planning. Their books are an exploration, a journey without maps, or one in which the map of events is a secret held by its characters, as Elizabeth Bowen explained:

> The novelist's perception of his characters takes place *in the course of the actual writing of the novel.* To an extent, the novelist is in the same position as the reader. But his perceptions should be always just in advance. The ideal way of presenting character is to invite perception. In what do the characters pre-exist? I should say, in the mass of matter that had accumulated before the inception of the novel.   (Allen, 1948: 109)

Characters arrive unannounced on page thirty-eight, plot-turns happen, and both must be dealt with as the journey unfolds. These fiction writers invite self-surprise, and it often shows in their writing. On the other hand, there are novelists who plan every page minutely; who scribe flow diagrams and maps of action as if they were storyboarding a movie. They leave little to chance, except chance itself. Even they must leave open space in their blueprints for serendipity.

Incubation

Planning and preparation overlap with the incubation stage, which can seem a contradiction: a languishing action. In this sense, a writer is always at work. In his novel *Old School* Tobias Wolff describes how:

> The life that produces writing can't be written about. It is a life carried on without the knowledge even of the writer, below the mind's business

and noise, in deep unlit shafts where phantom messengers struggle toward us, killing one another along the way; and when a few survivors break through to our attention they are received as blandly as waiters bringing more coffee.   (2005: 156)

We have already examined the importance of dreams, daydreams, unconsciousness, and writing badly; these are aspects of 'a life carried on without the knowledge even of the writer'. Incubation creates an incoming wave of the subconscious that washes over the pages you will write. Let this happen; wallow in it even, even when it feels like a form of depressive stagnation. This is a time for disciplined idleness, and not reading. Importantly, it is not a time for talking about your project, but for listening to it growing.

Beginning

A final work begins, as it were, *in media res*, literally in the middle. Do not begin with the intended *first* sentence of prose or *first* line of poetry. 'Get black on white' used to be Maupassant's advice, and that is what you should do. Writers agree that getting started on a new piece of writing is the most difficult of all the writing processes. Write any sort of rubbish that covers the outlines of what you intend: the plot outline; character sketches; description; a hackneyed sestina. Begin by freewriting and free-associating sentences until some patterns emerge that begin to intrigue you solely for the sound they make, their rustle of possibility.

There is no forward march: begin rewriting some of these into sentences or lines of meaning, and begin the forward stagger into writing. In writing, 'beginning' is a false notion, as is 'finishing'. You start writing by diving straight into its deeper ends, searching for structure. You will discover, later, that the true beginning for any artistic process occurs some way into its composition; all the rest was a kind of drumming of your fingers on the desk, a process that overlapped with incubation. This is the reason some creative writing tutors, when looking for the living words within a student's draft, experiment with the student-author's intention by striking out the first few paragraphs or stanzas.

You have now begun to walk within the open space of the page. The journey becomes an elaborate series of gambles, and there is no sense of forward progression as such; there is shaping and reconfiguring, stepping back, inking in and beginning over. The process of creative writing is analogous to the process of 'blocking out' a painting before shaping the details of the picture, allowing details to become clear within the murk of written material.

Flowing

If you keep to the discipline and habit of daily writing, then continuing will not present many difficulties, not least because you will begin to enjoy the exploration and actively look forward to seeing what happens next. This applies as much to poems and creative nonfiction as to prose fiction. Plot and character can hold you in a spell of anticipation. Within a poem, the adventure is more to do with language, sound and the depth-charge surprise of word combinations or images. This is where writing is the most fun you can have, and still call it work. At best, it feels like conducting an orchestra made of your senses and of language. The audience for writing is invisible to you while you are working; a conductor shows their back to an audience in order to give the best of their work.

I have suggested you maintain a steady flow of work, even a mechanical word count, putting in the hours, and writing quickly and uninhibitedly. 'Write freely and as rapidly as possible and throw the whole thing down on paper. Never correct or rewrite until the whole thing is down' – John Steinbeck. If you are finding this difficult, please turn to the Writing Game 'Improvisations'. Pick up your pen and take it for a walk.

Creative flow has been described by psychologists as a state of total absorption, a superfine focus in which the writer has clear goals but is writing at a stretch: at the limits of their intelligence, in fact. The act of writing becomes an end in itself. Flow can lead to a skewed sense of time; distractions and worries shift into a mental background. This is possibly why writing can become addictive, and also be perceived as therapeutic. However, it takes practice to reach that 'zone', and it is unwise to stay too long in it. As Joyce Carol Oates states, 'The practising writer . . . immersed in his or her project, is not an entity at all, let alone a person, but a curious mélange of wildly varying states of mind, clustered toward . . . the darker end of the spectrum: indecision, frustration, pain, dismay, despair, remorse, impatience, outright failure.'

Fluency is rapture, Virginia Woolf claimed. Momentum in writing is like a perpetual-motion machine, issuing words on words. Without impulsion, the enterprise becomes trudge; surprises grow rare or prefabricated. This pushing forward, even when your writing pushes three steps forward and two steps back, is the writer's natural rhythm and momentum, and you must find your own. Remember: you will rewrite everything. The best thing is to dash it down, and cover the pages, getting 'black on white'. By doing so you will achieve a fresh fluency which only arises through practice. Authors often say that books write themselves, and that invented characters have their own lives. As Seamus Heaney puts it:

Getting started, keeping going, getting started again – in art and in life, it seems to me this is the essential rhythm not only of achievement but of survival, the ground of convinced action, the basis of self-esteem and the guarantee of credibility in your lives, credibility to yourselves as well as others.

Writing Game

IMPROVISATIONS

Choose a time of day when you are free of commitments for thirty minutes. *Improvise* in prose, not poetry, on one of the following subject headings, all of which are adapted from ideas and titles in the Norton American literature anthologies (see Preface):

- A voyage around your bedroom
- Three heroes of your youth
- Adolescence
- A horrible truth about your family
- How to tame a wild tongue
- How to tell a story
- Five lies you tell about yourself
- I heard a fly buzz when I died
- Going to the movies
- When I read a book
- The missed chance
- A life history of your grandmother
- Effort at speech between two people
- Thirteen ways of looking at a blackbird
- Building a fire
- Remembering your last birthday
- Reading the mind of your friends
- Pulling weeds
- Scene in a waiting room
- On observing a large red-streak apple
- A conversation with your parents
- The emperor of ice cream
- The real thing
- Thoughts on the present state of American affairs
- Midnight and I'm not famous yet
- One square metre of your soul
- Fates worse than death
- Owlwoman and coyote
- After a dinner party
- What it is like to be hungry every day
- Why you are wonderful

The average word count for each day should be about 500 words. Try to reach this number as best you can by writing fast.

AIM: This game lasts a whole month, and requires you write every day for thirty minutes on subject headings, some of which will make you 'write what you know' (such as 'Adolescence') or 'write what you don't know' (such as 'How to tame a wild tongue'). Improvisation is good practice, especially when you feel blocked, and provokes happy accidents. The point is not to create the free associations of free-writing, but to encourage concentration and improvisation on one subject, and to engender the *habit of fluency*, a little like practising scales before improvising your own melodies. Once you have completed this game, try making up your own subject headings and titles from the Norton anthologies, and improvise from them regularly. You may wish to play a guessing game of the origins of the titles given.

The silence reservoir

The writing process is not unidirectional, but a total, an organic process. It is unwise to imagine that 'incubation' wakes one evening; 'beginning' rises with the moon; and 'continuing' follows like sunrise. Each phase smashes, or melds, into the other. The process may be rapture, but sometimes feels like a sequence of ruptures, or even a series of running battles with language. For example, incubation is part of fluency and flow. You will often find your fluency naturally slowing in order to allow the reservoir of language and ideas within your unconscious mind to replenish. Leave the field. Stop writing. Finish for the day, and go for a walk. Give yourself the time to recover your eloquence through silence. Silence is itself a type of eloquence, for thinking about writing *is* writing. Idleness itself is also conducive, but less easy to get away with. You will find, as you do so, that the reservoir fills quickly, and words and phrases rise through it in shoals.

Breakthroughs and finish lines

One of the matters you will begin to apprehend is not progress, as such, but a feeling of completion, when form and structure click together sweetly in your mind. You will also begin to be able to gauge where your work has reached in relation to the target you set in the first place for this project. Writers operate on the same artistic plane for a time, working through several pieces of writing, or even several books. However, given sufficient fluency through practice, they make artistic breakthroughs and leaps while writing *one* particular piece – a poem or short story, say. One analogy comes from evolutionary theory.

In early studies of natural selection, palaeontologists could not understand the progression of fossil evidence for the evolution of a species, such as a horse. Instead of evolving in small and gradual stages (and leaving the useful remains in the mud like a chain of evidence), species seemed to 'jump' from one significant stage to another. This was called stochastic evolution, as if the species 'aimed at a mark'. Observed from outside, writers evolve their voices and styles stochastically, making occasional quantum leaps in the quality and authenticity of their writing.

However, once a writer has 'jumped' a stage, and made a breakthrough, they very rarely fall back to their former quality or practices. The whole landscape of their game has altered forever. Be aware of this as you are writing, and watch for such jumps and steps in the evolution of your talent. At these times, it will be hard for you to comprehend just how you wrote the piece. It will seem the work of another person entirely, and you may think it the work of some mysterious 'other' (as you will read in the final section of this chapter). Like a string of powerful love affairs, every book (as Joyce Carol Oates has written) will feel like *The Book* while you are writing it.

You will get used to all of this after a while – the apparent mystery of process will become clearer, and you will then want to set your objectives even further away from your new level. You will have the feeling of having completed a stage of development, although that does not mean you have finished. 'To finish is a sadness to a writer – a little death. He puts the last word down and it is done. But it isn't really done. The story goes on and leaves the writer behind, for no story is ever done' – John Steinbeck. For most writers, nothing is finished; it is abandoned, for nothing is perfectible in language without killing it. A novel is finished many times. A poetry collection is sorted and resorted, ordered and reordered, until it finds some provisional shape. Many writers revise their work even after publication. Sometimes the thorniest issue to finalise is the title.

On titles

What does a title perform? What does it do, sitting there on its own like a little crown prince of your continent of writing? The title offers a first impression to readers. Like it or not, it may tip the balance between your work being read or not, and it might form part of what is graded within a writing course. You must make your title work as hard as all the words in your piece – harder, in fact, for the title is a door for the reader to open, or a little window through which they peep at the interior, an intrigue making them question whether they should enter or take part. A lazy or imprecise title can damn an entire book.

This applies to poems, stories, novels and creative nonfiction. Spend a great deal of *conscious* time on your titles, and produce many maquettes of it:

several versions and variations that you can trial on your fellow writers in your workshops, or your tutors. Use a working title to begin with, even if you dispense with it later, since evasions like 'Untitled', 'Story' or 'Poem' carry no charge. You might borrow a phrase from a well-known literary work, but make sure there is a precise resonance between the phrase and your own work; or go through your own piece and locate a phrase that either summarises it or captures its spirit. It may be that one of the character's names, the setting, or the time, contains that spirit too, as might your theme, or some overriding idea, or trick of structure. Titles require a reader's eye, and many titles come to their authors a long time after composing, when writers can become a reader *of* themselves again. Choose wisely and, if you do not have that leisure, at least choose precisely.

The writer post-performance

Rewriting

Actually, the performance has yet to begin. Writing it down is just the overture. *All* of what we write needs planing and pruning and, as all writing is rewriting, so all rewriting is another form of writing. 'The most essential gift for a good writer is a built-in, shock-proof lie detector. This is the writer's radar and all great writers have had it.' – Ernest Hemingway. Or so you hope. Many of us are wedded to our work even when we know it is under-performing, and that goes for other art forms. Writing of musical composition, Johannes Brahms declared, 'It is not hard to compose, but it is wonderfully hard to let the superfluous notes fall under the table.'

Rewriting your work requires a quite different state of mind from creating it from nothing. We work so hard on some sentences that we find it impossible to part with them. Or: we find something inappropriate in one part of our writing, but it glistens too beguilingly. However, we must become self-editors, remembering that striking phrases contaminate with their beauty and we should excise them. Various qualifying words and phrases do not tug the momentum of the book forwards. They are easily identified, and adjectives and adverbs are the first to feel the spotlight of redrafting. Any word or phrase that distracts the attention of the reader from the book is redundant. Any word or phrase that diverts the reader by its exoticism or literariness is also in peril: clichés, archaisms and inversions must earn their place or suffer deletion.

There are certain simple procedures that all writers can try for themselves. I have already stressed the importance of reading your work aloud. It exposes the errors or niggles of sound and sense; it shows up where your language is forced, flaccid or affected. You may also benefit by asking someone else (for example in your workshop) to read your work aloud to you. This offers even greater distance. You should imagine that you are not the author and listen carefully for where the reader stumbles over words, and make note to rewrite them. A ruthless but useful technique, suggested by Ursula Le Guin in *Steering the Craft*, is to cut one of your narrative exercises by half: 'Severe cutting intensifies your style, forcing you both to crowd and leap' (1998: 147). Begin by cutting every adjective, then the adverbs.

Another procedure is to watch out for where a piece of work *begins*. You will find the first paragraph or even paragraphs of a piece of nonfiction or fiction redundant. Attempt to mutate your work through various versions. For example, with poetry, try reading the draft from the second line onwards, then the third line, then the fourth, and so on until the thing rings right. Try reading a poem backwards, line by line, or stanza by stanza. Mix the stanzas about in different orders. Practise this with something of a cold eye, until you begin to feel the work has some recognisable life. Keep copies of all these mutant versions of the original. Who knows? More than one may be 'right', or even some conflation of two mutant versions. Keep copies of everything; maintain an organised paper trail from first to final draft should you need to salvage something.

Writers rewrite 'endlessly, endlessly, endlessly . . . even after it's published' – Frank O'Connor. You look at the writing again. Some of it holds up. You sense your words have their own life and music, and it would be dangerous to tinker. The part that holds up is the board and bind of the natural-language pressures meeting the artificial, mathematical human choices *you* took in turning and transforming the words. In rewriting, you create new, knottier pressures, holding the superstructure of your story or poem in place. However, there may still be some uselessness stuck in your work, undermining it as more and more readers are exposed to it. This is a very dangerous moment, with little of the excitement of fluent composition. Take stronger words away – you would watch the thing crumble. It would unpick itself – your story or poem would actually unmake itself before your own eyes. There is a feeling of *in*ability and even panic: Can I walk away from this one? Can I leave it as it is? There is shamelessness, too: Does my name carry enough weight that I can get away with this half-made work?

Failing, and failing better

If you ever ask yourself questions like this, then you have become too involved. You require some indifference: either the eye of time or somebody else to look it over. Put the work away for three weeks, then revise it, or give it to a trusted member of your circle. Indifference allows savagery. Tobias Woolf likens the process to learning how 'to keep gnawing the same bone until it cracked' (2005: 156). Cut and compress. Rearrange and rewrite, adding and subtracting as you go. Condensing a piece of prose requires one of two approaches. You could plan the entire content in detail, allocate a given number of words and then try to keep to those limits as you draft, or work without regard for length and then slash and burn. While poets tend to tinker word by word (and sound by sound), many prose writers adopt the slash-and-burn approach, in which they draft without thinking too much about length, and then hack back as necessary. Slash and burn has a cut-your-losses logic all of its own. Never forget the possibility that your writing does not work. Say the unsayable: it has failed. You will try again. There is merit in abandoning a mediocre piece, and starting again with a blank sheet and a savage sense of accomplishment gained by decisiveness: by learning from error rather than rewriting versions of the same mistake. Samuel Beckett nailed it: 'Ever tried. Ever failed. No matter. Try again. Fail again. Fail better.'

Deadlines as lifelines

One huge aid to the writing–rewriting dynamic is the deadline. It forces savage action. Like form or design, the deadline is not a prison to creation. It offers a promised release from the self-created prison of indolence, of not writing. It is as liberating as form, despite the sensation that it makes time weigh upon the act of writing. But that weight is not just the weight of expectation; it is also the weight of anticipation. Deadlines are good for us, stern though they may seem.

A deadline is like a supervisor who tells you impolitely to get on with it. The deadline pays heed to your writing; it does not pay heed to your life. The deadline set for the submission of a student's portfolio of writing pays little heed to the different ways that students write, learn and live. The date is the same for everybody, and only illness or accident can provide excuses. The deadline is a necessary falsification of time. What's more, somebody else has usually placed it in your calendar, which can make it feel almost like a physical threat. The threat is that some reward will not come your way should you fail to meet it. Those rewards can include the score your work receives or an advance of money. It may include promotion, sales, or the praise of a tutor, editor, critic or reader.

In the writing business, deadlines are a fact. Writers working in the media, especially, write against them daily, even hourly, and the practice of journalism provides outstanding training not only in punctuality and brinkmanship, but also in economy and clarity. Hemingway received his training on the *Kansas City Star*. 'On the *Star* you were forced to learn to write a simple declarative sentence. This is useful to anyone. Newspaper work will not harm a young writer and could help him if he gets out of it in time' (Phillips, 1984: 38).

Deadlines demand concision and conclusion; at some point, a piece of writing is as complete as it can be. The threat and the reward hanging over that final process are usually external factors. Academic years trot their tidy schedules; newspapers net their copy; publishers pump out books on schedule, in tandem with the schedules of their marketing and sales departments. In the middle of these demands, the writer sits with their stalled or stilted creations, with both eyes on the clock. I suggest you seize back the initiative, and use the power of time as a motivation to write. By setting your own deadline (it must be earlier than the official deadline), you take control of the process psychologically. You will also learn to appreciate how your deadline then gives *form* to the way you write and even to how you conduct your life around that, as we explored in the section on discipline.

Your challenger

Drafting requires objectivity of a sort, so you may choose to disembody yourself; become impersonal; or even play somebody else, some other writer that is used to overcoming this moment and pressing on with the next draft. You might even view the creative act of drafting as a journalist turning in their copy. Having a real deadline imposed by somebody else is useful here. Writing then becomes a job, not a chore, not yet an art – which is liberating. The reward is completion combined with a fee or, in a student's case, what you hope will be a good grade. It is tough, in the beginning, to motivate yourself by inventing some reward for completing your work by a deadline. In which case, have someone external to yourself devise and set that deadline in order to have the reward of their approbation. Writers often use their partners for this role, but these relationships must be demonstrably robust to survive such role play, especially if the stakes are high. I know many writers who are unremittingly cruel in this regard. How you do this will depend, therefore, upon the trust between you and your challenger (a better word); and the level of obsession you are able to bring to the table, and the level your challenger is willing to put up with.

Precisions of process

Most of the ways we express ourselves in prose and in speech are imprecise; tangential at best to what we intend to say and mean. We all know the frustration of not having said what we intended; of not having communicated what you felt was your version of a truth. However, writing gives you time for rehearsal, and time to get your words as right as possible. Clarity is crucial; it is a desirable quality in writing.

As Strunk and White declare, 'Although there is no substitute for merit in writing, clarity comes closest to being one' (2000: 79). Clarity is of the first importance. When we use words, we have to use the right words and the right words in the best order. When we examine and fossick the world for material for our writing, we must be precise about what we really see, hear, touch, smell and taste. The garden of language is the same; so much language claims our attention and thought that we must be precise in what we choose, in where we place it and in the overall and particular correspondences of those placings.

Our perceptions and apprehensions are, of course, partial and particular, but we can train ourselves to perceive more imaginatively and empathically through practice. Knowing that the world is wider than our thought leaves people with a choice either to find out more about that world or to find the worlds inside you. Both are positive choices, since they are active. An easier life is available through a wilful ignorance of the self and the world around you. This option is not available to us as writers.

A writer will want to balance these choices but pursue them both simultaneously. There are various ways to get out of oneself and into the world. Experience plays a part, and our notebooks allow us to arrest the motion of experience and record it for our use, but engagement with knowledge plays a part also. Forms of knowledge carry their cargoes through language. We can borrow these languages, we can burrow into these forms of knowledge, but it is our duty to do so honestly and learn their precision and, with that, their power.

Writing Game

SHAKESPEARE'S FIELD TRIP
Rise before dawn one day. Make your way to the nearest green and open space, or woodland. Carefully observe the process of the dawn through its natural consequences on animals, and on the way trees and flowers react to the light, and the action of the different declensions of light on water. I also want you to observe the surface of a stone wall or a rock very closely, making notes on everything that you see. Make nothing up. Do not impose your own aesthetic judgement, emotions or mood on what you are writing. Your task is to build a poem or story out of what you observe or, more precisely, to let the observations, the things, the life, make a poem or story from you. When you have finished, go

back to the place with your writing, and place it somewhere where it can be seen by other visitors; or hang it from the branch of a tree.

AIM: Try being entirely self-effacing in this writing, as the best poets, naturalists and scientists are, but also playful in how you 'perform' your work. By placing your poem or story in the 'publication' of a natural space, you are echoing a moment in Shakespeare's *As You Like It*, when a lover hangs sonnets from the trees of the Forest of Arden:

> these trees shall be my books,
> And in their barks my thoughts I'll character
> That every eye which in this forest looks
> Shall see thy virtue witnessed everywhere

(For your interest, this workshop was pioneered in a remnant of the ancient Forest of Arden in Warwickshire, England.)

Raiding the languages of elsewhere

Names have great power, and here we encompass not only the names of people, places and countries, but also the scientific and local names for fauna and flora. We might learn the terms for natural phenomena created by geography, geology, astronomy and oceanography, and the terminologies of the synthetic world from fields of architecture, information technology and engineering. Moreover, we need not stop at names and terms; by entering into an engagement with traditionally non-literary fields of knowledge, we open their languages (and even their sometimes-opaque jargon) for our use as writers. By doing so, we release fresh themes and subjects for our imagination to scrutinise, turn over and play with.

The American poet Marianne Moore wrote poems the design of which depended mostly on syllabic count and intricate judgements concerning space and line breaks. The language and subject of her poetry almost seemed to spring from the language and subject of a clear scientific paper. As William Logan puts it, 'Moore found the poetry lying asleep within prose, in manuals and monographs, advertisements and government reports' (2005: 89). Here is the opening of 'The Icosasphere' (Moore, 1968: 143):

> 'In Buckinghamshire hedgerows
> the birds nesting in the merged green density,
> weave little bits of string and moths and feathers and thistledown
> in parabolic concentric curves' and
> working for concavity, leave spherical feats of rare efficiency . . .

A reading of Moore's 'Notes' to her poems reveals a scrupulous regard for recording the source of her creations. They illuminate the extent of her library, the compendiousness and open-mindedness of her reading, her voracity for knowledge, the polyvalence of which appeals to a writer. With regard to the poem above, the sources throw light not only on the subject of the poem but also on the geometrical design of her work. Try writing a story or poem that contains her finding that 'a steel globe of twenty equilateral triangles – the greatest number of regular sides geometrically possible – could be grouped into five parallelograms and cut from rectangular sheets with negligible scrap loss' (Moore, 1968: 281).

You can discover precise, clear language of this type easily, and a good creative exercise is to 'find' such material and transform it into something of your own. Take any good field-guide you have to hand and open it at random. You will find precise, and sometimes magically incisive, description, and names that seem to fall from fairy tales, and a language as precise as it is strange to the ear. In the following example, I have broken some prose verbatim into counted syllabic lines; I have placed episodes of linked description into stanzas, and indented lines in a way which forces the eye to move around the page to find connections and answers. Nevertheless, it could also stand as prose given the right context; little has been changed (the italics are in the original text):

Found Poem: 'The European Larch'
The Alps –
   replaced by Norway Spruce
      in colder, wetter areas –
         with ranges
            in the Tatra and Sudetan
  plains and mountains of Poland.
      Long cultivated and abundant:
      in older plantations, shelterbeds
    and parks,
away from cities and the driest, drabbest areas.

Shape: spire-
   like, on a trunk straight up
      only in the finest, sheltered
         trees; often
         broad and characterful in age
in arid or exposed sites.
      The fine shoots *hang* under the branches.
        Blond in winter. More finely, spiki–
        ly twig–
gy – set against, say, the Ginkgo or, say, a Swamp Cypress.

We will look at 'found poetry' in Chapter Eight. You are encouraged to take what you can from other writers, but the argument here is that you should also take what you can from other *non-literary* writers, whether they are scientists, architects or even businesspeople.

Precision and voice

The right names and terms give your writing greater power and show you have done your work. Precise language wakes or rewakes the world and replicates it more immediately than a film ever could. Moreover, clarity finds its equal in simplicity – the hardest skill for a writer to master. The other property in writing that comes out of precision, clarity and simplicity is a natural 'sound' or voice to the writing (Raymond Carver and Robert Frost are exemplary in this respect). The 'ear' of the writer becomes unmuffled, and the language carries that quality too; in doing so it feels natural, it feels *of* the world rather than an artifice made *from* the world. As an example for possible imitation, read this extract from 'A Cold Spring' by Elizabeth Bishop:

> The infant oak-leaves swung through the sober oak.
> Song-sparrows were wound up for the summer . . .
> Now, from the thick grass, the fireflies
> begin to rise:
> up, then down, then up again:
> lit on the ascending flight,
> drifting simultaneously to the same height,
> – exactly like the bubbles in champagne.
>
> (Bishop, 1979: 56)

'Swung through the sober oak. Song-sparrows were wound up for summer. Fireflies lit on the ascending flight.' The trained field biologist in me wants to shout, 'Exactly!' and then discover what 'the same height' for fireflies is. Alert, evocative, precise writing of this standard is not too far from the best observational nature writing, or writing that arises from scientific inquiry. Obviously, an ethologist would not reach for the simile of 'exactly like the bubbles in champagne' while writing a scientific paper, but they might were they writing a popular nonfictional book on the life of fireflies. You may wish to learn this precision, too: by observing the world, and making translations from the natural world into your own creative writing.

Writing Game

Here is an extract from a poem about a snail by the Australian Les Murray from his book *Translations from the Natural World*:

> by the gilt slipway, and by pointing
> perhaps as far back into time as
> ahead, a shore being folded interior,
> by boiling on salt, by coming uncut over
> a razor's edge, by hiding the Oligocene
> underleaf may this and every snail sense
> itself ornament the weave of presence.
>
> 'Mollusc' (1993: 26)

As with Bishop's 'A Cold Spring', note again not only the precise observations, but also the naming ('Oligocene'), and the concise sounds within the language which simulate what the words are describing ('coming uncut over / a razor's edge'). Your game is to find a natural history field-guide, and locate a found poem or story within it. Write it out as your own, before altering it as you wish in order to make a final poem or short story that imitates the precision of language of a field-guide, and a precision of your own observation in the writing.

AIM: The language and syntax of Murray's poem seek precisely to imitate the movement, the inner world, the perceptual world, of the snail. This takes an alert writer: the poem must *be* a snail; the poem must 'itself ornament the weave of presence'. In language (to quote William Blake), energy is eternal delight, and the energy of your expression as a writer gains from precision: the right words in the right order.

Confidence and practice

It is not only important to practise a certain degree of ruthlessness as a writer; it is also imperative to practise confidence. Who is born confident? The possession of confidence says much about how a person was raised and educated; about how others treated them; and about their attitude to themselves. Confidence clambers over some of the same obstacles as talent, and the difficulty and complexity of those obstacles creates and shapes the writer. The absence of confidence tells its own tale. Many writers appear, on the face of it, to possess confidence; very often, they do not. It is an act, another performance to some degree, although it need not be pretence. 'The act of writing is an act of optimism. You would not take the trouble to do it if you felt that it didn't matter' – Edward Albee.

The invisible audience

When you, as a writer, sit down to work, there is always a certain amount of prevarication as you adjust to the condition of the task ahead, and for new creative writers that prevarication can be extremely uncomfortable because the condition is unfamiliar. The *role* is also unknown, and the role is difficult to understand because the writer performs at nothing, to nobody, to a notional audience, invisible to the writer – possibly an audience that does not exist, or has yet to be created.

An actor takes to the stage and views their audience; the audience's response makes and moulds their performance; and a good actor can smell when the audience is on their side, or when they need winning. A writer's audience, as Margaret Atwood says, 'consists of individuals whom he may never see or know. Writer and audience are invisible to each other; the only visible thing is the book, and a reader may get hold of a book long after the writer is dead' (2002: 43).

One of the benefits of a creative writing course is that you have a better idea of who the audience for your work might be, even if it is only the writers teaching the course. For many writers, the sheer habit of writing is what forces the performance, which is why discipline is so important. Another trigger is the knowledge that 'not writing' makes one feel a great deal worse than writing, which, when the performance is going well, creates euphoria in the audience *within* the writer. The writer-as-actor senses the invisible audience within themselves, willing them on to win that self or selves.

Suspensions of belief

A new writer should try to suspend belief in what they are: uncertain and unable. One of the processes offered by cognitive psychotherapy is to imagine a situation that causes you to feel awful; to hold that image in your mind; and then to shrink it as the opposite situation takes over. Let that image be you, the new writer, sitting down to work. Using your imagination, place the same situation in a positive light – a fine paragraph made, an electric piece of dialogue, a poem of precision. Hold that image in your mind alongside the first negative image. Then, gradually, enlarge the positive image and shrink the other, until only the positive one remains. Remember how you feel as you hold that image in your mind, and teach yourself to think and feel *that* way every time you sit down to write. You will begin to believe in your own possibility, and that creates confidence. Confidence affects the quality and style of your writing, and writing in this frame of mind will become habitual and addictive, as euphoria becomes familiar through practice. We become what we seem; what was performance becomes life; you inhabit the character of the writer without pretence. The action of writing can prove to be an *act* of writing, only there is nothing phoney about it. It would be glib and misleading, however, to think this is going to work all the time, especially if the writer suffers from self-doubt, as all do, or depression, as many do. Reversals to type will happen. To continue, we have to become somebody, or several people, other than ourselves.

Self's voices

Suspensions of belief are not always possible. Sometimes a writer's brain dries, in exactly the same way in which an actor's voice dries on stage, and the confidence to say, or write, vanishes. It feels a lot worse than it is because it feels like a loss of ability, a loss of voice. It shouts, 'You will never again write well.' It feels almost as if we have forgotten our speech, and that we have caught ourselves out in an embarrassing self-deception. Or: our body gets in the way of the practice of writing with illness, depressions and mood swings. Or: the price of precision can be perfectionism, an attitude that can result in freezing before the headlights of your own expectations.

At this point in a writer's career, the resilience of the personality has a great say in whether artistic progress is made or not. You either freeze or thaw. Everything experienced so far, everything written and read, decides that outcome. This happens repeatedly, at every stage, especially at the beginning. The consequence is ultimately decisive and life-changing. Moments like this can precipitate artistic crisis: writing careers can fall apart, the language becoming clinical or unravelled and worn-out. All the tricks show, and show the writer up. This is not writing block; it is disaster. This is the time to employ a metaphorical ghostwriter, to become your own ghostwriter in the employ of your writing self. It is time to discover your other writing selves.

Voice

Do you require crisis to make discoveries? Since writers lurch about in language, yes, you probably do. Knowing this is going to happen does not mean you can evade it, but it does mean you can use various guises of the self's voice to get by and take risk. Finding your voice might be only one stage on the way to finding your voices, or finding your style. Your style, above all else, is your aim, and it should show no sign of effort. But your writing voice must be distinctive; it must be differentiated from its precursors or your reader will stop listening.

Voice may seem mysterious not least because, in creative writing, it begins as a metaphor. To quote Novakovich, 'Novice writers go around looking for their voices just as people used to go around "looking for themselves"' (1995: 200). Voice is a three-way metaphor: for writing as you speak; for writing as you speak at your best; and for writing with rigour, stripping away all the unnecessary apparatus from language that stop you from speaking clearly, that stop you being phoney.

Say what you mean, and say it without pose, equivocation or elaboration, and, believe me, you will find your voice. This makes it sound easy, whereas what has happened is that I have been pithy and plain. Try writing as directly and actively as you can. The reader will always be able to tell when you are not writing in your voice, since your syntax will sound inauthentic. Although writing is often there to make a fiction of the world, and to convey fiction's greater truth, the voice makes the writing honest and authentic, truer than any relative truth.

Writing Game

PORTRAITS OF THE ARTIST
This is a class exercise. Make pairs. Each person draws or paints the other while simultaneously being drawn or painted. Draw what you see; invent nothing. Do not show the subject what you have drawn until they have also finished. Then exchange drawings, and write a poem of ten lines *or* a flash fiction (see Chapter Six) of two paragraphs as a direct and immediate response to (a) what you see as you look at this drawing of yourself, or (b) how it felt being scrutinised. Rewrite this piece and then fix it to the drawing. Now, sit down separately and draw a picture of yourself, without using a mirror. You can feel free to make things up about your appearance; this can be a realistic or fantastic representation, or one that combines both approaches. Pass this drawing to the other writer, who writes (as above) on the subject of this drawing. Fix this writing to this picture. Display both pictures, with their writing, in some public space.

AIM: Where is the truth of the self? Is it located in the observer or the observed, or in the act of observation or the act of observing? The self we see in the mirror, and the selves we explore in the mirrors of our writing, are always different. The self is mutable, and writing is a performance of one's self and selves. The self in the mirror is also quite different from how we are seen, for everybody's perception of us depends on the time of day, their view, and their skill at recording us visually. When we draw our own face, we also falsify truth; we offer a partial snapshot of a mirror. When we write, we sometimes write out of a discomfort with that parallax between the self and world, and self and selves. However, we write to improve on truth, not to tell the truth. This game objectifies that procedure.

"...THE NOTION OF THE OTHER HAS BEEN AS THEORIZED TO DEATH AS THE AUTHOR. LEAVING NOT ONLY THE AUTHOR DEAD, BUT THE FAMOUS OTHERS STALKING THE EARTH LIKE ZOMBIES."

Placebo selves

As I wrote, finding your voice may be one step to finding several voices, even to the point of 'losing your voice'. Writers work using different states of their own mind, and voices become a plural. The taste of your own self's medicine might be, at times, unnecessary or inhibiting to your development or you might even find your voice boring. In the way that a placebo-medicine can have the effect of real medicine, so the selves with whom you are communing may write as well as you, and sometimes better. All these selves lead to different personalities of voice, but they are not personae. They are placebos.

What I term 'placebo writing' often produces interesting work by people who have struggled to write anything with ease, energy or imagination. A 'placebo voice' takes them outside themselves, like a literary translation by the writer, but *of* themselves. Of course, the fastest way to slip on another's skin is literary translation, as we discovered in Chapter Three. What a placebo voice does, however, is reduce self-expectation, simultaneously earthing the negative charges of artistic and linguistic inhibition. Yet this is no 'performance'. These 'placebo selves' and voices already exist in you. As you carried out the Writing Games in this book, especially as you free-wrote, you began to realise that the self you know is not necessarily the self who writes, or the one who writes well. How many selves are there with which to play?

The Other

The idea of the Other is only a metaphor for a state of mind while writing. One of the troubles is that the notion of the Other has been as theorised to death as the Author, leaving not only the author dead, but their famous Others stalking the earth like zombies. It is best to keep it simple, and say that many creative writers experience the sensation that somebody other *in* them is at work while writing. A depressive person may well rely on this form of the Other in order to get by in everyday life. As the poet Edward Thomas puts it:

> I wait his flight.
> He goes: I follow: no release
> Until he ceases. Then I also shall cease.
> 'The Other'   (1978: 33)

This is not a mystical notion, although it was once interpreted as a muse for whom the writer was a medium. Partly it is a leap of the imagination into the open space of somebody else, or even *something* else. Keats would write about taking part in the life of a sparrow or knowing what it must feel like to be a billiard ball! Like negative capability, the Other is a psychological notion, a disassociation within the sensibility of the self: a controlled bipolar sense, one that allowed the poet Arthur Rimbaud to speak of an 'I' that 'is an other': *Je est un autre*. Sometimes that Other feels disassociated to the degree that it is outside of you; in this case a creative daemon, a creature or person that stalks you, is tracked by you, but *is* part of you, a little like the figure of the Devil in James Hogg's novel *The Private Memoirs and Confessions of a Justified Sinner* (1824). The author lives with their *autre* as best they can, for who is brave enough to say which is which, and who is who?

Playing dead

A ghostwriter or, in this case, the persona of an *other* taken to extremes, has several advantages, one of which is they do not need to endure directly any of the experiences or passions that go towards the making of a book other than to take the dictation of 'the author'. This is not a schizophrenic exercise, but liberation of the self from the self: the art of losing your *self.* You do not write as *l'autre*; you write as though you were entirely absent, as though you were dead, as though you had no responsibility left to life, and no audience to please or pander to. This, like many other exercises in this book, is a simple thought-experiment, one that proceeds by metaphorising the process of the self at work. You *do need* to believe in it, at least while writing or beginning to write. However, do not take this role outside your writing room.

This is not a tone of voice so much as a tone of mind: the mind engages its own mortality in a porcelain language, language that is firm, but does not conceal the inherent breakability in its making. In late life, great poets and novelists can achieve that cold and clarifying self-obliteration: experience and ceaseless practice demand it of the voice. The effect of such self-characterisation is not self-dramatisation; it is a forensic, merciless honesty. The character and performance of the writer becomes posthumous, a colder and clearer way of expression, and one that requires a little less worrying about the temporal.

So, how can you, as a new writer, achieve what it takes a lifetime to know? Well, you can learn to care less about the whole received idea of writing as something mystical. Do it and, if you cannot *do* it, then act it. The point of this thought-experiment is to achieve a coldness and frankness of expression that is largely unavailable to either the writer who lives in the moment and in their appetites or one who cannot help thinking too much.

What I am urging is that you do not wait for age to confer such an attitude, nor long experience to clothe you with wisdom or material, but that you create a cognitive short circuit within yourself by playing both the attitude and the wisdom. You will risk sounding presumptuous, but risk is in everything you try. Play dead. Write as though a *dead* line lay so near to you that what you are writing is the final thing you will write. By doing so many times, it will become one of the habits of writing, and one of many self-roles of the dramatic personae within you. Remember: it is a tone of mind.

Playing others

You will begin to recognise that there is some heartlessness at the core of writing, despite its assertion and celebration of human values. The mother of the French novelist Gustave Flaubert wrote that her famous son's 'mania for creating sentences' had 'dried up his heart'. Writing can be as faceless and as masked a business as drama. The novelist Jorge Luis Borges diagnoses the talent in Shakespeare: 'There was no one in him; behind his face . . . and his words, which were copious, fantastic and stormy, there was only a bit of coldness, a dream dreamt by no one. At first he thought that all people were like him.'

Have you ever had the experience of thinking that all people are like you? By observing, remembering and imagining, you absorbed these others, as selves. They are sometimes masks behind which you write: *personae*. Borges can also think of himself as two people, as 'Borges and I', in which the other Borges

> is the one things happen to . . . I like hourglasses, maps, eighteenth century typography, the taste of coffee and the prose of Stevenson; he shares these preferences, but in a vain way that turns them into the attributes of an actor . . . I do not know which of us has written this page.   (quoted in Burke, 1995: 339)

Borges claims that he lets the 'first self' go on living, so that the other self can create literature, and that this writing justifies the existence of the first self: 'my life is a flight and I lose everything and everything belongs to oblivion, or to him'. To paraphrase Margaret Atwood, in her book of essays on writing *Negotiating With the Dead* (2002), a writer also consists of individuals whom they may never see or know. The person and the writer are invisible to each other or they might move between selves, characters of themselves, while they are writing. Indeed, this facility is one of the engines for development of characters in fiction and creative nonfiction, or of voice (and voices) in writing more generally. As Samuel Beckett said, 'I write about myself with the same pencil and in the same exercise book as about him. It is no longer I, but another whose life is just beginning.'

If this disposition is extreme, it can be perceived as extrovert, a mild schizophrenia even. When in the flow of writing, it is almost as if the writer

"...MANY CREATIVE WRITERS EXPERIENCE THE SENSATION THAT SOMEBODY OTHER *IN* THEM IS AT WORK."

has gone native with their created personae or characters, like an actor staying in role to explore their stage or movie character to its fingertips. Once upon a time, this faculty might have come within the realm of sensibility: sympathy for the other, or others. It did so with Charles Dickens, a veritable sponge of selves, through his facility to 'transport' into the mind, body and history of observed people and look out from within them. In this example, from 'A Visit to Newgate', he writes from the point of view of a real man he has seen for a moment (not a fictional character), condemned to execution in Newgate Prison:

> Seven hours left! He paces the narrow limits of his cell with rapid strides, cold drops of terror starting on his forehead, and every muscle of his frame quivering with agony . . . He suffers himself to be led to his seat, mechanically takes the bible which is placed in his hand, and tries to read and listen. No . . . The book is torn and soiled by use – and like the book he read his lessons in, at school, just forty years ago! He has never bestowed a thought upon it, perhaps, since he left it as a child: and yet the place, the time, the room – nay, the very boys he played with, crowd as vividly before him.   (NE2: 1344)

Writing Game

'METHOD' WRITING
Each member of the writing group elects to be another person within it for one week. They follow their routines; they even exchange rooms, parents, house keys and writing habits. After one week, they bring either a new story or poem to the group, which is written from the point of view of that other, or from using the other's style or voice.

AIM: Our world is too much with us. Sometimes we need to slip into somebody else's life, or even their skin, to understand our own aims and processes better, and possibly even to write better. Method actors sometimes live as their characters before playing them on stage or screen.

Being others

One can use versions of oneself to create writers, each of which is a persona. You are not creating fictional page-bound characters; you are creating artificial people, real to everybody else except yourself. For example, the Portuguese writer Fernando Pessoa invented four writing selves, each of whom published under their own name and had their own style of writing (1974). They were, however, all Fernando Pessoa. We contain multitudes (or maybe four . . .). You write *in* character, another self so far away from your nature psychologically that they follow a separate but fictional existence. You invent heteronyms, and hetero-existences.

Why would you do this? Firstly, it allows you some distance on your own practice as a writer. Secondly, it gives complete freedom to write as you wish, because it removes responsibility for the work's reception from your name. Thirdly, it encourages you to explore different styles and voices, which can be allotted in any fixed combination to each of your heteronyms. There are also practical and political considerations, some of which are strategies for survival. Women have published under male names in order to conceal their gender at a time when publication for women was near impossible, as Virginia Woolf explains in 'A Room of One's Own':

> It was the relic of the sense of chastity that dictated anonymity to women even so late as the nineteenth century. Currer Bell, George Eliot, George Sand, all the victims of inner strife as their writings prove, sought ineffectively to veil themselves by using the name of a man.
>
> (NE2: 2179)

For similar reasons, some writers from minority cultures have published using names from the dominant culture in which they live. Some writers have published anonymously or under assumed names in order to conceal their identity from society or to create curiosity about their work. Walter Scott, for example, published all his novels anonymously.

Effacement

'One can write nothing readable unless one constantly struggles to efface one's personality' – George Orwell. That said, a writer is going to end up saying a lot about their personality over the two hundred or so pages of a novel, or the eighty or so pages of a poetry collection. Some writers try to remove themselves, or any of their selves, from their writing by self-effacement of voice. One of the purposes is to throw the personality of the writer into the background entirely. What is said is what is held out to the reader: the message, never the messenger.

Self-effacement creates an illusion of objectivity, for it is itself a deliberated posture, an action of the personality, and a choice of style. In non-literary forms, such as scientific writing, impersonality of this type is taken to an extreme, and the active voice and the personal pronoun had no place until recently. The problems created are the *illusion* of impersonality (who is saying this and why are they deliberately absenting themselves?), and the risk of seeming somewhat cold or aloof in tone. Creative writers might take note that many scientists are now being encouraged to warm up the self-effaced passive voice of their communications, and return to a more active, first-person engagement with readers who are, after all, their fellow scientists as well as members of the public. It would be a challenge to write a story in which effacement of personality ran up against its opposite in a twin style of telling.

Using depression

Many writers suffer depression – the manic phase often delivers their writing, while the depressive phase that follows bouts of creativity is misinterpreted as a failure of creativity. Some writers mistake depression for the real thing, and there lie padded rooms and early graves. Sigmund Freud was wrong: writing is not a neurotic activity, but a natural activity that takes pleasure in the contemplation of relations, and associations and disassociations of form in language.

Literature is not by its nature destructive; the practice of creative writing, like any art form, is on the side of life. However, some writers view the practice of writing as a confessional business, or a paper trail of suicide notes. The process is both more subtle and cleverer than to cut your wrist, and a world away from the arch deliberations of self-effacement. This is 'writing cold': to look at yourself from outside, as our ghostwriter must, and make objectively simple what is subjective and complex. *You* become your daemon. We may come to see that this apparently severe experiment in self-perception can have the result of making our writing more honest. It may even make us more honest, more aware of our flaws. If you are depressive, this is one means of using the depressive phase constructively. It may sound strange, but depression can be a useful tool for a writer if they know how to play with it.

Change your life

In his *Letters to a Young Poet*, the poet Rainer Maria Rilke has this to say about the perceptions and exactions of the literary life (advice that applies to new writers of any genre):

> You ask whether your verses are any good. You ask me. You have asked others before this. You send them to magazines. You compare them with other poems, and you are upset when certain editors reject your work. Now (since you have said you want my advice) I beg you to stop doing that sort of thing. You are looking outside, and that is what you should most avoid right now . . . Go into yourself. Find out the reason that commands you to write; see whether it has spread its roots into the very depths of your heart; confess to yourself whether you would have to die if you were forbidden to write. This most of all: ask yourself in the most silent hour of your night: must I write? Dig into yourself for a deep answer. And if this answer rings out in assent, if you meet this solemn question with a strong, simple 'I must', then build your life in accordance with this necessity; your whole life, even into its humblest and most indifferent hour, must become a sign and witness to this impulse.

Different states of mind are useful for writing; learn to engender the states that best suit your working rhythms. Some writers, famously, have used alcohol or drugs to reach these preferred states; for others, it is a kind of self-hypnosis. What I am advocating is less intense: self-acknowledged play-acting. With constant practice, the role becomes a reality through simple discipline and repetition. However, if a new writer cannot access one of the others within themselves who can perform these placebos of voice and self, and be the first audience to that writing, then there may be no option than to stop writing or to change their life. What I am advocating, after all, is really no more than a kind of individualistic drama, and these states of mind can be very enjoyable in themselves. If a new writer cannot take the steps of experimenting with different states of mind or practice such as 'suspension of belief', 'the Other', 'playing dead', 'playing and being others', 'translation', 'self-effacement' or 'writing cold', then they must review the question of writing at all.

If the answer in the small hours to the question 'Must I write?' is 'I must', then they must change their life. They must begin over as a writer, reinventing a self that will be as unfamiliar to their friends as a person who has gone away for a long time and returned with a fresh history and a different face. For some writers, this takes place several times in one lifetime, and produces differing but noticeably fresh artistic phases of development. For some, it requires the writer to abandon familiar surroundings and people and begin over; or that they give up writing altogether, although they may return to it later in life when time and experience have had their say on them and they have something to write about or against.

For a few, though, answering Rilke's question signals the end of the game.

Writing Game

CHANGE YOUR LIFE

After your creative writing class has been running for three months, exchange all works of fiction in progress with other members of the group, handing over a hard copy of this work and a version on disk. Rewrite this other person's piece of fiction as if it were your own. Strip it of any over-writing, and weigh each sentence and paragraph carefully by reading it aloud to yourself. Transfer all alterations to the saved version on disk, and print it out. Return the new version, on disk and paper, to its author, and explain why your changes were appropriate.

AIM: One of the quickest ways to rewrite is to get outside your writing and, obviously, it is easier to do this with somebody else's work. However, doing this regularly is excellent practice. You grow used to giving as well as receiving constructive comments, edits and criticism, and can begin applying these lessons to your own work.

Recommended reading

Many books probe the process of literary composition as well as practices that encourage fluency. The novelist Anne Lamott's *Bird by Bird: Some Instructions on Writing and Life* (Anchor, 1995) draws brilliantly and provocatively from experience, and offers sensible instruction on everything from index cards to writing groups. *Self-Editing for Fiction Writers: How to Edit Yourself into Print* (HarperResource, 2004) by Renni Browne and Dave King is genre-specific but a very clever sharp and amusing take on the planning and *planing* needed for writing a novel. The notion of selves and others is wittily explored by Margaret Atwood in *Negotiating With the Dead: A Writer on Writing* (Cambridge University Press, 2002). Arguing that a writer cannot really begin their work until they have a voice of their own, the critic Al Alvarez contends in *A Writer's Voice* (Bloomsbury, 2005) that voice – as distinct from style – is what makes a writer great. *Writing: Self and Reflexivity* (Palgrave, 2006) by Celia Hunt and Fiona Sampson is an expert synthesis of the critical and creative theories for voice, authorship, characters and selves, and the question of an essential writer's 'self'.

Chapter 6

The practice of fiction

You can't start with how people look and speak and behave and come to
know how they feel. You must know exactly what's in their hearts and
minds before they ever set visible foot on the stage. You must know all,
then not tell it all, or not tell too much at once: simply the right thing at
the right moment. And the same character would be written about
entirely differently in a novel as opposed to a short story.

EUDORA WELTY (Plimpton, 1989: 166)

Fiction writers know a lot about point of view. One thing they know is that,
from the point of view of their publisher's accountant, commercial success has
considerable edge over artistic truth. This is frustrating for authors who serve
their art scrupulously but make little return on it. Unfortunately, loss-making
writers give the impression that if you sell well, because you can 'turn plot and
character', you are a lesser species. Many new writers find themselves at this
crossroads of literary choice.

When you are starting to write, choose the road more travelled by. For simplicity, I use the term 'story' throughout this chapter to describe your writing,
although I am aware you may write something that does not have a traditional
form or structure. Any recommendations I make about wordcount are for guidance only, and are in no way prescriptive. Your job is to create 'story'; that is,
to make believable prose narrative and characters. Accept Orwell's proposition
that 'Good prose is like a window-pane', and then proceed to build your story
straightforwardly and without frills. Later – even in a later drafting – you may
turn the House of Fiction upside down and smash all its windows. The truth is
many writers secretly desire the cultural cachet of literary fiction while not so
secretly yearning for the popularity (and royalties) of a great storymaker. There
lies your challenge. For new writers, the best way to make story is by knowing
what forms are open to you; by taking a thread of narrative and letting it lead
you; by dreaming your scenes into verisimilitude; by building credible characters and placing them in situational conflict; and by asking your story the
question: What if *this* happened?

Writing literary fiction

As John Updike says, 'Fiction is nothing less than the subtlest instrument for self-examination and self-display that mankind has invented yet.' Literary fiction is the customary objective for an apprentice to creative writing – the making of novels, novellas and short stories, as well as the modes of flash fiction and anti-narrative. Some question the legitimacy of this. Why not teach them to compose pulp fiction? The answer is that some writing schools *do* teach commercial genres, and there is every chance that many more will follow: the teaching of children's fiction, after the success of Philip Pullman, Jacqueline Wilson and J. K. Rowling, waxes exponentially. The argument to teach literary fiction comes down to an analogy with a rainforest. Like poetry, we value some species of writing for reasons other than their price within the free market. We value them because they are luminous, protean and give pleasure. More than any other function, they allow language to live. Our languages get flattened, ossified, drained of life by people who do not care about variety or luminosity. Such 'villains' – among them politicians, bureaucrats, and the media – are like loggers working language's forests to the roots, replacing their depth and strangeness with monocrops. Someone needs to cultivate the spaces; regrow them; and even surprise new species into happening. Like rainforests, you never know when these species of literature might prove useful, even essential, for the evolving life of language. Such literature even brings with it the possibility of prediction.

Writing Game

A MINIATURIST TALE
Write a whole story from the narrative point of view of an adolescent ('I'). The subject can be either a date or an evening with friends. Use the present tense, and deliberately use precise language, tiny details and slang in the dialogue. The setting should be a suburban park. Begin the story minutes after something extremely dramatic has happened there (for example, a fight or an arrest). Write this entire tale in 500 words.

AIM: You will probably write 1,000 words before cutting this story to its elements, and the lesson in economy can be applied across your fiction. This exercise will get you used to some of the basic principles of story quickly.

Flash fiction

Flash fiction (or short-short) is a subgenre of the short story characterised by limited word length of anything between 250 and 1,000 words. Indeed, the entire action may take place within the space of a page. Think of them as prose-haiku. The shortest versions are called nanofiction and are popular on internet publishing sites. Despite their experimental brevity, write your story using a protagonist, conflict, obstacles and resolution; even use a beginning, middle and end. Some aspects should be alluded to or implied, like sticky threads thrown wide around your piece in order to capture and reel in external connotations and resonances. This saves words. More than any other type of writing, a short-short should be written and redrafted in one sitting; part of their energy arises from that concentration of nerve. As Don Paterson writes, 'The shorter the form, the greater our expectation of its significance – and the greater its capacity for disappointing us' (2004: 189). Flash fiction is popular with new writers: it makes for immediacy, but can become a displacement activity to avoid longer-haul tasks. Ron Carlson comments, 'I'm all for short good writing with no sagging in it at all, but I'm also for good long writing with no sagging in it at all . . . the boom in short-shorts has more to do with precious page space than with attention spans . . .' (Shapard and Thomas, 1989: 312). Carlson has a point. Is brevity a virtue? The various *Sudden Fiction* anthologies edited by Shapard and Thomas provide models and challenges.

Writing Game

THE NOISE OF STORY
Four games in one! Write a short-short using words of one syllable only. Then write a short-short of 400 words, in which every sentence has exactly 8 words. Then write a short-short of 300 words which is entirely one sentence. Write a short story of 2,000 words using no adjectives or adverbs and which can only be understood clearly when it is read aloud by two disembodied voices.

AIM: Professional oral storytellers vary the speed and rhythm of their voices to capture and maintain our attention. The page is no less demanding an arena than the ear.

Short story

Although the marketplace for short stories is difficult, many new writers choose to begin with writing them, almost as a rite of passage, a place for honing language, testing their narrative nerve over a shortish distance and organising a palette. Later, these abilities find release across a novel's vasty fields. The short story is a place of order, resonance and closure. Language, imagery and form are super-concentrated. 'All high excitements are necessarily transient', wrote Edgar Allan Poe, and the short story enacts that intense transience. Richard Ford suggests in his introduction to *The Granta Book of the American Short Story* (1992) 'there's a rage for order in certain of us, a fury which nothing but a nice, compact little short-course bundle like a story can satisfy':

Or maybe story writers – more so than novelists – are moralists at heart, and the form lends itself to acceptable expressions of caution: You! You're not paying enough attention to your life, parcelled out as it is in increments smaller and more significant than you seem aware of. Here's a form which invites more detailed notice – displaying life not as it is, admittedly, but in flashbacks, in hyper-reality, with epiphanies and without, with closures, time foreshortenings, beauties of all sorts to please you and keep you interested.   (1992: xvii)

The short story offers restriction in length of anywhere between 7,500 and 20,000 words, and can be read in one sitting. Writing a good short story may take several sittings. Concision is everything. To begin, create a single character or two characters. The classic structure begins with a significant event involving your character that precipitates the story, followed by rising action until a climax, a fall in action and a denouement. Short stories take place over a short period; endings are often abrupt or open.

Imitate the concisions of previous writers. Read, study and imitate influential historical models such as Edgar Allan Poe's 'The Tell-Tale Heart' (NA1: 1572), Nathaniel Hawthorne's 'Young Goodman Brown' (NA1: 1263), Herman Melville's 'Bartleby, the Scrivener' (NA1: 2330), Ambrose Bierce's 'An Occurrence at Owl Creek Bridge' (NA2: 452), James Joyce's 'The Dead' (NE2: 2240), William Faulkner's 'Barn Burning' (NA2: 1790), Katherine Mansfield's 'The Garden Party' (NE2: 2423) and Ernest Hemingway's 'The Snows of Kilimanjaro' (NA2: 1848). The anthologies edited by Ford (1992) and Bradbury (1988) offer solid introductions to the modern notion of the form, and your understanding of the form's possibilities will be further extended by reading short stories by Honoré de Balzac, Anton Chekhov, Vladimir Pushkin, Ivan Turgenev, Gabriel García Márquez, Guy de Maupassant, Jorge Luis Borges and Isak Dinesen.

Writing Game

CREATING CHARACTER IN SHORT STORY
In 400 words, write part of a whole short story that takes as its subject a contemporary news item. Write your tale from the point of view of a person involved in that news, using the third-person point of view ('he' / 'she') and the given setting of the event.

AIM: This five-finger exercise encourages you to fictionalise a single aspect of reality. It allows you to get to grips with writing a story because you have already been given setting and, to some extent, character.

Novella

Some new writers choose the novella form to find their voice before writing a full-length novel, gathering maybe three or four novellas together between one cover as a means of setting out their stall. A novella is a short novel, commonly fifty to a hundred pages long. This allows greater character and theme development than a short story, without the intricate structural exigencies or the Niagaran tightrope walk of a novel. It offers the concentration of a short story and the wider compass of the novel's form. Some critics have imposed a word count on where the novella stops and a novel begins. Thinking about numbers is counter-productive when writing a novella – 'an ill-defined and disreputable literary banana republic', as Stephen King calls the form – although 40,000 words seems a sensible target for a new writer.

Novellas are similar in structure to short stories, in that they often open with an event, but may then move backwards in time to give background material. They also frequently place a change of direction, such as a reversal of fortune or a new event, within the rising action. Again, it is wise to read, then imitate, aspects of some of the most numinous models, such as Henry James's *The Beast in the Jungle* (NA2: 524) and *The Turn of the Screw* (1898); Joseph Conrad's *Heart of Darkness* (NE2: 1958); Franz Kafka's *The Metamorphosis* (1915); Virginia Woolf's *Mrs Dalloway* (1925); Thomas Mann's *Death in Venice* (1912); George Orwell's *Animal Farm* (1945); Carson McCullers' *The Ballad of the Sad Café* (1951); Truman Capote's *Breakfast at Tiffany's* (1958) and Anthony Burgess's *A Clockwork Orange* (1962).

Novel

It is as useless to define a novel by its length – there are trilogies and tetralogies – as to define a mountain by its height, but the new writer is looking at an extended prose narrative with a great deal more characters, varied scenes and a more open-handed coverage of time. In such a longer form dramatic structure is almost certainly a mark of the voice, and the new writer should play safe with that structure in their first efforts. Like bouldering in the Alps before hitting the Himalayas, some novelists write two or three short 'trial novels' before they attempt their first novel. What is imperative is to keep at it, getting the first draft down as fast as possible, and 'not leaving the room' in Ron Carlson's phrase. I make no recommendations as to reading, since it is extremely unlikely that your wish to write a novel is not already based on reading hundreds of them.

As we discussed in Chapter One, how can we know what is genuinely new unless we are familiar with what has gone before? Many would-be novelists suppose that the novel form is fully explored. For a beginning novelist, a challenge would be to take up one of Milan Kundera's four appeals in *The Art of the Novel*. Kundera argues for the creation of novels that explore what he calls 'missed opportunities' in the genre's history, such as playfulness; the fusion of dream and reality; the novel as a vehicle for philosophical thought; and the enigma of collective time, a novel that attempts 'to overstep the limits of a temporal life' (2000: 15). We explored some of these ways of thinking about writing in the first five chapters. The point is that there are still many open spaces.

'The literary novel' is, of course, a prickly term, used to distinguish it from commercial or genre novels (such as science/detective/horror). Its qualities include psychological depth, subtle characterisation and attentiveness to style. It denotes seriousness and profundity to some readers and critics; it can also seem slightly po-faced to others. I suspect that most of us enjoy a story, and that story is one of the things that drew you to reading and writing as a child. That does not mean plot and narrative are put aside as childish things. Let us be clear: because a novel is popular, it does not follow that it is junk. About teaching and learning to write fiction, John Gardner contends in *The Art of Fiction*, 'what holds for the most serious kind of fiction will generally hold for junk fiction as well' (1983: x). Think about these issues, but then forget them while you write (but less so while you are rewriting). Do not let any of these matters intimidate or skew the way you write a novel. The only way forward is to write for yourself. One thing you will begin to recognise in fiction is that, although worldly experience can be drawn upon to make setting, character and scene believable, you will write more easily using your own imagination, especially if that imagination is fired up through research. Find things out, or imagine them, and afterwards check your facts. But trust in your own judgement at first – do not get hung up on reality. It is astonishing how much you will 'get right' (say, with setting) by simply following your nose and by reading up on the subject. Fiction's predictive power comes from this ravelling of intuition and research.

Writing Game

FISSURES IN FICTION
Read any story or any novel and locate the moments when a fissure has been planted in the narrative – some gap between scenes, for example. Your aim is to write a story that fills that gap, stays with the original subject, and to do so using the author's narrative style and the point of view.

AIM: Imitation of style, subject and point of view are useful training. Writers leave room for the reader to do some work, to negotiate a deliberate fissure and write their own experience into that space. Filling these fissures allows you to share this sense of fiction's 'continuum' with the reader. You can replicate the effect in your own work. This game is also one way to begin creating a new story, 'in dialogue' with a known story.

Form and structure

In Chapter Three, we introduced the practical notion that design leads to more surprises in writing than free expression, and that form, such as patterns and restrictions, liberates creativity and imagination. Form in fiction can be as specific and as conscious a decision as choosing to write in the form of a journal, a blog, or letters (epistolary), or emails between characters, or by choosing not to use the letter 'e' in your story. Form is simply a decision about the way your piece is written, and your final decision may take several drafts and unsuccessful trials before you realise which suits the material best, and carries the story inevitably. Did you know that Jane Austen initially wrote *Pride and Prejudice* as an epistolary novel?

Deciding your form

Some writers use the terms 'form' and 'structure' interchangeably because it is almost impossible to separate them in the act of writing. The structures of literary fiction allow you to frame your decision: the architecture of all the action; how you place incidents, and when; where you position and resolve conflicts; whether you write the piece as a third-person narrative, or as a rapid-fire burst of taut first-person narratives from the point of view of each of its several characters. The most important matter for a new writer is that they understand the structure they have chosen, and wide reading will help develop this.

The categories of fiction (which many writers also call the 'forms' of fiction), such as novels, short stories and flash fiction, are like different species of a literary genus. Although many understand these forms to mean differences in length, they also refer to differences in structure, and the demands made by them. In this way, they mirror some of the expectations and restrictions set up by using verse forms in poetry. However, calling one form of fiction by a name is not an exercise in Linnaean classification; each form flows quite fluidly through another. As Ailsa Cox explains in *Writing Short Stories*, there is obsession among creative writers about the classification of literary forms because of a 'question of status. Historically, the novel has been the dominant form, and it is still difficult to establish a literary career based purely on short fiction' (2005: 3). However, this business of status is not your war – not yet.

One challenge is that you might not know at first which forms are the most appropriate for your story. Again, you must trial several to find the one that works. You might well have some notion beforehand. For example, if you feel your story is thorny with events, swarming with characters and powered by a succession of conflicts, then you are probably writing a novel. If you wish to write about a moment of significance, some life-changing event that deals with, say, one character, then your miniaturist instinct is creating a short story. If you want to hit-and-run the reader, and then quickly shift out of view, flash fiction fits the action. Experiment with all of them. Like poetic forms, the choice you take with the form and structure of fiction will automatically begin to shape what you can do, eliminating multiple possibilities at a stroke.

Writing Game

FLASH FICTION TO SHORT STORY
Write a story in exactly 1,000 words, no more, no less, taking no more than 100 minutes. When revising, cut the story by precisely one tenth of its length, leaving a final version. Take all the words/sentences from the 'cut tenth', and begin rearranging them so that they take on a rough internal logic. Then take the key character from your flash fiction and make them the protagonist of a short story of 3,000 words. The 'cut tenth' must find their way into your short story, either as description or as monologue/dialogue. It must in no way 'shape' the narrative thread of your short story.

AIM: Writing to these restrictions precipitates a controlled free fall. Reusing a character is useful training for developing a longer narrative thread, say in a novella. Recycling deleted work is an exercise in developing verbal cunning.

Subverting the form

Your decision will also shape the reader's expectations even before they absorb the first sentence. You might wish to play with such expectations. You will remember from our discussion of form in Chapter Three that it provides a useful tool in so far as you can break with it, subvert it and even shatter it. One way to think about this is to allow the structure of a piece to 'ambush the story' (in Ian McEwan's phrase) so that the structure tells a different story from the one the piece is telling.

Anti-narrative techniques in fiction disrupt and subvert the forward momentum of a story, and even the sense of time and place. Some short stories appear to be assembled cunningly from several apparent flash fictions, which are cut up and collaged into a longer narrative. This produces jump-cuts in time, and rapid switches of scene like viewing the world from a fairground waltzer. For a powerful example, read, then write an imitation of, Robert Coover's 'The Babysitter', in Ford (1992: 350).

Dreaming a fictional continuum

In *On Becoming a Novelist*, John Gardner states, 'Good fiction sets off... a vivid and continuous dream in the reader's mind' (1985: 39). In Chapter Four, we saw how Les Murray spoke of 'the painless headache' of writing as 'an integration of the body-mind and the dreaming-mind and the daylight-conscious-mind. All three are firing at once, they're all in concert.' Writing fiction may induce this trance of composition, and of reading, but technique will maintain it for you, and for the reader. As Gardner goes on to say, 'If the writer understands that stories are first and foremost stories, and that the best stories set off a vivid and continuous dream, he can hardly help becoming interested in technique, since it is mainly bad technique that breaks the continuousness and checks the growth of the fictional dream' (1985: 45).

Plots and scene

Short-term, short-haul pieces of writing do not suit the novelist. A novel is a long haul, and a creative writing workshop will not miraculously generate a whole one (a doctoral programme in creative writing presents a modus operandi). Writing Games often make miniatures or set pieces, such as character sketches, exercises in style or point of view. You cannot simply stitch together these set pieces to make extended fiction unless you have decided on a 'brave' (and probably clunky) experiment. A fiction writer depends on something larger: the dream or fantasy of scenes that are true to life or, at least, carry verisimilitude however fantastic the setting or story. This tone of mind is not really required by poets, except when they are stitching together long poems or thematic collections. It is necessary for the writer of fiction to make this dreaming of scenes a virtual habit for their imagination.

One matter that checks that trance or dream is a misunderstanding of plot. Even a professed outsider figure like the novelist Stephen King calls plot 'the good writer's last resort and the dullard's first choice' (2000: 189). Plot is *not* the story. Plot is a series of events you have devised, and these events may not even occur linearly. In the first paragraph of Chapter One, I asked you to think of the page as an open space. Writing a story creates a four-dimensional landscape in that space. Space and time become one – a continuum. Within that continuum, you must choose one strand of narrative that you intuitively feel will lead you through the landscape. Please notice that you will be *led* for, as Isabel Allende contends:

> It is not I who choose the story; the story chooses me . . . Writers imagine that they cull stories from the world. I'm beginning to believe that vanity makes them think so. That it's actually the other way round. Stories cull writers from the world. Stories reveal themselves to us. The public narrative, the private narrative – they colonise us. They commission us. They insist on being told.   (Rodden, 1999: ix, 3)

The insistent strand of narrative is your plot, and it will lead you through the maze of narrative possibilities that open, move around, and close behind you in a sequence of discrete but connected scenes. King playfully argues, 'I believe that plotting and the spontaneity of real creation aren't compatible . . . I won't try to convince you I've never plotted any more than I'd try to convince you that I've never told a lie, but I do both as infrequently as possible' (2000: 188).

Some writers prefer not to work this way despite the illuminations of discovery. Instead, the writer plans their story as if they were teasing out an academic essay or storyboarding a movie, sketching microcosmic plots for each part, or chapter, of their story. They then know precisely what will happen on the next page, to whom, and create time lines for these actions. This might suit you as an approach, but it is less likely to engender surprise and inevitability, unless your style is sensational. If there is no surprise for you, the writer, then there is a possibility there will be little surprise for the reader either, for your fiction might feel predicted and thus predictable. If you tie everything neatly, what is the writer's or the reader's role?

As you should beware of clichés of feeling, or kitsch, in your writing, you should also be aware of clichés of plot, not that following a traditional plot structure is a bad thing. Gardner nutshells the traditional plot as 'A central character wants something, goes after it despite opposition (perhaps including his own doubts), and so arrives at a win, lose or draw' (1985: 54). In *The Seven Basic Plots* (2004), Christopher Booker suggests there are seven standard stories in the world that all fiction uses and recycles. These are summarised as

'Overcoming the Monster', 'Rags to Riches', 'The Quest', 'Voyage and Return', 'Comedy', 'Tragedy' and 'Rebirth', although Booker does extend the franchise to include 'Rebellion Against "The One"' and 'Mystery'. Booker believes that stories tend to have the same structure because they follow the contours of human development: initial success followed by crisis, then lasting success or failure, arguing that:

> in storytelling the underlying archetypal structures are so constituted that they must always work towards that concluding image which shows us everything in a story being satisfactorily resolved. The mark of a well-constructed story is that every detail in it is contributing in some way towards that final resolution.   (2004: 462)

This is interesting but very much open to debate. It is based on the outside-reader 'looking in' to plot and psychoanalysing a function, rather than being its co-creator. However, just as retelling myths and legends offers a good Writing Game, your first efforts may mirror these templates. As Toby Litt says, 'The truly great stories are the ones you already know but want to know again.' You have to start somewhere. However, you may later choose to play variations, combine them, or confound them. Remember: plot is not the story, but an Ariadne's thread you follow through a labyrinth of scenes.

The units that light the pathway of the novel in particular are its scenes, the stages on which small dramas unfold. They show the reader one part of the story, as a frame or picture, but they do not tell. Scenes are often perceived beforehand by the writer as they dream their way through the story. They are usually a location in which characters are seen and heard at close quarters, and they accomplish some action which has an outcome directly bearing on the forward movement of the story. Every scene moves some, if not all, of the elements of your story forwards. Each scene leans into that momentum, however gently, revealing to your reader some further revelation of character. As a rule of thumb, the events that are most crucial to the story will be those that lend themselves to be carried by scene; narrative carries the rest.

Writing Game

RETELLING
Think about some aspect of your everyday life and personal history, and try to match it against a legend or myth you know about. To begin, take the story of Little Red Riding Hood and retell it so that the events of the tale take place in your time and in a real place known to you.

AIM: We freely adapt stories from our lives, and our world, but many stories can be adapted on to ancient templates, such as fairy tales, legends, Greek myths and biblical parables. They borrow structure, character, scene, point of view and power from these origins. James Joyce's novel *Ulysses* (1922), for example, takes Homer's *Odyssey* as a template.

Character is story

To paraphrase and extend something John Gardner once wrote, character is the heart and mind of your story – it is what makes it live. Setting offers character a stage; it can even help character to be defined; but setting, at best, is really another character in your story, as Venice is to Henry James's *The Wings of the Dove* (1902) and Egdon Heath to Thomas Hardy's *The Return of the Native* (1878). Dialogue expresses character in speech, in idiom and their manner of speaking. What people say is as revealing as their actions, especially when they do not do what they say they are going to do. Plot allows your character to act on that stage, but is still only a means for character expression. As for the philosophy of your fiction, or your theme, these are merely summations of how characters 'behave' in the face of conflict. Theme emerges as the story proceeds. As we saw in Chapter Two, few good writers begin with a theme or big social idea, and then write to its order. As Gardner says, 'what counts is . . . the fortunes of the characters, how their principles of generosity or stubborn honesty or stinginess or cowardice help them or hurt them in specific situations. What counts is the characters' story' (1985: 43).

Writing Game

BELIEVING IN CHARACTER
Write a short portrait of 600 words on an imaginary character. Do not bother to use plot or dialogue; rely entirely on a description of the person, their setting and their mood, as if you were capturing them on camera and they could not see you. Although you know what the character is feeling, do not mention this in your writing. Attempt to convey their emotions by personal details, their appearance, and their setting.

AIM: To show a character honestly and without authorial prodding requires precise and sometimes uncomfortable observation. Use this mode of observing real people within your notebooks, as you go searching for characters. It is a silent rule that you never tell your reader what a character is feeling. Detail conveys this information with subtlety, surprise and force.

Finding characters

Where do you find your characters? As a first-time writer you would do best, as always, to start with yourself by fictionalising your own character or creating a character from an aspect of your own personality, and you will now be used to the habit of keeping such observational notes in your notebook. Your characters can also be assembled from various elements of observed (but real) people. For example, during fieldwork, when you spy somebody who interests you, make observational notes and try to interpret their appearance and possessions as aspects of character, but also ask yourself what the person's *story* is. How did they get to this moment in their lives, and where are they heading next? In other words, try to 'read' them.

I would warn you not to use people to whom you are professionally close (for example, within your workshop group). Go wary of caricaturing somebody real. Do not 'copy' *complete* people but create composites from several, not out of moral discretion, but out of artistic cunning. Absolute reality writes fiction badly. The *Oxford English Dictionary* defines fiction as 'that which is feigned or invented; invention as opposed to fact'. Fiction creates parallel universes to the actual: the relative closeness to reality enthralls us. Save actual reality for writing creative nonfiction. Finally, characters can simply be invented, but you will also find with practice that characters *arrive* in your imagination as you work on a piece.

Character history

We have discussed the importance of rewriting in Chapter Five. However, more than any other genre, *prewriting* is essential to create believable fictional characters. Prewriting allows you to get inside them. Before you even know the storyline, you should create grids of information about not only who your characters are, but also what they do, and what they value and feel. These issues will say a great deal about them to the reader; and to you, the writer, for they will push your story in unexpected ways, and your characters will even begin to spring surprises on you – more so than in life, character is destiny in fiction. As the epigraph of this chapter from Eudora Welty reminds us, 'You can't start with how people look and speak and behave and come to know how they feel. You must know exactly what's in their hearts and minds before they ever set visible foot on the stage.' Your characters will only surprise you if you know them inside out.

How do you do that? Create a character history for every one of them in your notebook – a dossier. Take each character and write about their type, gender, age, name, their relation to other characters, appearance, mannerisms, speech patterns, personality, background, private and professional life, strengths and weaknesses. What are their passions, professions, obsessions? Where do they live? Who do they live with? What family did they come from? Are they happy? Why not? What is their nickname, pet name, or street-name, and what are the reasons and meanings behind them? The character history should also include the details of life: physical appearance, clothes, speech, likes, dislikes, body language and personal habits. Adapt your style of writing to the subject matter of this information; that is, let your character lead the way. No amount of information is going to jolt your Frankenstein monster into sudden life on the page. It is important, however, for *you* to know this information. Most of it will never appear on the page at all; it is the invisible part of the iceberg to a work we discussed in Chapter One.

Writing Game

CHARACTER DEVELOPMENT
Most of us have some sort of bag where we keep daily belongings. Open it and make a list of every item. What do these items say about you? Now, take a friend's bag and do the same; then write a character description of the person based on those items. Think of two characters you wish to create. Make a list of all the belongings in their bags before they go out together to a wild party. Make a list of their belongings the morning after. Without making any reference to the party, write a flash fiction based around the 'before and after' of these lists.

AIM: As any forensic psychologist would say, information of this type shows you, not tells you, and is as indicative of character as any long-winded description.

Main and viewpoint character

Your main character is the person who your story is about, and your narrative follows them around from place to place. They might be likable or awful; yet we generally sympathise with them because they are likely to be the person most hurt in your story despite their power to act, and the writer creates situations that hurt them in order to make the reader care for them. The viewpoint character may or may not be the main character; nevertheless, we see and hear the story through them, and there may be more than one such viewpoint character. They are the narrator. Generally, you rely on them to move the story along and tell the truth of it. However, you may invent what is called an unreliable narrator, usually a character who we monitor and soon learn to distrust, however much fun they are.

Believability

Information and history allow you to know your characters better; they provide you with elements of their back-story; and let you know their motivations and needs. You will then have some realistic notion of how they will react to conflict and situations, and whether their motivations drive the story or, better still, drive the story *for* you. A recurring question in fiction workshops concerns problems of believability in characterisation, as in 'I do not believe X would do/say this.' Character history does not provide with an alibi, but it will prevent you creating bogus moments of behaviour and speech, or help you correct aberrations in the next draft.

Storymaking

Storytellers take pre-existing tales, memorise the key moments, and then retell them with variations, almost like beautiful but innocuous lies. Few of their variations make a serious difference to the continuum of the original tale. Fiction writers are not really story*tellers* in method. They are storymakers and shapers, as poets are makers and shapers of poems. The final value of fiction rests in that making and rewriting. Made well and shaped well, fiction becomes believable – more like life than lie – and far less innocuous. In order to show well, rather than tell, you need to be clear about issues of position.

Where do you, the writer, stand in relation to your created characters? What do you, the writer, want your readers to know about them, and who tells the story? As with character, you decide the point of view of your story before you begin to write, and prewriting several points of view will help you decide which of them, singly or in combination, carries the story most honestly. David Lodge reminds us, 'One of the commonest signs of a lazy or inexperienced writer of fiction is inconsistency in handling point of view' (1992: 28). Getting this right allows the reader to be captured by the story. Getting it wrong wrecks its continuum.

Point of view and narrative voice

These are important choices; points of view are the visualising verbs for making a believable continuum for fiction. They include first, second and third person, that is 'I', 'you', 'he/she'. Second person is less common, although offers the challenge of speaking with yourself, such as a schizophrenic other or a youthful or elderly version of yourself. It also allows you to address the reader, although it must be clear, always, who this *you* represents. 'You' is more distant to the reader than 'I', yet 'you' always feels like it could be conversation.

A first-person narrative has a purpose-built narrator, 'I', and 'I' can be the writer, a person spinning a story, the main character (the protagonist) or another character. The trick is closeness; a reader will read the word 'I' and come to the story through the *eye* of the character. They become the character, and the story may even begin to feel autobiographical, so wrapped up is the reader in the relationship. Thus, first-person narrators offer the simulation of reality and utter subjectivity and are therefore able to tell somebody else's story extremely authentically. They tell the story of the main character because they are observing the person. They are the witness of events or the reteller of them. How reliable they are is up to you.

The third-person point of view can be as objective as a camera, recording only what is seen or heard and never engaging with the thoughts or feelings of characters; or it can be as engaged as if the characters were dear to you. Camera-like objectivity can be too distancing for the reader so, generally, you should elect to talk about your characters as if you know them. The narrator is not usually a character (although they have been known to show up in postmodern fiction), and what the narrator does not know about all the characters is not worth knowing. However, this godlike authorial viewpoint, or Third-Person Omniscient, popular among Victorian novelists, can seem strange to us now. The reader finds it hard to identify with a Creator loitering on the edges of the world of their book.

You may therefore opt to write from the point of view of the Third-Person Objective, in which the narrator does not know everything, only what they have observed at first hand. If well written, the reader will pick up resonances and inferences from what the characters do and say, although their thoughts and emotions remain unwritten. One final option is the Third-Person Limited point of view, in which the narrator perceives the fictional world through only one of its characters. This is the most flexible and common point of view; it can carry most stories and cope with almost any situation. Never switch a point of view without making some break in the action – say, a section or chapter.

Narrative voice has little to do with 'finding your voice', although you might choose your own natural voice for your first stories. It is the voice of the character who tells the story, and that will include their dialect, idioms, manner of speaking, and their choice of language. Although neglected, *tone* is as important to capture correctly. Tone is the story's attitude to the world of the story and its events and characters – the attitude and style of the narrator, too. It will greatly affect the way a reader perceives the story. When, in a workshop, a fellow writer says that a story 'does not quite work', usually it is best to examine tone and narrative voice, before working on the more obvious fault lines within point of view.

Writing Game

POINT OF VIEW

Write a short story, based on an event in your own life, but write it in the Third-Person Omniscient. Redraft the piece from the point of view of the First Person and show it to somebody who knows you well, who played some role in the event and who appears in the story. Ask them what they think the story is about. Take *their* character from the piece and redraft it from that point of view, Third-Person Limited. Ask them the same question.

AIM: Learn to use point of view consciously. Test its impact on your perception of a reality made fiction, and on another person whose point of view is as an objective witness to your own perception, and to your own fiction.

Beginning

To the question How do I begin? the answer is, What is the story and how do you want to tell it? 'The story is not in the plot but in the telling' – Ursula Le Guin. Readers choose to enter the alternative universe of a fictional narrative, and that choice is active; they can always say no. Your first page is a threshold you wish the reader to cross, and its mirroring of reality is one of the aspects that entices. How can we make a reader walk straight through that page's mirror into our world? That page is also a door. When you begin writing, think about what you place behind it (a scene), and who opens it (a character), and what can be heard behind it (a dialogue). Do not open the door with a flourish (a dead body); such tricks distract and create distrust. Many editors talk of the need for a 'hook', some striking moment that drags the reader into the story. This is a trick, and it can seem amateurish. If you choose to use a 'hook', then make sure it is invisible, otherwise you appear insecure.

Confidence in writerly voice is the hookiest (yet least obvious) hook. Your story begins where reality's drama ends. As we said in Chapter Five, we begin in the middle. Create a scene or mood with economy and lucid concrete language – with narrative, an image or dialogue – just enough to show the life of your language and the presence of an alternative world. The novelist Philip Pullman always begins a work with a powerful image or disconnected pictures or scenes that he develops further – 'That means I don't have a plan, because it would prevent more than it allows. There has to be a lot of ignorance in me when I start a story.' That ignorance is a beguiling but intangible factor for the reader, for it affects them unknowingly, making them as curious as the writer. The choice of a beginning locks down everything else: the mood, subject matter, and even the ending. Pullman believes, 'The opening governs the way you tell everything that follows, not only in terms of the organisation of the events, but also in terms of the tone of voice that does the telling; and not least, it enlists the reader's sympathy in *this* cause rather than *that*' (2005: 4). The entrance and exit of a story frames the journey of the entire drama.

Writing Game

BEGINNINGS
Skim the anthologies recommended in this chapter, and write down at least ten opening sentences of stories you have not yet read. Then, without reading further, write 200 words of narrative using those openings as starting points.

AIM: There is no formula for beginning and this will help you practise. This game allows you to create narrative but also to subvert it or play satire against existing models.

What if?

You can provoke your story into creation by looking at everyday circumstances and events and asking them this question. In creative nonfiction, writers often take two aspects of life and lean them against each other so that they become more than the sum of their parts. Similarly, poets sometimes take two elements from life (such as a recollection and an object) and usher them towards each other to explore a greater dimension and resonance. Fiction writers ask 'What if?' of their characters, of their story, of their subject and of their own everyday life. Anne Bernays and Pamela Painter offer a whole book of writing exercises with this question as the title. They argue that this constant interrogation of the story lends it not only the beginning but also forward momentum and framing. Follow their advice if you have trouble finding or telling your story:

> Look in your files for a story that seems stuck . . . Next, write at the top of a separate sheet of paper the two words *What If*. Now write five ways of continuing the story, not ending the story, but continuing the story to the next event, scene etc. Let your imagination go wild. Loosen up your thinking about the events in the story . . . one of the what ifs will feel

right, organic . . . and that is the direction in which you should go . . .
You just have to allow your imagination enough range to discover what
works. (1991: 99)

Conflict and crisis

When reading novels as a writer, you will immediately notice the importance
of conflict as the engine of fiction. Fiction, especially novels, depends on situational conflict – a moment of chance or change – as a triggering event.
Characters are thrown into this predicament as into a whirlpool or maze, and
your job as a writer is to observe them work themselves free, and not to assist
them. With your first story, select (or, if ambitious, combine) two types of
situational conflict. Your characters might find themselves in a crisis which
they did not choose, and which requires their action, or they may find themselves in a self-made predicament. Remember that, for most people, it is only
during a crisis that we discover how little we know of ourselves, and of others, and basic qualities of character are always the first to emerge. Your story
reveals the flaws and revelations, and the rapidity with which characters react
to unfolding events. Thus, danger and crisis allow you to get into characters,
but they also throw a reader headlong into your story. Use your notebook
as a repository of crises and conflicts, in your personal life and in the wider
world.

Setting and time

Although setting is a stage for character, it is four-dimensional and can be used
as a character – that is, it must convince; it can never be generic or a backdrop.
Even if the setting is fantastical, Pullman argues, 'It isn't interesting to write
about if it isn't real, if there isn't a dimension of reality there, particularly a
psychological reality.' Place is more than location; it is mood, history, other
people's lives. A recognisable cityscape is something a reader understands;
gaining their trust, they move towards your story. You may then choose to
make that city a place of strangeness, or to allow it to offer your story local
colour. A carefully observed and vivid natural landscape carries its own precise
connotations, edges for wildness and the unpredictable. In some fiction, you
might write the setting as an antagonist. Time and weather affect setting, and
will affect character, but they are not the 'machines of the gods'. Do not use
them witlessly. Nevertheless, as the creator of the place's weather and time,
you will learn when best to use them to move your story forwards or to shade
its atmosphere without playing God. Remember, the place, time and weather

may be inessential to your story but you, as the writer, must know where your characters are and what conditions they inhabit; what year it is and even what the time on the clock is. That information may never even enter the text, but it will implicitly affect the behaviour and mood of your characters, just as it affects you.

Rewrites

We explored rewriting in Chapter Five. With fiction, once again the best test is to read it aloud, and read it to somebody (Flaubert would invite friends and admirers to marathon sessions of this type). This will reveal problems and longueurs; it will also test whether speech and dialogue is alive on the ear, and if it animates your story. If you find that some of the writing seems flat, shift sentences and paragraphs around to see what sounds more true to character; what order of words makes characters more emotionally honest; and what intensifies description. If this does not help, begin thinking about altering the verbal tense of the piece, or the point of view. Ensure that the narrative moves forward, and that you excise cliché words and clichés of feeling, or mutate their language into something fresher.

Your next step is more drastic: to let the story rest; to put the story aside for a considerable time and not to look at it again until you have almost forgotten you wrote it. As Stephen King explains, 'How long you let your book rest – sort of like bread dough between kneadings – is entirely up to you, but I think it should be a minimum of six weeks.' This will give you the necessary distance to edit your story into some final shape, as King believes it is 'like reading the work of someone else, a soul-twin perhaps . . . It is always easier to kill someone else's darlings than it is to kill your own' (2000: 252–253). Annie Dillard in *The Writing Life* remarks, 'It is the beginning of a work that the writer throws away . . . Painters work from the ground up . . . Writers, on the other hand, work from left to right. The discardable chapters are on the left. The latest version of a literary work begins somewhere in the work's middle, and hardens toward the end' (1989: 5). When you look again at your story, do so with a cold eye. It is very likely you will soon be deleting some of it, so it is best not to get too chummy with your old friend. The novelist Ursula Le Guin comments in *Steering the Craft*:

> Anton Chekhov gave some advice about revising a story: first, he said, throw out the first three pages . . . I really hoped he was wrong, but of course he was right. It depends on the length of the story, naturally; if it's very short, you can only throw out the first three paragraphs. But there are few first drafts to which Chekhov's Razor doesn't apply. Starting a

story, we all tend to circle around, explain a lot of stuff, set things up that don't need to be set up. Then we find our way and get going, and *the story begins . . .* very often just about on page 3. (1998: 148)

The end

Writing on why even great novels can have disappointing endings, the critic James Wood (2005) cites the Russian formalist critic Viktor Schlovsky's praise for Chekhov's 'negative endings', which 'frustrate our sense of tidy form by refusing to end: 'And then it began to rain.'' Wood states that the novel 'is a form that doesn't want to end and that generally contorts itself into unnatural closure. How often we feel of long novels . . . that their last 50 or so pages are mechanical and overwrought, that the rhythm of the book is speeding up as it reaches home . . . Perfect endings of the open Chekhovian kind, or of the positive and closed kind, are rare.' Some novels offer more than one ending. I suggest you keep your objective simpler.

When completing your story it is sound practice to have written several versions of the final page before you reach it. You might have an ending that offers closure and conclusion, or an open Chekhovian image, or something else. As you approach the harbour of your story's close, you will probably know which of these permutations best suits the *rhythm* of your narrative's journey. It will also mean that the rhythm of these closing pages is guided by the simple necessity to furl your sail, as it were. You can then tack the gap skilfully by knowing beforehand the nature of your landfall and the speed of the story's currents.

Recommended reading

There is an embarrassment of riches when it comes to books about writing fiction; some jewels shine more honestly than others. Some offer a systematic ABC approach at odds with the open space of creative discovery. I do not have space to list them all, even those I enjoyed as much for their style as their subject. What the best of them agree upon is the centrality of character to the making of story. John Gardner taught Raymond Carver among many others and his *On Becoming a Novelist* (HarperPerennial, 1985) and *The Art of Fiction* (Vintage Books, 1983) are exceptional in their urgency and drive, and refreshing in their exaction and psychological depth. *On Writing* (Hodder, 2000) by Stephen King is honest, clear and practical. It is also exemplary as a species of creative nonfiction, a novel-length reflective essay on his aims and processes. Ailsa Cox's succinct *Writing Short Stories* (Routledge, 2005) focuses on an important form for writing students, and does its reader a further service by also looking beyond literary fiction towards genre fiction, science fiction and cyberpunk. Fiction writers will also find a highly useful demonstration of formal craft in *Writing Fiction* by Janet Burroway (Longman, 2003), Ursula Le Guin's *Steering the Craft* (Eighth Mountain Press, 1998) and David Lodge's *The Art of Fiction* (Penguin, 1992). Milan Kundera's *The Art of the Novel* (FirstHarperPerennial, 2000) is useful on suggesting fresh possibilities of theme and idea for novels. While travelling the world's creative writing departments, the most common book I have observed is a well-thumbed copy of *What If? Writing Exercises for Fiction Writers* (Quill, 1991) by Anne Bernays and Pamela Painter. *The Seven Basic Plots* (Continuum, 2004) by Christopher Booker is a fascinating introduction to the templates of universal plots, useful to the writer in that they can copy or confound them. The modes of flash fiction are introduced in the anthologies edited by Robert Shapard and James Thomas: *Sudden Fiction: American Short-Short Stories* (Norton, 1986) and *Sudden Fiction International* (Norton, 1989). No creative writing classroom or new writer should go without two great anthologies of modern short stories: *The Penguin Book of Modern British Short Stories*, edited by Malcolm Bradbury (Penguin, 1988), and *The Granta Book of the American Short Story*, edited by Richard Ford (Granta, 1992).

Chapter 7

Creative nonfiction

the permanent importance . . . lies in its being the meeting point of an impersonal art and a very personal life story . . . Obviously Nabokov's method would lose all sense unless the material were as true an account of personal experience as memory could possibly make it. The selective apparatus pertains to art; but the parts selected belong to unadulterated life.

VLADIMIR NABOKOV, *Speak, Memory: An Autobiography Revisited* (2000: 239)

A story grows from real and imagined experience. Creative nonfiction usually takes reality as its origin, but that does not mean we dispense with the mind's natural skill for story. Creative nonfiction deals with realities truthfully – experiences, events, facts – yet the drive of the writing is the author's involvement in the story, and writers use every literary device in the book to tell that story well. Carol Bly offers a precis in *Beyond the Writers' Workshop*: 'All you have to do is be truthful, tell things in your personal voice, and have your modus operandi be revealing your own life circumstances through anecdote or narrative and revealing the meanings you attach to those circumstances, rather than arguing the point' (2001: xvii). Readers are drawn in by this personal engagement, the author's literary style and passion for the telling. This chapter introduces some of the introductory elements of creative nonfiction, and some basic literary tools. We then look at some of the more common projects that new writers and creative writing students can carry out to get them started in this fascinating supergenre.

Reality's literature

Time makes stories of us all; history rewrites us. Creative writing explores the narrative of humanity moving through time, and creative nonfiction makes those realities readable. In his work in this field, the writer Barry Lopez sees his mission as bringing the observed together with the imagined, to achieve a steady state of consciousness in writing, 'a state in which one has absorbed that very darkness which before was the perpetual sign of defeat' (1986: 414). With such vigilant aims, you can see that creative nonfiction shares many of the perceptual and philosophical possibilities of poetry and fiction, but it reaches out even further to readers: it teaches to some extent; it has a purpose beyond entertainment or art for art's sake.

Earlier models

Try to think of creative nonfiction as simply an evolved term for something that has been with us for some time, but that we called by other names such as 'belles lettres', journals, memoirs and essays. In order to see the variety and possibility of creative nonfiction, read earlier models such as Dorothy Wordsworth's 'Journals' (excerpts in NE2: 385); Charles Lamb's essay 'Old China' (NE2: 505); William Hazlitt's 'On Gusto' (NE2: 510); Henry David Thoreau's *Walden, or Life in the Woods* (NA1: 1807) and 'Walking' (NA1: 1993); Frederick Douglass's *The Narrative of the Life of Frederick Douglass, an American Slave, Written by Himself* (NA1: 2032); John Ruskin's *The Stones of Venice* (excerpt in NE2: 1432); Virginia Woolf's 'A Room of One's Own' (NE2: 2153), 'Professions for Women' (NE2: 2214), and the excerpt from her autobiographical essay *Moments of Being* called 'A Sketch of the Past' (NE2: 2218); George Orwell's 'Shooting an Elephant' (NE2: 2457); and the excerpt from Keith Douglas's vivid account of a battle in *Alamein to Zem Zem* (NE2: 2538). The truth is that well-written literary journalism, biographies, autobiographies and histories have always found audiences, alongside stylish investigations, profiles and travelogues. However, when the author Tom Wolfe in the 1960s named a fresh wave of fact-based literary writing 'the new journalism', he largely kick-started what we now write, read, teach and learn as creative nonfiction but which, until that point, traded under many titles.

Accuracy and art

If you think about the normal nonfiction you have read, you will probably be picturing books that place and explore the apparently solid world of facts. Such books speak *to* you and *at* you, and this can produce an arid, and even a distancing, experience in some readers. Writers of creative nonfiction try to close that distance between reader and writer while also dealing in the factual. They are not creating fiction, poems or journalism, even though the writers may also *be* novelists, poets or journalists.

Creative nonfiction draws general readers with the twined attractions of accuracy and art. Consider journalism. You may be thinking about journalism in terms of factual reportage, balance of opinion and informational impact. For creative nonfiction, subjectivity of approach is fine; the writing does not have to be structured for maximum information in minimum space; and balance is not required. Indeed, journalists may sometimes recast their reportage as creative nonfiction. Writing on nonfiction as literature, William Zinsser contends that he has 'no patience with the snobbery that says nonfiction is only journalism by another name and that journalism by any name is a dirty word . . . good journalism becomes good literature' (2005: 99). You should hold that ideal in your mind, not so much when you write, but when you redraft and revise your work.

Writing creative nonfiction

Creative nonfiction exercises an almost incredible gravity. Playwrights, novelists and journalists are pulled into it along with popular scientists, psychologists and mathematicians. Poets use their perceptual and linguistic precision to create exact and resonant pictures of reality. It catalysed the movement called 'self-inclusive scholarship' in which academics place themselves into their work and talk personally about their role within the research process, even though, to the real world, scholarship and criticism has always been a personal endeavour. History scholars discover untapped public audiences for their knowledge as 'narrative historians', while academic connoisseurs of the arcane beguile readers with books on singular, or single, subjects such as silk roads or salt. If you have a story to share, you will use any device of literary craft to tell it well, or at the very least clearly.

Devices

In creative nonfiction, these devices will include many of the characteristic methods of the practice of fiction. These might include story-like qualities such as 'hooking' the reader with the first sentence (the device is more permissible than in literary fiction); developing convincing real-life scenes and characters; using linked events and narrative; writing description vividly and tautly; creating and maintaining a believable point of view and setting; and using speech and dialogue compellingly. Reality must be transformed into literature, but remain recognisable and grounded in life and vivid detail.

Obviously, the range of creative nonfiction is vast. To give you an idea of range, here are two contrasting examples from radically different experiences – war and nature – by two young writers who are both writing close to their worlds, with absolute precision.

From *Alamein to Zem Zem* by Keith Douglas

Control now instructed us: 'Open fire on the enemy. Range one zero zero zero. Give the buggers every round you've got. Over.' With, I think, some relief the various squadrons acknowledge: 'One O. K. off'; 'Two O. K. off'. 'Three O. K. off'. I ordered Evan to fire. 'I can't see a muckin' thing,' he protested. 'Never mind, you fire at a thousand as fast as I can load.' Every gun was now blazing away into the twilight, the regiment somewhat massed together, firing with every available weapon. I crammed shells into the six-pounder as fast as Evan could lay and fire it . . . The turret was full of fumes and smoke. I coughed and sweated; fear had given place to exhilaration.   (NE2: 2538)

From *Walden, or Life in the Woods* by Henry David Thoreau

I say, beware of all enterprises that require new clothes, and not rather a new wearer of clothes. If there is not yet a new man, how can the new clothes be made to fit? If you have any enterprise before you, try it in your old clothes. All men want, not something to *do* with, but something to *do*, or rather something to *be*. Perhaps we should never procure a new suit, however ragged or dirty the old, until we have so conducted, so enterprised or sailed in some way, that we feel like new men in the old, and that to retain it would be like keeping new wine in old bottles. Our moulting season, like that of the fowls, must be a crisis in our lives.   (NA1: 1819)

In the first excerpt, the poet and soldier Keith Douglas recreates the action of desert warfare in a vividly experimental narrative. This memoir of World War II *Alamein to Zem Zem*, written when the author was in his early twenties, has the momentum, precision and honest perception of an improvised spoken monologue. Douglas was killed in action before the publication of the book. Thoreau was also in his twenties when, in 1845, he built himself a wooden hut on the edge of Walden Pond, near Concord. In *Walden, or Life in the Woods* he recounts his two-year experiment in self-sufficiency. He assays himself and his daily life with intimate attentiveness and scrupulous honesty. Ask yourself: How did these authors make their particular so general? In your own writing of creative nonfiction, begin paying attention to the worlds to which you are closest, and maintain a logbook of your experiences.

Basic structure

We will discuss topics later; first, we look briefly at a basic structure for your creative nonfiction. In a creative writing class, it is simpler to concentrate on shorter forms of writing such as a memoir, rather than a whole autobiography, or an article that explores some aspect of the world around you. We use the essay's form as a basis for writing articles, and even memoirs. Think of your creative nonfiction articles as simply creative essays – essays with literary panache, essays that employ narrative.

The structure of essays depends on stylistic intention and the function of the piece, but the first draft takes a straightforward shape. Use the first paragraph to set up your theme and tell the reader why it is significant for you and for them. Follow this with a series of paragraphs, each of which should present at least one complete idea, argument or demonstration of an aspect of that theme, and which maintains the forward momentum of the piece. There is usually logic to the order of these middle paragraphs, even a sense of narrative and certainly of scene-building. Conclude with a final paragraph in which what has gone before is summarised. This is the indispensable structure known as introduction–body–conclusion. It offers your piece structural clarity; however, it is simply the starting point.

Subverting the structure

In subsequent drafts, play creatively with the order of narrative, and inject your writing with energetic details and devices. For example, if you have not already woven speech or dialogue into the piece, now is the time to do so. You may also wish to subvert the structure, jump-cutting between paragraphs or making the narrative move backwards. You might interrupt the flow of prose with inner monologue, or poetry even, or hold the reader in suspense by removing information from one paragraph and withholding it until close to the end. Examine your piece to find a framing device that supports the story's structure. Bear in mind also that audiences are fickle – they are always searching for something new and stimulating – and only by surprising yourself will you surprise them.

As an example of structural subversion, read aloud *Fates Worse Than Death* by Kurt Vonnegut (in NA2: 2183). Listen to how Vonnegut plays with the focus of this piece, and is constantly undercutting serious points with dark humour and self-deprecation. He mixes the registers of the vernacular with the factual-scientific, and collages his ideas, bringing in dreams, genetics, politics, asides about *the New Yorker*, and religious history. This piece is intended to be a spoken lecture, and was originally delivered at the Cathedral of St John the Divine in New York City. Vonnegut uses the setting in the piece; then he plays with his audience (rather than playing *to* them), buttonholing them with apparently spontaneous remarks, weaving in and around the title subject. The order has the semblance of logic, but it is the logic of a freewheeling conversationalist with something on his mind. At one point he pulls back the focus entirely, and pulls the rug from under himself, declaring, 'So I haven't had much luck, have I, in identifying fates worse than death.' Yet the point is to turn and return the audience, to cajole and tease them, to the real subject: that racism not only allowed and allows slavery; it also encourages a slavery of the moral mind, one that can celebrate the incineration of innocent people through nuclear attack. The man had something on his mind, and this frames the whole piece. Be sure to read your own work aloud also, testing it on the ear for euphony, textual colour, emotional honesty and impact. Try to replicate some of Vonnegut's literary and rhetorical effects in your own work.

Speaking with the reader

The attitude of the work should not merely echo your writing voice; it should *be* your voice, even to the extent of it being your spoken voice, and an honest voice at that, for – as in all writing – honesty is a craft. In 1933, the poet Osip Mandelstam, writing in his great nonfictional account 'Journey to Armenia', wryly supposed, 'It must be the greatest impertinence to speak with the reader about the present in that tone of absolute courtesy that we have for some reason yielded to the memoirists' (2002: 200). Yet this is exactly what the best writers of creative nonfiction do. Like good novelists and poets, they aspire to speak *with* the reader, and the only impertinence for some commentators is that the genre is so popular that it even appropriates the word to describe some of its parts – popular science, popular philosophy, and so on.

However, speaking with the reader is more than a fireside conversation over a few pages. Speaking with the reader often takes the form of speaking up on behalf of an important personal, social or environmental issue. Writing is a matter of responsibility, and there is much to be said about writing well about the concerns of your time, such as social and political injustice or the environment. In fact, *Journey to Armenia* is a superb example of that very form of address, dealing as it did, obliquely, with the harmful realities of Soviet collectivisation even though the aim for its sponsors was propaganda disguised as literary travel writing.

Passion and involvement

Creative nonfiction differs from nonfiction by its very literariness, by the quality of expression and construction and, as Lee Gutkind argues:

> when people are discussing essays, articles or nonfiction books, they use words such as *interesting, accurate,* perhaps even *fascinating. Passion* and *intimacy* are not words that are often attached to nonfiction; they sound too spontaneous, emotional and imprecise . . . But passion is what is required of a creative nonfiction writer . . . A passion for the written word; a passion for the search and discovery of knowledge; and a passion for involvement.   (1997: 8)

Try not to view memoir writing as a place for confession, since real-life details 'confess' much more in being shown to the reader than you ever could by 'telling all'. Try to write to entertain as well as inform, but design your work in subtle ways to teach by demonstration, not assertion. The information carried in creative nonfiction is accurate and scrupulously researched, but you deploy creative devices such as narration, edited (but real) dialogue, characterisation and well-developed scenes to maintain a reader's attention. However, the sharpest creative devices remain your personal engagement and emotional honesty. Sometimes the writer is in fact partly the story; sometimes the writer's style is a large part of the story; and sometimes, as in autobiography, they are the story.

Writing about yourself

Writing a memoir engages both memory and memory's natural selectiveness. As I said in Chapter Two, new writers are often told to write what they know, but the problem is we do not usually know enough about what we 'know', because we do not know ourselves clearly enough. Many students appear to be finding it harder to connect themselves personally with what they know. Writing of this type helps to reconnect them to both self-knowledge and knowledge.

The face of life

One of the reasons for finding difficulty at first in writing what we know seems to be that we now gain so much knowledge in a relatively frictionless manner, such as the Internet and television. Children and teenagers living in affluent countries, for example, may not experience much in the way of physical work, such as agricultural or industrial labour, and the knowledge this brings. Therefore, although new writers might possess a range of information that would seem incredible to their forebears, it is sometimes uncoupled from physical reality, and does not carry distinct details mined from the face of life, from real landscapes, and from weathers unmonitored by any thermostat.

Remedy this by setting out to gain experience, even if that simply entails interviewing members of your family and getting experience second-hand. The paucity of real detail, or the forgery of detail, can undercut a memoir. It will read like a forgery of life, or simply under-researched, unless the details are real, and you have some experience of them (through travel or work, for example), or are ready to find and interview people with real-life experience (see 'Writing about people and the world' below). For example, in the cartoonist Art Spiegelman's account of his father's experience of the Holocaust, *MAUS* (1986), the author makes the interviews with his father an important and poignant part of the story, in that they reveal both the best and worst of their relationship, and the son's changing reasons behind the desire to tell his story.

Writing Game

WRITING ABOUT YOURSELF: WHAT YOU DO

At the end of Chapter One, we wrote about what we know about ourselves, using real-life details taken from our present day. Use the same technique, only this time think about an aspect of your life that involves action and activity, such as physical work. It should be something you know thoroughly, something 'you could do with your eyes closed'. Make rapid notes about this, especially any routines, concrete details, co-workers, working conditions, the boss, etc. When you write, do not introduce your own emotions or value-judgments at any point; stick with real-life description and dialogue. Write about 2,000 words using the first-person point of view. You do not need to have a 'story' within this piece; the narrative will be carried by the very physicality of your description.

AIM: This writing reveals itself in telling detail. You will also astonish yourself by how much more you know about something you thought you knew backwards, and how observant we are even when we are working. In your second draft, try switching this to third-person point of view and redraft accordingly. This will provide practice for writing about subjects 'you do not know' and which require observation and research.

You are a story

I said at the beginning of this chapter that time makes stories of us all. But we also make stories of ourselves. We are our own fictions even if most of the time we do not wish to understand ourselves in this way. Nevertheless, we allow ourselves to be *read* in this way, and we guide our 'readers' – whether they be our friends, employers or lovers – with no small amount of care, even when we are 'telling the truth', possibly even more so. Aspects of our lives are stories waiting to be told, and we already have some idea of how to tell them. Margaret Atwood believes that 'Our memories are much more constructed by us than we often admit to ourselves and they are certainly much more edited by us. I think every individual is his or her own novelist in a way' (1996). You will recall the neuroscientific notion from Chapter One that 'story' is a basic principle of the way the mind organises the information you take in. Memory is dynamic and selective; it can delete whole days, or magnify everyday happenings so that they become mythic. Toby Litt says, 'We shape our memories in the same way as a writer shapes their stories, leaving out the parts they do not care for and embellishing whenever the occasion calls for it.' These shaping processes should suit creative nonfiction, since stories and memoirs are themselves dynamic and selective. As the epigraph to this chapter by Nabokov reminds us, 'The selective apparatus pertains to art; but the parts selected belong to unadulterated life.'

Memoir and memory

So: felicity to reality can make for good art but only because, to some extent, our reality is partly an art. When Nabokov was writing the first version of his autobiography *Speak, Memory*, he claims he was 'handicapped by an almost complete lack of data in regard to family history, and, consequently, by the impossibility of checking my memory when I felt it might be at fault' (2000: 9). You need to collect the data of your own life before you begin playing with it, or subverting it, artistically. However, the truth is always stranger than fiction. For many readers who do not care overmuch about art, the truth is always *stronger* than any fiction, too – dangerous, even.

Begin by writing down what you consider the first memories of your own life. These might include rites of passage, such as birthdays. This will be written as a scene. Try to remember details, such as your clothes, ornaments in your house, the weather, sensations, landscape, and any speech. Try to recall images from that time. Then interview somebody – a family member, for example – and ask them to remember the same occasions. Examine photographs from that time. Weigh all this evidence, and test to what degree you already make up your pasts.

Your next step should be to compose an account of some moment of your recent life in which some conflict occurred. Write this as a series of scenes. We have seen in Chapter Six how conflict and action serve to engender and shape fiction. Just as fiction tends to deal with the exceptional rather than normal, so your memoir should trade on real life but with the boring scenes excised. Does this misrepresent your story? Not in the least. As you will begin to see, honesty and self-knowledge are crafts.

Writing Game

WRITING ABOUT YOURSELF: CRISIS AND CONFLICT
Think of something which has caused you pain, fear or doubt and which has led to crisis or conflict in your life. It could be something like a phobia, an addiction, illness, or a painful childhood memory. Use this as a starting point. Write the topic in the centre of a page, and write notes around it, including images, scenes, dialogue and associations. Research the topic; find out what other authors have written about it; and carry out at least one interview with an expert. Begin drafting your piece using a chronological framework of vivid scenes. Make nothing up; write from life and keep it simple. When did it start? How did it precipitate conflict or crisis? In subsequent drafts, subvert the order of the scenes, and leave the conclusion open-ended.

AIM: In Chapter One, I mentioned that some writers find creative writing therapeutic. Some writers of creative nonfiction write essays as a direct response to crisis, especially their own illness or the death of someone close. Although the main point of this game is to create a vivid autobiographical memoir that deals with an issue, you may find the process of writing about conflict liberating. It may not solve the conflict, but it can lend it perspective and clarity.

Pulling back

You may sometimes have experienced the dislocating sensation that you are starring in a film of your life. Begin to practise the writerly trick of freeze-framing moments of your life as they are experienced, fixing them sharply in your memory (it helps to write them down in your notebook), and ceasing to be merely a passenger in your journey through time. However, do not practise this self-consciously to the degree that it begins to change the way you live or behave.

It is all too easy to become snared in nets of self-awareness by asking too many questions, such as how well any of us know ourselves, and how well any of us know how others perceive us, or think of us. Be serious: you are not going to know the answers to all of these questions and, if you did, it would not help you or your writing. Mirrors and photographs offer you an external take, skewed by light levels. When a camera 'sees' us, we cannot help but perform a little. Your voice, when recorded, distorts the burr or drawl you hear through the bones of your own head and body. It is the same with writing: it conducts, reflects and transforms. That does not mean that it lies. Indeed, it often clarifies.

School yourself into the idea that few people are more knowable to yourself than you are, but that you *are* a story. Like a story, how you are perceived depends on a point of view. For readers, nothing is worth knowing about you unless you tell the story memorably. To write about yourself requires ego, but so does all writing. However, the risk with this kind of writing is *egotism*. You may possess the most fascinating set of experiences in the world and still be a bore. The first business of one who practises creative nonfiction is to get rid of self-conceit because it is impossible for anyone to begin to learn that which they think they already know.

As you make notes on yourself, remember that you are open space. You are many influences. You are many points of view. There are many versions of you. And you change with time. When you are writing about yourself, you are creating a story that tells *one* of several versions of the truth about yourself. You are creating a version, and everybody knows that. Do not distract yourself or your reader with egotism. The best creative nonfiction manages this balance of self-involvement and impersonality. The critic Northrop Frye said that literature was a disinterested use of words. There is a cancelled phrase in John Keats' notebooks that captures the attitude of the writer of the self very precisely: 'The feel of not to feel it'. Use both these notions as talismans while you are writing.

Knowledge is self-knowledge

The way you *choose* to tell your story will carry precise but subtle messages about your philosophy and experience, about the essential truths of your character – and its falsenesses. Write with emotional candour, even though candour might feel slightly unnatural or showy. Do not be in a hurry to disguise your own flaws in your own story. They add depth – even truth. As Jean Cocteau urged, 'Cultivate your flaws. They are the truest thing about you.' In *Therapeutic Dimensions of Autobiography in Creative Writing* (2000), Celia Hunt presents research showing that writing fictional autobiography as part of an artistic apprenticeship not only helps to extend literary skill and the finding of voice, but also benefits the writer therapeutically. Remember again that many readers read for self-instruction. They may appear to read your personal narrative to find out more about you, but what many of them are doing is trying to discover more about themselves and their own flaws and life-lessons.

To do this well, you must get outside yourself during the time of writing, looking at yourself as dispassionately as you dare. In his classic nonfictional study of the Far North, *Arctic Dreams,* one of the insights that Barry Lopez unfolds is that self-knowledge and knowledge are a continuum. For him, creative nonfiction offers an arena for their reconcilement, for *Arctic Dreams* is also partly memoir:

> The edges of the real landscape became one with the edges of something I had dreamed. But what I had dreamed was only a pattern, some beautiful pattern of light. The continuous work of the imagination, I thought, to bring what is actual together with what is dreamed is an expression of human evolution.   (1986: 414)

Most of what we meditate upon is external to us, and we need to get to know ourselves better so we can better respond to the world and the people around us. Nobody is an island; our lives are the people we meet. If we can learn to write clearly about ourselves, then we earn permission to explore more openly the patterns and stories of the people in the world around us.

Writing Game

WRITING ABOUT REAL PEOPLE: CHARACTER SKETCHES
As with flash fiction (see Chapter Six), a character sketch is a tightly written and highly focused form of around 500 words, and an extremely effective exercise for new writers of creative nonfiction. It allows for no excess verbiage, and can be written within the time of a workshop. The quickest approach is to write about somebody known by everybody in your group – for example, a member of the workshop, the tutor, or an interesting member of your wider community. It is probably best to concentrate on one characteristic of the person, and use vivid but concrete detail and snippets of speech.

AIM: This short form forces wit to its surface and one of the challenges of character sketches is to sublimate a desire for self-display in order to capture the essence of the subject and one aspect of their character – for example, their generosity, vanity, heroism or modesty. Several character sketches can be woven together to create longer works, or adapted and threaded into nonfictional work. They are also useful exercises for creating believable characters in fiction.

Writing about people and the world

What obsesses you? What do you want to explore? What might you investigate? Make a list. William Zinsser declares that new writers ought to begin their writing lives with creative nonfiction because 'They will write far more willingly about subjects that touch their own lives or that they have an aptitude for' (2005: 99). For creative writing students from academic backgrounds such as the sciences, creative nonfiction comes into its own, and 'writing what you know' might prove to be writing about your own studies or research (see 'Creative writing in the creative academy' in Chapter Ten). Those new creative writers who worry that writing about external matters is less authentic a project than writing about themselves ought to be relieved by the certainty that the style of any piece of writing is going to reveal as much about the writer as it is about the subject. However, the way you write will also reveal inauthenticity, especially if you get facts and details wrong through lack of familiarity.

Finding a topic

If you find it difficult to locate a topic, then write a trial piece in which you take a subject that you know a great deal about. Again, test out its promise and literary integrity by writing it as a scene, or a series of scenes. Many new writers begin with what is on their doorstep: family history. They then choose some discrete aspect of family history, one that they know very little about, and which requires a small amount of research. They shift from the panoptic to the microscopic focus. Tight scenes have much greater light and energy than any vague, large vision.

Mirror this shift of focus in your creative nonfiction. Choose an aspect of the world or people that you know reasonably well, and then choose some aspect that is new to you and needs fieldwork. Your task is to connect them without them seeming slung together haphazardly. For example, you might wish to write a personal essay about one of your grandparents, but then use the impact of age on memory as a hook on which to hang the essay. A similar strategy is to take two aspects of life, and lean them against each other so that they become more than the sum of their parts. For example, you could write a piece that combined your love of a sport with foreign travel. Or combine public and private narratives, such as an issue of public injustice with some crisis in your family life.

Ask yourself what touches your life now, or who touches your life, and excites you into expression. Is there a current issue you know intimately and wish to share? Or is there an issue, place or person that you are desperate to find out more about? Choose your topic with some care; make it contemporary; and keep it current. If it does not possess and excite you, then this will show in the writing. It is a good idea to run at several ideas for articles simultaneously, until one of them takes on its own life. Once you have chosen the topic, write down everything you know about it in note form, and then think about at least five questions to probe the subject. The answers to these questions will need research but, taken with the notes, they will form the first draft of the article using the basic essay structure.

Writing Game

WRITING ABOUT REAL PEOPLE: INVESTIGATIVE WRITING
Working in teams of two people, carry out an investigation into the world of work in your area. Choose an occupation or profession that is relatively unknown to you. Using telephone directories, locate workers in that field locally and arrange to interview at least two of them. Discover their motivations and daily routines, and try to gain permission to shadow them on a daily basis for at least a week. Write a fly-on-the-wall article about their work, and include your own experience of it.

AIM: The details of work are interesting to many readers; it allows them to experience another life vicariously. People are not defined by the work they do, but working life is central to people's concerns, and to the way society runs. This game introduces you to interviewing and research. It also accesses a huge amount of telling detail that you may use at some other point in a piece of fiction.

Fieldwork and interviews

Research will involve carrying out Internet searches on your subject, and checking library databases for books and articles on the same or similar subjects. Importantly, check whether your subject has already been covered, and what gaps are left between subjects that are ripe for research and writing. Try also to read a national newspaper at least twice a week to keep up on current affairs, and maintain what writers call a 'futures' file of press clippings in your notebook. These clippings may touch on your subject or contain matters you may wish to write about later. If you are writing about local or family history, then you need to become acquainted with record offices. Most cities and towns possess excellent archives of official documents, papers and records. Talk to their archivists and librarians about the kind of information you are seeking. Third-party help of this type can allow you to access materials it might take many weeks to find under your own steam. Research might also include interviewing an expert in a field simply to get information. However, interviewing people about their own stories is a different matter.

Interviewing people is an art form in itself but it comes down to three matters: being interested in what a person has to say; becoming a good listener; and recognising which materials to select from an interview. Choose your interviewees with care, and make sure you are well prepared. Try to formulate your questions so that they do not 'lead' to predictable responses, but that they elicit long answers that may even take the form of an anecdotal story or joke. Nurture the relationship with a subject; this promotes mutual trust but also allows you to take in more than mere surface information. It allows you to know people better – their values, attitudes and thoughts. It should also lead you to make fewer factual, or moral, mistakes.

It is your judgement whether you should use a notebook or recording device during an interview. Some writers of creative nonfiction find that these produce a distancing effect between interviewer and subject, and that the writer is less likely to listen attentively and sensitively, probing deeper into certain answers, if they have the fall-back of a recording device or the 'screen' of a notebook. Some writers use nothing but their memories. Once the interview is over, they simply write down as much as they can remember. If you use quotations from interviews, especially if you have compressed or doctored them to fit your piece, it is only fair to allow interviewees 'sight of copy' (the final draft before submission), so that they can either corroborate the manner in which their words have been used, or request changes.

A literature of hope

You are writing during the silver age for creative nonfiction. It is probably the most communal, idealistic and open-ended of literary genres – 'If I were asked what I want to accomplish as a writer, I would say it's to contribute to a literature of hope', states Barry Lopez in *About This Life* (1999: 15). Creative nonfiction is now an international supergenre encompassing memoirs, history, autobiography, biography, travel writing, nature writing, popular anthropology, film and music writing, popular philosophy, ethnic studies, journalism, writing on religion, literary studies, and more. It contributes to the boom in popular science and a greater public awareness of the work of scientists. It expands the continent of creative writing, presenting complete pictures of a subject and fresh ways of looking at the world around us. Its permeable open space continues to grow and capture ever more subjects, writers and readers, especially through weblogs (see 'Electronic performance' in Chapter Nine).

We discussed in Chapter Five the metaphor of an invisible audience that stands behind poets and novelists while they are writing. Such writers are often writing in the dark to an extent, and only begin to refine or change their work once it is finished and they begin to have a clearer idea of who might read it or attend a performance of their work. Remember that your creative nonfiction generally has a less phantasmal relationship with its audience since it often takes their real world as its subject. However, unless you have been asked to write specifically for a small and known faction of readers, do not be misled into thinking that you must tailor your style and subject to suit anybody. To make your work new and challenging you must still write primarily for yourself, and that remains a huge challenge to any notions you may have for telling the truth and showing the shape of truth by using art.

Writing Game

WRITING ABOUT THE WORLD: TRAVEL WRITING
Research the history of your neighbourhood using record offices, your local library and local history archives. Try to gain the trust of older members of your community, and then interview them about their experience of life and work. Create a collage of these interviews and histories, and thread a narrative through it that holds the work together. Use as much of the interviews as you can, but be selective.

AIM: The local is global. You do not need to be a world explorer to write well about travel. Close study of your own area, even your neighbourhood, will reveal many mysterious aspects, hidden histories and fascinating people and stories. Apply this technique next time you travel to somewhere that is strange and new.

Recommended reading

As a cautionary tale about the liberties and licence of a certain type of journalism, and the importance of a creative nonfiction writer's fidelity to reality, Janet Malcolm's *The Journalist and the Murderer* (Granta, 2004) remains indispensable. William Zinsser's stripped-down exposition of nonfiction's provenance in *On Writing Well* (Collins, 2005) teaches by example. This early guide to writing nonfiction (first edition, 1976) carries introductions to writing about science, technology and sport. Research and craft are emphasised in Philip Gerard's highly useful *Creative Nonfiction* (Story Press, 1996). The novelist and filmmaker Lee Gutkind edits *Creative Nonfiction*, which is highly recommended, as is his *The Art of Creative Nonfiction* (John Wiley & Sons, 1997). In the UK, the best international creative nonfiction is published in the magazine *Granta*; and *The Granta Book of Reportage* introduced by veteran editor Ian Jack (Granta, 2006) is an excellent representative anthology. *Autobiographical Writing Across the Disciplines*, edited by Diane Freedman and Olivia Frey (Duke, 2003), reveals the remarkable breadth of the intellectual movement toward self-inclusive scholarship. With primary texts, begin at first by reading some of the earlier models listed at the start of this chapter. You may also gain by reading the autobiographies and biographies of any writers you admire. Rather than landing you with an extensive and probably partial list of exemplary books, I suggest you follow your enthusiasms at first, not so much for authors but for subjects that interest you. However, in your first attempts at the genre – and within the time constraints of a creative writing course – you will learn a huge amount about the different available styles, and gain by their imitation, through reading nonfiction and essays by writers such as Martin Amis, John Berger, Truman Capote, Bruce Chatwin, Richard Dawkins, Joan Didion, Annie Dillard, Maureen Dowd, Louise Erdrich, Martha Gellhorn, Stephen Jay Gould, Ian Jack, Ryszard Kapuściński, Barry Lopez, John McPhee, Norman Mailer, Janet Malcolm, Blake Morrison, John Pilger, Steven Pinker, Oliver Sacks, Iain Sinclair, Lewis Thomas, Hunter S. Thompson, John Updike, Gore Vidal, Eudora Welty, E. O. Wilson, Tom Wolfe and Tobias Wolff.

Chapter 8

Writing poetry

Behind several theories of what happens to a poet during the writing of a poem – Eliot's escape from personality, Keats's idea of informing and filling another body, Yeats's notion of the mask, Auden's concept of the poet becoming someone else for the duration of the poem, Valéry's idea of a self superior to the self – lies the implied assumption that the self as given is inadequate and will not do. *How you feel about yourself* is probably the most important feeling you have. It colors all other feelings, and if you are a poet, it colors your writing. It may account for your writing.

RICHARD HUGO, *The Triggering Town: Lectures and Essays on Poetry and Writing* (1979: 67)

Where does rhythm come from? The cellular life of a poem is its language. All language naturally possesses rhythm, even non-human languages. Rhythm is made of beats, whether of a skin drum in a frog's throat, or a hoof's thrum. For living creatures, rhythm is used to create and defend territory, and communicate. Song is modulated in order to carry it best through resistant matter, as whale song is through the soft walls of ocean, or an owl's call spooling through woodland. The languages of most animals on our planet are based on sounds, and the sound carries the meaning. Rhyme and rhythm are not as artificial as you might suppose – they are natural mnemonics, occurring in birdsong and animal calls. Slow a skylark's song and you will hear a sophisticated thematic development of beats within just one second of song, yet the bird sings continuously in real time as you pass beneath. What is the secret of poetry?

Listening to language

Metre and rhyme

Surprise in language is poetry's open secret. When you were a child you probably loved poetry without knowing why. The rhythm of language is what engaged you, and rhyme may also have surprised poems into your memory:

Sing, cuccu, nu. Sing, cuccu.   *now*
Sing, cuccu. Sing, cuccu, nu.
Sumer is i-cumen in –
   Lhude sing, cuccu!   *loudly*
Groweth sed and bloweth med   *blooms / field*
   And springth the wude nu.   *buds / wood*
      Sing, cuccu!

Poems are made up of lines of words that do not usually reach the far side of the page. Words themselves possess a small amount of music because they are made up of syllables, which are themselves made up of short and long speech sounds, and gradations between, just like birdsong. You can guess-measure this length by saying them aloud. As you speak them, you will also hear how we breathe out harder on some syllables than others; we stress certain syllables more than we stress others, and all the gradations between. This lends spoken language its rhythmic coloratura.

There is no final science about this; stresses change when we catch our breath, and every language has its own music – every accent too; and even the mood we are in affects the way we speak. A lover may sound their words rather differently than a murderer, although a good poet might play on this distinction. Yet, as we speak, our larynx, teeth and tongue – even our upbringing and intention – inject stress patterns into the words we speak, the beats of rhythm. Poetry raises the voice in language, and sings, says, whispers and shouts – intentionally. If poets possess verbal cunning, then, like dramatists and novelists, they exploit the lively variousness of speech too.

For ease of conversation, we talk about lines of poetry having a 'metre' which counts these stressed syllables and arranges them in patterns called 'feet'; and we give terms to various patterns of stress (such as a 'spondee': two stresses one after the other). These patterns reveal themselves in speech without the need for śtress márks urging *hark! – a spondee!* The most common stress pattern in English verse is called iambic pentameter. An iamb is a 'foot' with an unstressed syllable followed by a stressed syllable. It mákes the kínd of nóise this séntence mákes. Yet even as I speak the sounds will change. A lump of stress is catching in my throat. As you can hear, no two iambs are the same. And, given the fluidities of language and speech, stress patterns are always approximations to the real thing.

Poets play with these patterns, often intuitively, in order to create verbal effects because they have trained their ears to listen for these effects not only in speech but in listening to the rhythms in the world. Boisseau and Wallace offer an excellent example from the first line of Richard Wilbur's 'The Juggler':

A ball will bounce, but less and less.

The iambic line (of four stresses) imitates the ball. As they put it, 'Within regularity or, rather, because of it, small differences in stress give the effect of less and less force and so seem to imitate the way a ball slows to a stop in smaller and smaller arcs' (2004: 54). Poetry is a form of creating such epiphanies through making lines of language, the internal musical arrangement of which, as with Wilbur's ball, carries the poem into memory.

In the same way that paragraphs of prose have the effect of herding words into a point, lines of poetry are gathered into stanzas to make a triangulation of meaning, sound and shape. We sometimes use forms of poetry to shape lines and stanzas. Many of the traditional forms had their origin in song and the oral transmission of poems. Regular metre, rhymes and forms help you to remember the poem. Memory has its metres, and various verbal strategies glue words into place. Alliteration, for example, alerts us that language has a larynx, and offers an afterlife through being stickily memorable:

No trembling harp,
no tuned timber, no tumbling hawk
swerving through the hall, no swift horse
pawing the courtyard.
from 'Beowulf' (NP: 9)

These word strategies are terrifically important and primal. After all, poems once carried the stories of our species through time. In Aboriginal culture, song-poetry governs the mapping of territory and sacred sites. Of course, some of the newer forms of poetry have their origin in speech, or even visual appearance. However, the form known as *free verse* is still a shaping pattern for poetry's language; and the form called *syllabics* is shaped by speech's mathematics. Forms and patterns are shaping devices whose purpose is not to restrict but to create units of time for language, and to provide open spaces for saying and transmitting. You should try them all.

'Rhyme' and 'time' sound the same to my ear, but only because my verbal memory blends them so. As words, they look very different, and a thousand years ago many words would not have sounded the same way, as the poem about the cuckoo demonstrated. Rhyme emerges from listening to the music of language, as do line, metre and form. Like them, rhyme is elastic and subject to change. This is why poets have always exploited the range of rhyme and the essential plasticity of verbal sound. A 'full-rhyme' like 'full time' can be played on by a half-rhyme like 'fall-time' or 'full room', and many gradations between.

Repetition devices, like restrictive devices, are ways of shaping a poem, and carrying a poem forward as speech. They plant avenues of words to help drive a poem forward; they plant a simple repeating pattern to serve out rhythm; they plant a simulation of rhyme also:

> I am the womb: *of every holt,*
> I am the blaze: *on every hill,*
> I am the queen: *of every hive,*
> I am the shield: *for every head,*
> I am the tomb: *of every hope.*
>   from the Irish, sixth century

Hearing your own nature

Poetry is more natural an art form than you might have been led to believe. Lines in your poetry are units of your time. Those units of time operate with the rhythm of language, the beat of your species and of *you*. It may be what drew you to creative writing in the first place. The heartbeat of your mother heard by you in her womb; then the nursery rhyme, the children's song, the rhythmical poems and speech of childhood – all these lodged in your memory because of their rhythms. They are locked into you by many early synapses; and they were made because of your perfectly natural sensual pleasure in them. The music of language was your first teacher. This was the birdsong of your species; of you as a species of one individual. That song marked the territory of your perceptual world, one that grows if you keep developing the talent and ear. Poems can be seen as charms, as modulated enchantments, but they are also weapons made of speech.

Now, imagine somebody standing before you, and a fire between you and him. He places a poem and a thousand-dollar bill in the flames. How does this make you feel? As Richard Hugo suggests, how we feel about ourselves may colour how we write poems, and even account for poetry being part of our lives. It is a fine line; a question of value. As you will see, this chapter oscillates around this line. There are cherished values in writing poetry. For example, many poets teach the technical apparatus of metre and versification. I endorse such an approach unequivocally (as I hope I have shown rather than told), but only when the student has decided they are *already on the side of poetry*. In my experience, a purely technical focus in the early stages can make a beginning writer run for cover, leaving them with a somewhat exoskeletal idea of poetry's structures and forms. The task here is more inward and basic. It is to invite you to see writing poems as an activity worth your time and attention, so that you may eventually feel like reaching into flames on a poem's behalf – you may then find one day you are also that poem's author. In the remaining part of this chapter we unfold some maps for finding our way into the language of poetry; explore some introductory modes for making poems; and explode one or two myths that may otherwise hold you back from reaching ever more deeply into language.

Writing Game

METRE AND RHYME

Write a poem of twenty lines in iambic pentameter, without rhyme. Then write a poem in iambic pentameter of fourteen lines in which you use full-rhyme. Finally, write a poem in iambic pentameter of thirty lines in which you only use half-rhyme.

AIM: It is useful for any poet to get to grips with basic metres. If, during drafting of any of these poems, you feel that the rhyme or metre is getting in the way of the poem's success, then consider altering it, even if that disrupts the metre and rhyme-patterns.

Finding language

Processes

Poetry is the opposite of money in many fundamental ways. On the surface, it does not make its writers rich or chic; and, to publishers, poetry is a surefire get-poor scheme. As Robert Graves said, 'There is no money in poetry, but there's no poetry in money either.' In poetry, the notion of 'success' is extremely relative compared with other arts. Success can simply mean sculpting one perfect quatrain; as Derek Mahon wrote wryly:

> I have been working for years
> on a four-line poem
> about the life of a leaf;
> I think it might come out right this winter.
>   'The Mayo Tao' (1999: 66)

As this poem indicates, quick gains are not made painting the room of a stanza. Other forms of compensation arrive eventually; and nowhere else is the experience of creative process, especially drafting, more of a love–hate relationship.

Poets place value on language above every other literary consideration. It can be argued that poetry is one of the crucibles, along with research science, in which language crackles and transmutes. As I remarked early in this book, the fastest-evolving species is language. Poetry sets its camps on the shifting dunes of language, and sometimes trespasses beyond those known borders. The flux and flow in language can create a sense of continual crisis when writing poetry. Given these conditions, you will have to get used to feeling that you will not really know when you have got a poem 'right'. You may sometimes feel fraught as the language in your poems reacts against itself during rewriting. However, as you will see, reading other people's poetry helps you find such alchemies easier to understand, if only marginally more possible to control. But sometimes the language in your poem is reacting against itself because it knows better what shape it should be taking than you do.

Writing Game

KENNINGS

A kenning is a compound poetic phrase that takes the place of the name of a person or thing. It comes from the Old Norse, to express a thing in terms of another. In Old English, the sea would be called a 'whale-road'. A book could be called 'a word-hoard'. Create some kennings and use them in short poems or haiku.

AIM: Kennings exist today in everyday speech – for example, 'railroad'. Compression of image and language is important to poets, and kennings are an effective game for creating new images and metaphors, for finding fresh ways of seeing the world through language.

Inside poems

Poems are verbal contraptions: perpetual-motion machines made of words and, as Kenneth Koch reminds us, 'Each word has a little music of its own'. In writing poems, you hear, see and feel every word, space and punctuation mark intimately. You may even find your voice in the spaces between words, or the open space around the poem. Why do we create these little self-sustaining machines made of words and their noise? Some poets write to preserve moments of significance, often small and apparently trifling instants or perceptions. As Wisława Szymborska says of a butterfly's shadow passing over her hands:

> Seeing such sights I lose my certainty
> that what is important
> is more important than the important.

(1996: 57)

Observation and memory are as talismanic to poetry as character and story are to fiction. Poems create little worlds of perceptual and temporal clarity. Robert Frost described a poem as 'a momentary stay against confusion'. As Sylvia Plath put it:

> a door opens, a door shuts. In between you have had a glimpse: a garden, a person, a rainstorm, a dragonfly, a heart, a city. I think of those round glass Victorian paperweights . . . a clear globe, self-complete, very pure, with a forest or village or family group within it. You turn it upside down, then back. It snows. Everything is changed in a minute. It will never be the same in there – not the fir trees, nor the gables, nor the faces. So a poem takes place.   (Herbert and Hollis, 2000: 146)

Plath is right that our poems try to create a small and clear world that goes on recreating itself every time somebody reads it. Plath also wrote fiction. Like the best short stories, writing poems is one of the few open spaces in literature where you have the opportunity to make something resonant, complete and independent, even if that happens only a half a dozen times in your writing life. What of the world around a poem? Denise Levertov believed, 'Insofar as poetry has a social function it is to awaken sleepers by other means than shock.' What does it feel like to awaken in this way?

Writing Game

WISHES AND CURSES
Write two poems in free verse but using repeated phrases as a restrictive device to pattern your poem. Write one poem using the phrase 'I wish that . . .' at the beginning of every line. Write another poem in the form of a curse – choose something that has upset you deeply and curse it with this poem, each line of which begins with the phrase, 'I curse you with . . .'

AIM: These are good beginner exercises. They produce vivid and energetic phrasing, and establish the use of a patterning device such as a repeated phrase.

Awakening language

Meaning and being

Language is made to live through poems, but the living language of poetry does not simply begin and end with the meaning of your words, and those words combed into lines and stanzas. As we discussed in previous chapters, words are sticky with meaning, history and association, and these elements are brought to life through their choice and combination – and by chance, especially the chances created by metre, rhyme and form. There is more to it than that. Poetry's precision of expression, its accent on the sounds of language, draws the writer taken by the clatter and tilt of words. As Ted Hughes said:

> Words that live are those which we hear, like 'click' or 'chuckle', or which we see, like 'freckled' or 'veined', or which we taste, like 'vinegar' or 'sugar', or touch, like 'prickle' or 'oily', or smell, like 'tar' or 'onion'. Words which belong directly to one of the five senses. Or words which act and seem to use their muscles, like 'flick' or 'balance'.   (1967: 17)

It is important you develop a generous lexical awareness, and a feel for the sensuality of words. This lexical adventure can sometimes lead new writers astray, tempting them with wordiness or obscure diction. However difficult they might seem to be, your poems should not need to hang on a gallery wall with an abstruse explanation beside them. Any difficulties we feel we have with poetry are usually difficulties of expectation and, sometimes, mystification. There is no need to make more difficulty for the sake of it.

Expectations and mystifications are usually to do with the apparent *strangeness* of poetry – for example, what we think of as its language, subject and address, and even the fact we write it *in lines*. Yet, poetry has no 'special' language or subject of its own, at least not any more; and it is not addressed to a closed circle of chosen listeners. Poems do not have to mean anything significant, nor justify their existence in social or political terms. As Archibald MacLeish wrote in his poem 'Ars Poetica' (NP: 1381), 'A poem should not mean / But be'.

'It should not mean but be' sounds implausible if you are schooled to read poems as autobiographical or cultural documents, or as material for literary analysis. For a critic or student of literature, meanings may indeed be readable into poems. There are illuminations to be had through a critical approach so long as it does not turn readers off poetry; lead them into thinking that poems exist only for this reason; or make new writers feel they must manufacture poems that fit a critical mode of reading. 'A bad poem is one that vanishes into meaning' – Paul Valéry. And worse still, and even more truthful in its devastating brevity, 'All bad poetry is sincere' – Oscar Wilde. A poem, in its incubation phase, will run away from you if you proposition it in this way. For any good poet, it is simply impractical to try and charge a poem-in-process with significance (I will not say a 'greater' significance) or feeling (I will not say 'genuine' feeling). Wrestling the words into place is more than enough to be getting on with.

Writing Game

MAKING A SMALL TRUTH
Instead of electing to write on a high-minded subject in a self-consciously poetic way, let something small and everyday choose *you*. This could be a thing or even a word. Write the word or place the object in the centre of a sheet of paper, and write notes freely around it. Think about where it has come from and where it is going to; make notes on any memories it triggers in your mind; compare it to other things using simile, or transform it into something else through metaphor; use all your senses to describe it – do not use only visual description or comparison. Now freewrite about it, and underline any unusual phrases that occur. Try to combine all this material by using the form of address of a letter, but writing in lines. Think of the object or word as a *cause* for celebration that you are asking somebody else to share, and do not stray off the subject.

AIM: An obsessive and concentrated effect using something concrete and recognisable allows greater flexibility than writing about something abstract. In a sense, you are writing about what you know. However, there is latitude for discovering a lot more along the way, and you can learn to allow this sense of uncovering the mystery of what you *think* you know.

Subjects and ways of saying

The poet John Redmond believes that many new writers limit themselves by writing what he calls the 'default poem': 'a simple lyric formula: an 'I-persona' describing its state of mind and feeling as though chatting with the reader across a coffee-table' (2006: 17). He is right that a contemporary poem can of course be far more adventurous and bold in address – in the way the poem is expressed and to whom it is said. And it can be pointed out that, historically, poems have not behaved themselves in their registers, and could also be promiscuous about their intended audience. They have been known to swagger; slander; rave; lilt; boast; play; yarn; rage; and seduce. If you want to explore these possibilities, open *The Norton Anthology of Poetry* (NP; see Preface) and read, then try imitating – respectively – Lord Byron's *Don Juan* (excerpts, 837); John Wilmot, Earl of Rochester's 'The Mock Song' (552); Christopher Smart's 'Jubilate Agno' (excerpt, 678); 'Green Grow the Rashes' by Robert Burns (747); Walt Whitman's 'Song of Myself' (excerpts, 1060); Edward Lear's limericks (1041–1043); Robert Frost's 'Home Burial' (1228); 'Do Not Go Gentle into That Good Night' by Dylan Thomas (1572); and John Donne's 'To His Mistress Going to Bed' (312).

It is what your poem is, not what your poem says, that makes it work. That also goes for subject matter. There is no subject off limits, as the examples above show. Yet it is not what you write *about* that matters most; it is how you write it. And because poetry takes many drafts to get right, it is how you *re*write it. A poem about, say, tomatoes, written with verbal panache, will deliver greater energy than a high-minded but clumsily written poem about angst. You could argue that too few poets make their cause *poetry* because too many are chasing hearses and ambulances, or using a poem as a kind of mirror on which they breathe their own feelings.

The problem is that some new writers have been taught to view poetry through over-serious and personal spectacles; and they have also been taught that poetry has an association with conveying truth, the whole truth and nothing but. This association is partly a result of its strong relationship with the spoken word; partly through the persuasiveness of certain poets, critics and teachers; and partly because poets in some cultures were indeed regarded as the community's shaman. Good poems, of course, capture elementary truths, or allow these qualities to refract through certain tropes of language. Precise and playful images, for example, are prisms emitting the light of observation over and over again during reading, even if all the images are doing is celebrating something as mundane as the *tomatoness* of tomatoes, as in Pablo Neruda's famous ode on that very subject.

Shaping language

Form

As with the forms of fiction, the choice you make with the form and structure of poems will inevitably begin to shape what you can do with them; and it will shape the expectation of your reader even before they begin reading. Suppose you were blindfolded and handed a vessel shaped like a wine glass but containing water. Your mind prepares itself to expect wine and, depending on the fluting of the glass, even a type of wine, or champagne. When you take your first sip, part of your mind still tastes that premonition of wine.

It is the same with poems: the shape before a reader disposes them to expect a shaped experience, even if the words in the form's vessel are water. A sonnet shape sets up quite different expectations from a haiku. The thirty-nine-line sestina tastes quite different to a terza rima of the same length. But forms are not vessels that shape language passively. As Theodore Roethke asserted, "Form' is regarded not as a neat mould to be filled, but rather as a sieve to catch certain kinds of material' (Kinzie, 1999: 345). For the writer, the glass is broken; it must be melted and reblown every time you write in its form.

Rather than walk you through examples of metre and form, I direct you to the excellent books on form in my Recommended reading, and to concise examinations of these matters in NP (2027) or *The Norton Anthology of English Literature* (NE2; 2928). In my experience, the clearest and most thorough text for writers is a book intended for 'aspiring readers . . . of poetry', which seems a very strong place for us all to start: Paul Fussell's *Poetic Meter and Poetic Form* (1979).

Free verse

There is nothing free about free verse. It will not liberate a country or open a prison, and to write in free verse well is often harder than writing in form. The 'free' in 'free verse' refers to the freedom from fixed patterns of metre and rhyme, but writers of free verse use poetic devices like alliteration, figures of speech and imagery. As James Fenton puts it:

> Free verse seemed democratic because it offered freedom of access to *writers*. And those who disdained free verse would always be open to accusations of elitism . . . Open form was like common ground on which all might graze their cattle – it was not to be closed in by usurping landlords . . . But if the land looks overgrazed, one should feel free to move on.   (2002: 107)

Unfamiliarity breeds contempt. Any ingrained antagonism to form in poetry is usually an indicator that the poet hasn't read very much poetry. Free verse has a long history, and is as ancient as Anglo-Saxon verse. To move on, let me say that free verse can be written quite brilliantly, but I would argue that good free verse is harder to write than good formal verse. At best there should be no sense of a disjunction between the old shapes and the new, or apparently new. Fenton also points out that D. H. Lawrence stands out as a practitioner whose unmetred poetry was clearly better than his metred poems (see NP: 1284). There is a no-man's land between where his poems stop and where his prose begins. For examples to imitate, read 'Snake' (see NP: 1286) and 'Bavarian Gentians':

> Reach me a gentian, give me a torch!
> let me guide myself with the blue, forked torch of this flower
> down the darker and darker stairs, where blue is darkened on blueness
> even where Persephone goes, just now, from the frosted September
> to the sightless realm where darkness is awake upon the dark . . .
>
> (NP: 1291)

Syllabics

You can try writing in syllabics right now by creating a haiku – a three-line poem of seventeen syllables in which the syllable count of the lines is five–seven–five. Read this poem by the author about a bird called a 'Redpoll':

As if she had spilt
from cherries, from holly, from
a shake of nightshade.

The line break between line two and line three 'shakes' the nightshade-bush of the poem as the bird flies from it. Haiku are small open spaces for precise, often resonant, observation. Syllabics as a whole are a means to organise your lines of poetry by using a strict number of syllables in a constant and continuing pattern. It is a means to organise a poem into being. The 'found poem' 'The European Larch' in Chapter Five uses syllabics. Rhyme can be used with subtlety, as in the syllabic masterpieces of Marianne Moore (see NP: 1328).

Writing Game

SYLLABLES AND SENSES
Choose a place as your subject – for example, a school, a church, a town, a shop, a restaurant, a mountain. Freewrite on this subject, then transform what you have written into a seven-line poem, each line of which has seven syllables. Choose an emotion as your subject – for example, love, envy, anger, sorrow, hatred. Ask the chosen emotion these questions and answer them in lines of poetry (do not mention the emotion): What colour is it? What animal would it be? What weather is it? What time of day is it like, and why? What does it smell/sound/look/taste/feel like? Transform your answers into a seven-line poem, each line of which has seven syllables. The final stage is to *push the two poems together* to make one poem of seven lines, each line of which is seven syllables.

AIM: You will need to lose fifty per cent of each poem. This is an exercise in precise patterning; in knowing what to leave out; and in leaning two ideas against each other to make something quite new leap from that pressure.

Subverting form

New writers will do well to get the hang of a form before gunning it down, although it is an effective workshop exercise to create a poem in which the structure ambushes the subject. The structure of the poem could, as it were, tell a different story from the poem's words. While the sonnet is generally associated with love as its subject today, a good sonnet about contemporary war would surprise and subvert the form. A series of drastic limericks would similarly turn that form inside out.

Writing Game

DARK SIDE LIMERICKS
Read the limericks of Edward Lear (NP: 1041). Write a sequence of fifteen strict limericks which deal in the darkest or most taboo types of human behaviour; or with a subject matter, such as terminal illness, which would conventionally be realised through a 'serious' form, or form of address. Test these out by reading them aloud to people; if they do not get a laugh, you have succeeded.

AIM: Some forms of poetry, such as the limerick or triolet, become associated with a humorous mode of address. By turning the tables on the subject matter you introduce a tension into the form that will both incense but also compel readers.

Shaping a sequence and collection

Shorter poems are sometimes set in a sequence, unified by one or more threads, such as narrative, form and theme. This unity need not be frictionless: the shorter poems may be dissonant with each other in some ways. For example, each part might take a different point of view, and the sequence as a whole provides the arena for this variousness. Taken further, some poets order their collections carefully so that the poems in it, individually and as a whole, resonate in some way with each other and with the title of the book. In this way, the book itself becomes a type of poetic form (although you should be warned that many readers simply and naturally 'dip' into a poetry collection rather than read it as they would a novel).

Begin reading your poems with these ends in mind. For example, do some of the poems share the same concerns, or even images, and might they be brought together in some way to make a more powerful piece? Are there leitmotifs in sound between poems that would be clearer if the poems were grouped in some sequence? By shuffling and reshuffling your poems, is there some kind of narrative running through them, and might this be a sequence, or the best order, for your portfolio of coursework or first collection? If so, what title might illuminate these connections, or even challenge and subvert them?

Writing Game

A PERSONAL ANTHOLOGY
As we discussed in Chapter Four, writers often use their notebooks as 'commonplace books' to collect pieces of writing that impress them, show them something new, or speak to them emotionally and to their own need to write.

When you have assembled at least 200 poems of these types, make copies of them, and begin looking at them all with the view of creating your own anthology. What unites them? Are they mostly in form or free verse? What is the gender and background of the authors? Is there a theme or themes? In multiple permutations, try ordering these poems so that they speak to one another in sequence; and ensure the final order has inner logic from a reader's point of view.

AIM: This is excellent practice for examining poems from many angles, and for developing discrimination. You will find it helpful for when you order your own poems into a portfolio, poetic sequence or first collection. Later, should you become a poetry editor (as many poets are, however briefly), this practice will be of use in creating a poetry magazine or a published anthology of poems.

Playing with language

You can write poems in form and poems in free verse, and many variants between. You can write poems that are confessional and poems that are cold-eyed. You can write poems that tell stories, and poems that lock on to one object and express it to its very atoms. Your task is to find the poems you want to write; the ones you are capable of writing well; and, if you want to become a poet rather than a 'writer of poems', to find poems which nobody else could compose.

Volcano and diamonds

To do this, you practise several modes of writing poetry, until you reach a way of writing where subject and form 'click' together, as Robert Frost put it. This destination cannot be reached without your reading a great deal of poetry. There are billions of poems in this world, and thousands being written every day. Most of these are bad poems that contain clichés of feeling and imagery; clichéd or archaic writing; prosaic, dishonest or forced expression; inelastic or inappropriate form, however 'free'; or just common-or-garden dullness.

A volcano explodes tonnes of ash and waste on to its flanks, but the process might yield diamonds among this scree. You read a lot of poetry to develop your discrimination. Voracity shapes – it does not narrow – taste. If you possess received ideas about poetry, try unlearning them by reading more poems, and also reading poems in translation. There are many species of poem. Christmas carols; nursery rhymes; some forms of prayer; lieder; prose poetry; the blues; and concrete verse – all these are different and highly colourful species of poetry. As you will see in Chapter Nine, there are even poems that look like paintings; some poems are sculptures in gardens; and others which exist solely in electronic form.

Reading, reading aloud and memorising poetry will help you discriminate between poems that work and those that do not, and you can then exercise that discrimination on your own work. The best advice, as the poet Denise Levertov might have said, is to read until you 'waken'. You may then feel compelled to reproduce your first excitements about poetry within your own work, since it appears a wholly natural progression that readers who are wakened in this way by poetry wish to try writing it. Therefore, make a habit of reading at least five poems every day, and make time for them (and I do not mean five haiku!). As you begin to get comfortable, begin reading whole collections at one sitting, and then try to read the entire output of one poet over a week.

Many contemporary poets limit their literary awareness by only reading other *contemporary* poets: a circling and encircling strategy offering low possibilities. Read backwards in time, and across languages. When seeking models for style and diction, try to be broader in your reading than poetry. As I pointed out in Chapter Five, some fiction writers read poems in order to gain a sense of the compressed sonic mathematics possible in language. You can even find 'found poetry' in some very peculiar prose, such as museum labels or office memos. Good fictional prose can also present you with ideas and language for poems – the best prose can be read as another type of poetry. As the poet Robert Lowell commented, 'I felt that the best style of poetry was none of the many poetic styles in English, but something like the prose of Chekhov or Flaubert' (Herbert and Hollis, 2000: 108). Qualities you can borrow will include a sense for narrative and character, but you can also learn to relax – and to pace – some of the tension in your lines by seeing how a paragraph of good prose might work as lines of a poem.

Writing Game

FINDING POETRY

Take a sample of unusual or idiosyncratic prose from an obscure source, which might include labels, instruction manuals, business memos, science books, magazines about arcane subjects, or even this book. Freely adapt the prose into lines, using syllable count as the sole restriction. For example, you might break it into three quatrains, each line of which is ten syllables long. Then, read some short stories with the same end in mind, only this time create a longer poem, again using syllable count to break the prose into lines. Acknowledge the source somewhere in the poem or the title.

AIM: We looked at how we can borrow the precise aspects of language from nonfiction sources in Chapter Five. 'Found poetry' is a fine tradition. It seems like stealing. However, as T. S. Eliot reminded us, mature poets steal. Writing is always transformative. Some people condemn free-verse poetry as 'chopped-up prose'.

This game shows you how to chop it properly! Poetry, I said, is pervasive. This game also helps you to *see the poetry* in many different types of writing.

Writing poems requires a similar excess of exposure in order to create discrimination. Once again: a volcano vomits sky-high showers of ash, but there may be a small number of diamonds scorched into being. In the same way, you will probably *write a lot of poetry to get a little*. For example, read this poem by Donald Hall called 'Exile' (along with its footnote in NP: 1753):

Exile
A boy who played and talked and read with me
Fell from a maple tree.

I loved her, but I told her I did not,
And wept, and then forgot.

I walked the streets where I was born and grew,
And all the streets were new.

The footnote tells us that many versions of this poem exist and a much longer version has appeared in print. Imagine the ash and scorched earth of language around these six diamond-hard lines. If we were to replay Anatole France's analogy between carpentry and creative writing, the space around this poem is waist-high in wood-shavings. You might write and rewrite a lot of good poetry to gain something with which you are satisfied, even temporarily – and, even then, like Donald Hall, you might still change it. Nowhere is the editor's razor sharper and more frequently in use than in rewriting poetry. When that razor is not applied, the result can be shovel-loads of scree and ash. Think of the scholarly editions of the complete works of any major poet and the diamond-to-ash ratio therein. Yet weak, leaden or plodding poetry is the path to good writing, even though the ratio between them might seem horrendous at first. One way to make this process more palatable for you is to make it challenging and even entertaining, and playing with form and pattern is probably the best way forward.

Writing Game

DRAFTING LONG TO MAKE IT SHORT
Think about an experience that is lodged in your memory, possibly a childhood event that caused you some pain, or which matured your view of yourself. Make rapid notes in prose in your notebook, probably covering about five pages. Using these notes as a starting point, begin writing about this experience from the first-person point of view, breaking the narrative into rough lines. Write this

draft-poem continuously for about two hours or until you have written at least 150 lines. Place this draft-poem in a drawer for three weeks, then read it through, cutting it to five lines only. Discard the rest. There may be little connection between these lines but, by giving it a clear title, a resonant connection will become clear.

AIM: A powerful short poem, even if elliptical (as in 'Exile' above), is worth a hundred diluted long poems. Many beginning poets do not like to revise their work in the belief that the 'first thought is the best thought'. This drastic exercise in deletion and discrimination will teach you to distance yourself from your draft-poems, and regard them as *potential*, rather than final. Play this game every week in order to generate material and ideas for short poems.

Poetry's reasons

In the history of literature, prose is a teenager and fiction a child. Poetry (like drama) is ancient, but just as sprightly. As you have seen, it is also primal. That does not make the genre any more virtuous, but it does not make it any less trivial, either. Poetry is as pervasive as it is marginal. Poetry was, and is, a part of speech. This offers the genre a unique sense of literary currency, and a quite different set of technical demands, especially in terms of the sounds and rhythms of language, and its rich and various formal possibilities.

If you possess a vocation, then you follow that calling but, if you do not, there are other significant incentives for writing poems. First, we live in a world obsessed with the visual and, as we discussed in Chapter Two, language can be mistreated and misappropriated. Poetry will help you listen for language's music, and reintroduce you to the pleasure of taking pains with it. Second, you might choose poetry as the first of your literary apprenticeships. It hones skill with language – especially precision, phrasing and image – and develops your mind so you find it easier to shift sideways into less condensed genres. As Charles Baudelaire said, 'Always be a poet, even in prose.' You will eventually grow accustomed to feeling fraught with language, and this quality makes poets a very adaptable species of writer – many good novelists were, or are, practising poets. Third, and significantly, poetry's pennilessness allows it to float free of the book-buying marketplace. This creates open spaces for latitude, playfulness and for acts of fabulously invisible integrity.

A place for the genuine

Let us hold the light over that final reason. Most poets need not write with one eye on a fickle audience and the other on the publisher's balance sheet. You can take longer to achieve the poems you *need* to write. Poetry is relatively clean in that sense. You do not have to 'fake it' in writing, even if you write from behind a mask or take on a dozen voices. Indeed, it is probably impossible to fake the real thing. As Marianne Moore wrote in 'Poetry' (NP: 1329):

> I, too, dislike it: there are things that are important beyond all this fiddle.
> Reading it, however, with a perfect contempt for it, one discovers in
> it after all, a place for the genuine.

Richard Hugo (in the epigraph to this chapter) is on to something in implying that, in poetry, some important *part* of the self is revealed. Elizabeth Jennings pushed this further, claiming that 'if lack of compassion, meanness of spirit, envy or cowardice are present in the poet's nature they will be evident in his verse. You cannot fake anything if you are trying to write serious poetry' (Curtis, 1997: 16). I am less certain about this, since poetry is also, as Wallace Stevens would have it, a kind of supreme fiction. Yet, if this quality of creative conduct attracts you as a reader, then poetry may possibly suit you as a writer simply because it will suit your character. However, do not get the impression that the pursuit of poems is purely a solemn or stern concern.

You can have a lot of serious fun trying out poems, and it costs nothing but reading, practice and experiment. You are given permission to 'fail again and fail better' without imperiling the livelihoods of others (obviously most poets do something else than write poems to get by). However, as I wrote in Chapter One, vocation is important to many professions, and the impulse to write and the desire to be a writer are not the same thing. Given poetry's nature, that calling becomes magnified. You really must be driven about poetry to stick with it, so long as you feel that making good poems is its own reward. Even performance and slam poets serve long apprenticeships; theirs is a hard industry, and only small minorities of poets visibly succeed. We now turn to the worlds of writing as performance.

Writing Game

ADAPTING EXPERIENCE
Think of a vivid childhood experience. Make a list of things you remember and adapt this list into a short poem. Then, attempt to wipe your mind of any experience of poetry or writing, and write a recollection of a childhood experience of language or reading. Draft a poem that introduces this experience of language and try to write it in such a way that it mimics the experience as exactly as possible. Try to bring these two poems together to make one poem.

AIM: It has been said that poems are adaptations of your own experience. These two small exercises attempt to remind the writer how individual and strange is our relationship with words and language, and how a writer's personal reading, listening and writing are intimately linked within any poem.

Recommended reading

As with fiction, there is a glittering hoard of handbooks about writing poetry, and the finest are written by good poets. In my experience, the leading texts are Michelle Boisseau and Robert Wallace's *Writing Poems* (Longman Pearson, 2004), and Mary Kinzie's *A Poet's Guide to Poetry* (Chicago University Press, 1999). The former provides an excellent and thorough introductory text which does not confuse the would-be writer with mystification or false promises. The latter offers a bracing and beautifully written introduction to advanced technical matters. Taken together, they provide a penetrating explanation and exploration of every facet of writing poetry, and a sense of progression in craft and art. Kim Addonizio and Dorianne Laux's *The Poet's Companion* (Norton, 1997) offers a confident and thorough survey, and is especially strong on the choices of subject matter. Both William Packard's *The Art of Poetry Writing* (St Martin's Press, 1992) and James Fenton's *An Introduction to English Poetry* (Penguin, 2002) are lessons in writing economically, clearly and yet personally *about* poetry, as well as having the effect of making the reader feel like they are meeting the possibilities of the craft for the first time. John Redmond's *How to Write a Poem* (Blackwell, 2006) is a small masterpiece of concision, and has a very interesting take on the 'address' and 'design' of a poem. Peter Sansom's *Writing Poems* (Bloodaxe Books, 1994) has been a gracious guide for many new British poets. Mary Oliver discusses the precisions and voice of poetry in *A Poetry Handbook* (Harvest, 1994). This is a strong text for a writer with little or no experience of reading poems. Should you be one of these unfortunate many, you can begin to fill that deficit by reading the generous *An Introduction to Poetry* (Longman, 1998) by X. J. Kennedy and Dana Gioia. If you need further enthusing, you will find yourself immediately converted to the cause of reading poetry by John Lennard's radiant *The Poetry Handbook* (Oxford University Press, 2006). Two fascinating books from quite different figures will introduce you to the angular psychologies of poetic practice: Clayton Eshleman's *Companion Spider* (Wesleyan University Press, 2001) and Richard Hugo's *The Triggering Town: Lectures and Essays on Poetry and Writing* (Norton, 1979). If you are ever short of Writing Games, you will find an open mine of them in *The Practice of Poetry* (HarperResource, 1992) edited by Robin Behn and Chase

Twichell. Writing Games based on form and design can be derived from many books, not least *The Making of a Poem: A Norton Anthology of Poetic Forms* (Norton, 2000) by Mark Strand and Eavan Boland, in which these two excellent poets discuss and demonstrate poetic form. Paul Fussell's *Poetic Meter and Poetic Form* (Random House, 1979) is a strong introduction to historical styles and practices with distinctive examples. Ron Padgett's *Handbook of Poetic Forms* (2nd edition, Teachers and Writers Collaborative, 2000) presents, explains and discusses more than seventy traditional and modern poetic forms, with examples and variations. Jeffrey Wainwright's *Poetry: The Basics* (Routledge, 2004) offers a rapid and persuasive set of demonstrations. In the brief but classic *Rhyme's Reason* (Yale Nota Bene, 2001), John Hollander provides a luminous survey of verse and verse forms, with examples supplied delightfully by the author; and Timothy Steele's *All the Fun's in How You Say a Thing: An Explanation of Meter and Versification* (Ohio University Press, 1999) presents a rigorous overview. The open-minded but scrupulous *Poetic Rhythm* by Derek Attridge (Cambridge University Press, 1995) provides a strong introduction to rhythm and metre. Some websites allow you to experience other 'forms' of poetry, including electronic poetry (see Chapter Nine). The Electronic Poetry Center is the place to begin (at www.epc.buffalo.edu). Listening to poems read aloud allows you to experience and understand their full performance, but readings may not be available in your area. There are many websites for the spoken word, but for poetry the Academy of American Poets (www.poets.org) and the Poetry Archive (www.poetryarchive.org/poetryarchive/home.do) carry online recordings, as well as essays by and about contemporary poets and links to other poetry sites. There are many rhyming dictionaries on the market. Rhyme tends to charm through echo and expectation rather than clang. Therefore the most useful resource is *The Oxford Dictionary of Rhymes* (Oxford University Press, 2006), whose radical organisation relies more on indirect rhyme, sound's side-tracks and echoes. Its lists of rhymed words not only blend traditional/ancient with modern/contemporary but also introduce place names and technological and scientific terms. Lastly, *Preminger and Brogan's New Princeton Encyclopedia of Poetry and Poetics* (Princeton, 1993) is the definitive, brick-wide handbook for working poets – it squats like a bookend alongside your dog-eared thesaurus and dictionaries.

Chapter 9

Performing writing

I found that it was quite a lot easier than I'd thought to get into the magic anthill – the place where people other than yourself might think you were a writer . . . There was . . . a coffee-house called The Bohemian Embassy, situated in a falling-apart factory building, where poets congregated once a week to read their poems out loud . . . It was, I found, quite different from acting. Other people's words were a screen, a disguise, but to get up and read my own words – such an exposed position, such possibilities for making an idiot of yourself – this made me sick . . . How would you ever know whether you'd made the grade or not, and what was the grade anyway?

MARGARET ATWOOD, *Negotiating with the Dead: A Writer on Writing* (2002: 21)

All writing is performance. Style performs our voice. Our syntax and diction perform language. As we have discussed, the first pleasure of creative writing resides in process. However, a book once published ceases to captivate its maker in the same way: the covers shrink around it making it seem a closed space. The writer wants rid of something with which they have become over-familiar. They wish to move on to another open space, another book usually. Yet, in its composition, the book was performed in the present; it was improvised on to a page after practice. Performance offers another chance to visit that improvised moment. It returns them to your voice, places them in the ear; or remakes them as sculptures or even film. This chapter looks at three performance modes: public events and readings; performance as concept and public art, crossing into art forms; and the modes of electronic performance.

Speaking and performing

The magic anthill

Writing in performance is an art form, just as drama is, and requires as much attention to detail. Yet, as Margaret Atwood astutely signals, it is a very different world to acting. As a new writer, you need to find a place where people other than yourself, your tutor and your workshop think of you as a writer. This 'magic anthill' of writing, performing and publishing is as much about permission and self-belief as it is about the validation given to your work by fellow writers, readers and audience. You must engage with performance if you are going to find an open space for your voice.

A new writer must *create* an audience, and reading aloud to audiences is an ancient practice worldwide. Like the world of writing, the world of literature in performance seethes with workers, drones and guards. As we discussed previously, teaching writing can also be performative, but the best teaching in writing workshops is more centred on students' writing than on the teacher's performance, although being effective in performance may prove useful to the writer in the classroom.

Of course, published creative writers return to their published work to promote it. An author takes their page-bound creation, and reads aloud to an audience, transforming a closed space into open performance. However, the radar of an audience is tuned differently to that of readers, even though some of them *are* your readers, curious to see what you look like and sound like. Publication is not everything, and book promotion is only a small part of creative writing in performance. You do not have to be a well-known writer to do public performances of your work, although you are obviously less likely to be paid for it.

Audience as reader

A book or portfolio of writing signals finality for its writer and potentiality for its reader. Live performance renders your writing into something provisional. The spoken performance of your language escapes books by this means and audiences read you as the messenger, not the message, of your writing. In that sense, *you* are being read as you stand before an audience.

Only twelve per cent of what an audience receives and understands is made up of the words they hear. The rest is made up of the performer's body language, dress sense, mood and tone of voice. This invites us to make fools of ourselves; but it also creates the potential for using performance as a further open space, in which acts of creativity fledge and fly. So: although live readings can be merely promotions, they are also entertainments, or an art form in themselves. They may also be one means for holding together a community or social group through the codes of performance, as in a Mushairas or slam.

In a concert, the music comes first; in a performance of writing, the words always come first. We can prepare as carefully for a reading as a musician prepares for a concert. We should aim, first, at clarity (as in our writing), then aim at bringing the listener into the work (as we would a reader, by sleight of style). Having worked so hard on creating work that carries the natural qualities and inevitability of speech, we need to give care to ensure these qualities can be *heard* as much as read. Practice is also essential if we have made aural or musical innovations within the language of new fiction or poems, or our work needs 'voices' to come across explicitly; dialogue is the simplest example. All these elements need to be practised, but not over-practised: a writer reading their own work is not the same creature as an actor reading it.

Live performance is about placing trust in the truth of language. Even fine actors have been known to over-emphasise the dramatic nature of a literary piece, delivering it tremblingly or urgently, as if an important message might otherwise get lost. The audience is a *reader* and, like the reader of a book, the audience is active. If you leave them nothing to do, they grow bored or embarrassed.

It is almost as though some actors cannot trust a poem or story to be *spoken*. It is as though they do not realise the language of a good poem or story already contains a number of buried charges, each of them timed to detonate when spoken aloud. Maybe it is because they know that (as we noted in Chapter Four) a persuasive performance can elevate the quality of substandard work. Yet, an affected reading can make our work seem dishonest: dishonest not so much in intent and content, but dishonest in its language. This can of course be funny, but also awful; the poem or story is itself what gets lost in this translation. Actors must learn to trust writing and realise it is not some sorry-faced relation of drama. New writers might do the same. For poets, Mary Kinzie alerts us to the 'two chronic errors in the audible reading of verse, sing-song and reading as if verse were prose' (1999: 486).

Creating an audience

We must allow the fact that books do not feature in some people's lives. That does not mean we cold-shoulder these people. If they choose not to go to creative writing, then we should do everything in our power to open creative writing to them. Some creative writers and promoters have written and argued the art form into a closed room where it is not permitted to entertain. It self-censors laughter and the ordinary pleasures of response, and takes vainglorious pride in the fact that audiences for live literature are tiny elites. They allow that writing may educate – it can even innovate – but it cannot clown, or simply create rapture in a live audience. Who was it invented the rule that good literature cannot be a branch of entertainment? Would Dickens or Shakespeare have been sympathetic? New creative writers need to reinvent the world where fine literature drew its audience to it, and did not look down on them.

Part of the problem with literature promotion is that we may have the imagination to create material, but not the imagination to transform it in performance, and part of this comes down to being too comfortable in certain surroundings. Many literary events take place in venues more suited to lectures, or in self-consciously avant-garde or cultural venues. There is nothing wrong with these, but consider this: your work might well be extending the territory of writing, but the territory may prove, culturally, a small pond aswim with other new writers. You may be preaching to the converted, even to the narrow extent of your audience being your fellow students and tutors. Take lessons from street theatre – give an apparently 'spontaneous' literary performance in unorthodox venues such as a public park or shopping mall. Be sure to stay the light side of the law (use humour), and most people will take it in good part. Your action will be remembered: you will have made your mark on them with your work. Who can predict where such an action might lead them next? If writing in performance seems like a direction for you, then the next section shows you some of the basic things you can do to help you make the best of yourself.

Voice work

The tongue's arrow

In all likelihood, you will perform standing rather than sitting. Before you perform, go to a private space, stand and reach your arms into the air as far as they will stretch, and breathe in deeply. Let your arms sag forward slowly while breathing out gradually, and bend your body at the hips to allow your hands to reach as far down as you can. You should have little residual air in your lungs. Now, reach back up again using the same movement; repeat the exercise. The third time you reach down, shake your head loosely, letting your lips and mouth go flaccid. Continue this until your whole mouth and lower face feels relaxed and your breathing is even and full. Tug your shoulders back; unbend your posture. Anything that allows more space within your chest cavity will help you read far better than you might usually.

Regularly practise the projection of your own voice. You need to do this whether you use a microphone or not. There are many exercises for actors; here is one for writers in which your breath, body and voice work as one. First, use the relaxation exercise above. Then, stand in a room with other members of your workshop or class. Take one phrase from Shakespeare at random; it should be a relatively short and uncomplicated sentence such as 'I will play the swan, and die in music'. Everybody should move around the room saying this phrase aloud, quite naturally, while having one arm raised before them as though being led through the dark. Now, cease moving and pass the phrase from one to another, raising your arm slowly to point at the person who will say it next, in effect loosing the phrase through the air between you.

When it is your turn, take a deep breath and, as you raise your arm, begin to exhale gradually saying nothing for one second, then emitting the phrase on the length of the remaining breath: the breath turning *into* sound. Try, verbally, to *throw* the phrase evenly, clearly and firmly across the room so it meets the ear of the next speaker with as much volume and clarity as if they were standing next to you. The phrase is not peeping out of your mouth; this is not muttering. You must push up from your diaphragm, below your stomach, using the diaphragm to control the exhalation of breath and, by default, the projection of the phrase. In *Your Voice and How to Use It*, Cicely Berry, Voice Director of the Royal Shakespeare Company, says:

> as you release the breath into sound the whole of your chest cavity will add its vibrations and resonance and contribute to the sound . . . your whole body becomes part of the sound, giving it solidity, firmness and edge . . . The voice will spring of its own impulse – like loosing an arrow.   (2003: 31)

Pools and stream of speech

Many creative writers use the page of a manuscript or book as a screen behind which to hide. They read *at* the page, and not *to* the audience, creating an unnecessary distance and bouncing their voice behind them. Before you read, *look* at the audience; even talk to some audience members in order to break the ice and get a few of them on your side. While you are reading, look up regularly; even look one or two of the audience in the eye for a moment, as you read. Try to look at everybody at least once.

A writer who looks up to their audience draws their audience to them. The way to do this is to read ahead in the text with the eye (if you have not memorised the piece). With a story, you should be reading one sentence ahead of what is coming out of your mouth; with a poem you should be reading two lines ahead of what you are speaking. This allows you time to communicate with the audience, and think about how to frame particular sentences or lines. It also avoids your being caught out by something surprising, then misreading and fluffing a line.

There are four verbal equivalents of 'looking up' at the audience; they are still pools along a stream of speech. Pausing places silences into your reading. Silence, even a short pause, makes the audience wait; when you resume speaking they will listen even more acutely. Use silence regularly and knowingly. Changing the pitch and inflection of voice will maintain interest (just as a monotone will kill it). Altering the pace of your speech between readings and commentaries and within pieces will keep attention, as will changing the volume of your voice in as natural a way as possible. None of these is an artificial or rhetorical trick. Pausing, inflection, pace and volume are simply the classic meters by which we unconsciously guide good conversation. Silence allows our conversational partner, the audience, the time to prepare their mental and emotional responses.

Stand with your feet flat on the ground. Stay still while you are reading; any tension will transit itself through the soles of your feet, but keeping your feet completely flat will make you feel grounded and stable, a trick used by actors and politicians. By keeping still, you do not distract the audience by body language or irritating gestures. You focus their attention on your mouth and your voice. As you read, be sure to use the whole of your mouth, as newsreaders do. Tongue, teeth and lips must all be brought into play, allowing clarity of delivery, for clarity and intelligibility exceed expression in importance.

Voice work for creative writers has the same purpose as for actors or professional speakers. It is not about correcting your voice; it is about allowing the natural flows of your speech their speeds and slows. If you ever find that your mouth is, as it were, in a tight corner of panic during performance, remember just this one trick. Actively move your lower jaw downwards and keep it in that position. This should go a long way to removing the muscular tension damming your mouth and lower face. It can even release the lock of stagefright or a stammer. If you stutter, as the author of this book does along with a number of writers, it need not bar you from performing your work. A stutter often vanishes in performance.

Reading a reading

I suggested in Chapter One that if you are not interested in reading the work of other authors, why should anybody be interested in reading you? The same goes for creative writing in live performance. You learn by going to festivals of new writing, and to live readings, and watching, hearing, then imitating, writers in performance. There is a breadth of working practice, from po-face to panache, from the amateur to the avant-garde. *Read* these performances: make notes on what works for you and for the audience. You will begin to recognise that reading your work aloud to yourself and your friends in a workshop is one matter, while reading to an audience of strangers sets the bar higher.

Writing Game

A MAGIC ANTHILL
This is a group game. Choose to perform in venues that are harsher about the place and purpose of creative writing; or create a situation in your real life that becomes such a performance (the more surprising of these appear to be spontaneous but need thorough planning). Take your performance into inner-city schools, or get permission to perform in a prison, amusement park, factory, train, public park or shopping mall. If you wish to create a public performance, then do not seek official permission: carry out a performance in a space where people would not expect it, such as an elevator, a public street, on public transport, a science and technology park, a sports arena, or the waiting area of a hospital or airport. As a class, create a list of local places in which you will perform and begin writing for permission, or planning your 'spontaneous' performance.

AIM: In the epigraph to this chapter, Margaret Atwood describes how she first entered 'the magic anthill – the place where people other than yourself might think you were a writer'. Your task is to create such a place for yourselves, and define and extend expectations of creative writing in performance in your area.

Reading techniques and music

A charm

Approach your own event with as much calm seriousness as you can muster. A good reading is like a charm: you plan and prepare in order to make the reality of it possess inevitable magic. Sift the work you are going to read and what you might say about it by way of introduction. Like playwrights, you may wish to create a 'performing version' of a work. What is on the page may not work so well on the ear alone. Intrigue the audience with some anecdote about a work's composition, but keep your commentary brief or you risk making it sound more interesting than the work itself. The length and language of this explanation should be economical; people prefer jokes and anecdotes. Overstate nothing; over-explain nothing. Understate the importance of your work: beguile by your restraint. With a novel or book of creative nonfiction, read short excerpts that tug on a reader's curiosity, or which are playful, relaxing the audience. With poetry, choose poems that resonate strongly with your own speaking voice; there is no need to play safe with simple or humorous work. An audience will rise to your challenge if you offer this as a game. If the language of your poem is dense, or its form is part of its pleasure, then consider distributing a copy of this poem to the audience. You will know how long you are expected to read; always undercut this time and never exceed it. Understay your welcome. It is always better to leave an audience wanting more than to leave them word-weary.

Space

The audiences to whom you perform inhabit their own dimensions, and both you and they are affected by the space in which the performance takes place, and by the moment. Make something of this space if you can; try to rehearse in it briefly beforehand; sit where the audience sits and explore the dynamics of your performance from that perspective before they arrive. If you wish to make use of music or visual display as part of your performance, it is vital this is arranged, set up and tested well before your reading. Does your work really need it, though? Keep it simple if you cannot make it professional.

Set

When you are starting out, rely on having a 'set', a standard reading that you tailor to fit to different times. If you are a poet, it is always much more striking to learn the poems by heart than to read them aloud from a book; it makes them seem an everyday part of speech. Having a performing version of your work is useful at first, but dispensing with the prompt of a manuscript or book encourages greater freedom in this new open space. You may wish to play variations on your work, to add or remove words or whole paragraphs or stanzas to suit that time, place and audience, something a popular or jazz musician would do as a matter of course. You might even improvise poems or stories on the spot, freewriting them aloud from prompts solicited from the audience. You could even make the audience do some writing, too.

A cold open

One way you can begin improvising with creative performance tactics is to try 'the cold open'. In the opening scenes of certain films or TV drama, the viewer is plunged straight into some action. It hooks them in, but it also gives them some idea of the pace and context; introduces key characters; establishes the mood of what follows and the expectations that the viewer might possess. Begin your reading with practised intent by launching into a longer piece only to bring yourself up short after a minute, and then re-begin your reading in a more orthodox fashion. For performance poets this would be a routine manipulation of audience; for literary writers it is something to which you might aspire. These kinds of literary guerrilla tactics – memorisation, oral storytelling, audience participation, variations, improvisations, cold opens – bring many non-readers to creative writing.

A silent rule

Remember: going to such events is not like going to the movies. Some audiences find literary readings heavy going. If the language of your work is allusive and compacted, then your commentaries act as breathing spaces between pieces, allowing the listeners to absorb what they have heard and prepare themselves for the next onslaught. Here is a silent rule of such events. The audience, having paid in time, money or both, to play the role of audience to your role as literary artist, is at least entitled to *try* to believe they have made a good decision. They are often determined to enjoy the event even if the work and delivery leave much to be desired. Your task is to assist with this illusion, to make the moment live.

A writer who is determined to play the role of audience to their work by themselves, commenting on work after it has been read or making a show of personality, sometimes breaks that silent rule. They remove the audience's role as reader, and reduce the momentum of the event. Consider other art forms in performance, and occasions when you have witnessed acts of self-regard in dance or drama. Not often, I expect. Study the manner in which a soloist, a string quartet or whole orchestra proceeds in its delivery, and mimic that determination and professionalism. Applause, if granted, should be left to the end of any event, unless it arrives impromptu. Silence around your readings creates spellbound attention. Be wary – this silence could also signal boredom.

Blending music

It is a truth universally acknowledged among arts programmers that poets tend to be better performers of their work than novelists. This is because poets cannot earn a living by their work alone, and must practise singing for their supper more regularly then novelists. Readings also go with a poet's territory because poetry is primarily an oral art. However, more poets cross over into writing novels than ever before, taking with them the skills of the impoverished troubadour. Writers, novelists included, are also growing more interested in the use of music as part of literary performance. The memorised story or poem may be interwoven with original music written for the occasion by collaborators, or sampled from existing musical artists. Again, you may wish to try something of this type with your own work.

Slam poets blend spoken word stories and poems, sometimes with live music, in high-impact, competitive performances. Their experiments have developed large appreciative audiences. If you play a musical instrument, or if you possess a good singing voice, consider breaking up your set with your own music or songs. You might even compose music (played on stage by somebody else) which adds extra layers of mood or meaning to a spoken performance.

Mushairas

The previous sections presented a modern Western description of literary performance. On a different note, a Mushairas is a highly public event in Pakistan and India, and is defined by being distinctively literary and cerebral. For the past 200 years, poets of the Indian subcontinent have vied with each other in public readings. The impact of a Mushairas arises from a combination of vibrancies: the audience's knowledge of literary design and poetic form; the respect by the audience for poets, often expressing itself in calls for the encore of especially effective work; and the fact that these readings are social occasions for entire communities. Mushairas used to be polite affairs, but they are evolving fast, with poets introducing comedy, song and movie-style rhythmic poetry (*filmi shairee*), which combines singing and clowning. New writers should consider putting on such an event, or a Western version that sets poets in competition on forms such as the villanelle, sonnet or ballad.

At their conclusion, a Mushairas audience does not divide and disappear into the night – they often dine and celebrate the successes of the evening. There are different types: for example, a Gujarati or an Urdu Mushairas may focus on particular poetic forms such as the ghazal, geet or qawwali. The event is a test of the poet's facility within a form, similar to the Welsh eisteddfod's test of facility with cynghanedd, the metrical system of multiple alliteration and rhyme within Welsh strict metres. 'Speak, that I may see thee', Ben Jonson wrote. Should a Mushairas poet deliver a stunning ghazal line or one with political sting, the audience rises to its feet and acclaims it, calling it back at the poet, who then repeats it before proceeding modestly, knowing they have been seen, and seen by the ear alone.

Writing Game

THE CREATIVE AUDIENCE

Put on a performance of writing, with all the participants in your class or writing group. Choose a director for this performance; then, as a group, decide on the pieces to be used, and think of ways to increase the impact of individual pieces by first reading them aloud, and improvising different approaches. Become your own audience at first. Try a creative blend of approaches:

- straight readings from the page with improvised introductions
- readings from memory direct to audience
- walking among the audience while reading
- using audience participation
- improvising to challenges made by the audience
- with visual background material such as slides or overhead projection
- original music accompanying work or interwoven with it
- acting out the work
- reading with two or more voices
- reading work in different tones of voice, such as offering directions or sympathy
- singing the work.

Your performance should entertain or intrigue as much as it challenges. Interleave your own work with short excerpts from writers whose work is important to you. Practise breathing and projection exercises in classes, and rehearse the whole performance at least once.

AIM: Audiences for new work must be created and maintained, and you cannot rely on any form of publication to assist you. You must take your work *to* its audience and persuade them it is worth their time, even if that means challenging them on occasion. This will also create challenges to your own work; it might even begin to change the way you write and perform. The project will also provide you with good practice should work become successful and you are asked to do readings, or you decide to pursue a career allied to writing such as literature promotion, arts programming, publishing or broadcasting.

Concept as performance

What is a book anyway? Some books never appear on shelves. This does not mean they have vanished on the audience's radar. Not all types of creative writing are created to fit the pages of a book. Writing can perform as a spoken or musical art, as a species of visual art, or as a form of electronic art. 'Books' can be downloaded from the Internet. Their process of composition and reception might depend entirely on this medium: hypertext novels writhe with multiple plots and endings in the layers of text hiding behind a link; poems move kinetically on the page of a screen, making and reinventing themselves. Their existence does not mean that the end of the book is nigh, as some cultural commentators claim. Their existence means there are more concepts possible for writers willing to exploit another open space.

Writing Game

PERFORMING YOUR WRITING AS VISUAL ART
Write a poem on a kinetic subject, such as 'hard rain then light rain', 'the flight of doves', 'cloud movement in storm', 'panther's attack', 'a clock'. Rearrange – and revise – the poem so that the words imitate the shape and action of this subject. The next step is to display your word-paintings. Create posters and postcards – you might even paint them on walls or sew them into screens.

AIM: Some poets arrange their poems so that their shape imitates the subject. In the past, these were displayed in public ways; they were even sewn into fabric. The French poet Apollinaire created 'calligrammes' that performed the same trick of blending the visual with verbal.

Subversions

Some authors will not commit to writing at all: their poems and stories are memorised for oral delivery. Some books do not even look like books. The novelist B. S. Johnson published a book as a box in which the loose chapters could be read in any order. Raymond Queneau's *Cent Mille Milliards de poèmes* plays a similar game, making the reader an active rewriter of a literary concept, a collaborator in experiment and design. Some ancient Persian and Hebrew poetry was composed of shapes and marks that formed visual images, such as a lion or rider with horse. William Blake printed poems within his own vivid visual representations of the poetry. Guillaume Apollinaire's *Calligrammes* contains poems that look like pictures made of words: arranged so they depict the image described, such as 'It's Raining' or 'Mandolin Carnation and Bamboo'. Kenneth Koch took this even further by creating poems as comic strips, 'storyboarding' the *action* of the poems. One of the most interesting developments is the rise of the graphic novel as a serious literary endeavour. Writers such as Alan Moore and Peter Blegvad meld powerful storymaking with resonant images. Any of these are bold literary concepts; performances in their own right. Some of these subversions have become so successful (graphic novels make for effective Hollywood movies) that they are part of the mainstream. You might think about concepts of your own, using the traditional architecture of a book as a starting point and subverting your reader's expectations.

Writing Game

STORYBOARDING AND DIGITAL FILM
Draw the cells of a comic strip on a page, and try to break one of your poems or short stories into small visual scenes as if they were storyboards for a film of that

work. With a resonant image or persistent motif, try to draw what the writer intended by maybe expanding it in the background across several cells of the comic strip. Now use this technique on your own poems and stories, especially in the period before pre-final drafting. You may wish to use this game as the first step to making short poetry films or adapting your stories into screenplays and filming them.

AIM: This game makes explicitly visual what is verbal; it also allows you to get distance on your work. It provides a way to revise your work because storyboarding will test every sentence and every image for its translatability in the reader's visual mind. This is also the routine by which any novel, story, play or poem is prepared for filming: a director must be able to visualise the action of the narrative throughout.

Performing your writing as public art

When an artist blends different art forms, the result is a hybrid, as if two different species of flower or fruit tree had been cross-fertilised. In fact, the best experiments do *not* seem like hybrids but more like a new species of art, or something simply possessing bold taste. The process also leads to your collaborating with other artists, something many writers find emancipating. For example, many writers work with visual artists such as photographers and painters. Their writing is a direct response to visual art, a process called ecphrasis. If you are working with a particular space, such as a sculpture, its *space* increases the restriction within which you work (as *time* would, were you writing for film or radio). As we discussed in Chapter Three, restriction itself is liberating of new ways of saying. Finally, many such projects are published outside books as temporary or even permanent installations in public spaces.

This form of publication raises your stakes; it might even make you write differently knowing the audience to be more diverse. It demands you begin to work *with* people, since such work best arises through partnership and community. You will find working alongside people and artists refreshing, less lonely and more democratic. It will also widen your philosophy and practice. Many things can be said in literature using words, but they can also be said using other arts, or by means of a building, or even a garden. It all depends on how you *place* your writing. You develop an eye for placing, as well as an ear for the language of a place.

The poet Ian Hamilton Finlay transformed his garden, Little Sparta in Scotland, with emblems, word sculptures and conceptual art, writing of the process that 'certain gardens are described as retreats when they are really attacks'. Is his garden a book or a cross-art hybrid? What looked revolutionary was actually part of a tradition. Augustan poets and thinkers attempted to transform landscapes so that they reflected ethical and aesthetic values. In the past, poets who sought 'a place to stand' assumed the role of gardener, and gardening was seen as an act of composition, analogous to writing. How might you do the same? Finlay comments, 'Gardening activity is of five kinds, namely sowing, planting, fixing, placing, maintaining. In so far as gardening is an Art, all these may be taken under the one head, composing' (quoted in Abrioux, 1994: 38).

This kind of approach to writing can make you think and work using a far larger compass than a page's four points. It makes you write with a cartographer's spirit of scale and multi-dimensionality, mapping a literary idea on to a place or space (be it a garden, park or city). With a project of this type, try to perceive your work 'from the air'. Your writing project might have bird's-eye perception, like walking the plot of James Joyce's *Ulysses*, superimposing a huge question mark on the street map of Dublin. It is a useful paradigm to see the place in which you live as an open book, one already written by its history, a palace of memory on which you can draw for ideas for this writing.

You should begin on a smaller scale, say by placing your work in various public spaces such as the corridors of your school, office or university – or even by placing them in unusual spaces such as supermarkets, the small ads columns of newspapers – or hand them out as leaflets. Then start thinking sideways about the vehicle that carries your writing. Make your *page* something unusual. It could be the windows of a building; sand on a beach; snow in a field; sidewalks that are 'read' as they are walked by its 'readers'; skywriting seen from below; or words made from pebbles, twigs or garbage. The very temporariness and apparent spontaneity are part of the final piece, as is the process. Both process and product must be public in some way and, better still, involve members of the public or schoolchildren in its composition. Digitally photograph or film both the process of composition and the outcome. Be sure to clean up afterwards, and leave any site exactly how you found it.

Writing Game

WRITING AS A PUBLIC ART
The task is for everyone in your group to create a short poem, the placing of which does not require the page at all, and the composition requires some other vehicle for its 'reading'. You may wish to work in small groups (for reassurance). This might involve using any, and more, of the following:

- Write a colossal poem on the sand of a beach, or in snow in a park.
- Use the windows of a large building as spaces for individual letters or words.
- Broadcast poetry through your local radio or cable TV station.
- Publish a fake poetical manifesto during an election and post it around your city.
- Graffiti a poem on walls or sidewalks, using chalk (hose it off) or packed snow (allow to melt).
- Bake a cake on which creative text is the icing, and hand it out.
- Write a removable tattoo poem on yourself or others.
- Arrange for the crowd at a sports event to hold up the letters of your poem in rows and columns.
- Photograph, and then make a montage of, public signage, such as street and hazard signs.
- Use quantities of naturally occurring objects to form words, such as pebbles, twigs, ice or grasses.
- Do the same using unnatural objects such as the garbage on a street (recycle this afterwards).
- Project slides or overhead projections of poems on to the walls in your city or campus.
- Bury plant-bulbs in the form of letters and words of a poem, so that they grow in an unusual place next spring.
- Arrange for a one-line poem to be skywritten.
- Make a poem from the phrases of interviewed people you meet, taking one line from each passer-by.

AIM: Although entertaining, these games widen your writing's franchise and audience. There are obvious messages in some of these techniques regarding ecology and conservation. These messages are carried subliminally by the process, or made explicit in their wording. Projects such as this are very open to civic and private sponsorship should you wish to make public and conceptual art part of your working life as a writer.

Electronic performance

As creative writers, the Internet is another open space for the creation and performance of our writing, or the digital or kinetic performances of poems and stories that are first written for the page. There are several kinds of digital writing including weblogs, hypertext fiction and poetry, kinetic poetry, code poetry, and writing that takes advantage of the programmable nature of the computer to create works that are interactive (see 'Recommended reading'). Some programmes also generate text, or involve sound, or use e-mail and other forms of network communication to build communities whose purpose is collaborative writing and publication.

Transaesthetics

Electronic performance allows huge room for experiment, especially in the technological melding with writing in live performance of other art forms, such as film, visual art or music, a phenomenon Margot Lovejoy explores as transaesthetics (2004: 270). The result can sometimes be seen as a new genre of creative writing, inasmuch as writing and the spoken word are at its roots. When these performances take place directly in cyberspace, such works are better thought of as electronic literature, somewhat like the OuLiPo's idea of potential literature. For example, in hypertext fiction the reader actively selects links to shift from one node of text to the next. The reader becomes a writer, arranging the story from a deeper pool of potential stories. An author's creative use of nodes, the self-contained units of meaning in a hypertextual narrative, can play with the reader's orientation and add meaning and play to the text.

Collaborative performance

In the virtual continent of electronic literature, the literary concept as a performance is often interactive and even collaborative. Creative writing students might begin with something as simple as an e-mail list for the class to which they all contribute new work and criticism, before developing a website that performs the same function more publicly. Using computers to produce your first anthology of writing using a desktop publishing programme is an outcome at which most classes should aim, but you should also publish it online. The next natural step is a website that performs the role of an online journal of your new writing, and that of other writers. To publish is to make publicly known, and computers and the Internet have changed publishing, lowering the cost, and allowing more people to publish, through desktop publishing, publishing on demand and Internet publishing.

Writing collaboratively using e-mail and the Web produces new, multi-authored poems and stories in a virtual generative workshop. Each contributor has the democratic right to add, alter and delete text. Writing becomes recursive: each change prompts other writers to make alterations. The process is accelerated if the group has a specific target. A strategy for discussion and communication is necessary for when disagreements arise. So, an editor or teacher should oversee these projects, and moderate their development, but many of them should be allowed to grow without being overseen once they are up and running.

Blogs: wide open spaces

Many writers and students maintain a regular weblog or blog: an online journal. I believe this form of writing is a huge ally to creative writing, and a massive open space for creativity and cross-art-form practice. Writing a blog provides excellent discipline, like keeping a diary or notebook. The difference is that this diary of experience, imagination and observation is online and public, and it alters the way you write, even though the audience is invisible, as when writing a book. Other positive aspects of blogs are that they need to be written concisely and entertainingly – they require the inevitable spices of art and ecomony to become very good – and they assist fluency and variation of expression, since they are in effect highly visible performances of writing. You can also rapidly incorporate photos, video clips and audio files, or send images straight from your mobile phone to a blog, adding text while you are on the move. Blogs are changing the face of international journalism. They are beginning to alter the face of literature – especially creative nonfiction – and the speed at which we write, read and respond to what we are reading, for many blogs allow for written interaction from and with the reader. Blogs may even begin to change the nature of global politics as the network of political and social thought grows locally, but spreads globally. All students of creative writing should maintain blogs; teachers of writing may consider setting up a blog for any course in writing to which tutor and students contribute.

Distance learning

Many universities, such as the Open University in Britain, teach creative writing through distance learning. Drafts of stories, poems and nonfiction receive online comments from all students as well as the tutor. This is a continual responsive workshop with common objectives for all its writers, and the performance of the process of writing is open to all its participants regardless of country or time zone. It allows students to set their own pace, and to log in when convenient. In these situations, the writing process *itself* is performative, an open space into which you step before an audience of your fellow students, but one in which you find them stepping up beside you, all bearing virtual pages. Obviously, you could use your own blogs to set up a virtual writing course or workshop for yourself and your fellow writers.

Writing Game

SETTING UP A WRITING WORKSHOP ONLINE

Take the e-mail addresses of everyone in your class or workshop and set up an e-mail list for them. Ensure that everybody sends at least one short piece of work to the list every month. Each participant should submit work when they wish within that month, but all should contribute criticism more regularly, and this should be sent to the whole group, as if they were talking to them in the same room.

AIM: You can of course set up a website cheaply that acts as a forum for discussion and presentation of work. Online workshops of this type have the virtue of taking place whenever it suits the individual and allowing a record to be kept of new work and discussion-threads. It also allows participants to monitor the progress of the group.

Recommended reading

For voice work, relaxation exercises and voice projection, new writers should read the invaluable work of Cicely Berry in *Your Voice and How to Use It* (Virgin Books, 2003) and Patsy Rodenburg in *The Right to Speak: Working with the Voice* (Methuen, 1992). What works for actors sometimes works for writers, and finding a public voice in this way may even help you find another literary voice through spoken art. This goes for visual art, too. John Hollander's *The Gazer's Spirit* (University of Chicago Press, 1995) is a fascinating investigation of how poems speak to silent works of art (paintings, sculpture) as well as an anthology of beautiful examples. It will give you powerful ideas for your own work. There are many fine examples of writing as public art. Recommended visits include the Peggy Guggenheim Museum in Venice, which holds fine examples of writing as carved or as illuminated sculpture; and the Wales Millennium Centre, which carries inscriptions on its copper portico, side by side in Welsh and English by Gwyneth Lewis: 'In these stones / Horizons / Sing'. The poet Ian Hamilton Finlay's visionary garden project can be visited at Stoneypath in Scotland, but first read *Little Sparta: The Garden of Ian Hamilton Finlay* by Jessie Sheeler (Frances Lincoln, 2003). For new writers, a stimulating exhibition of Finlay's writing and public art is *Ian Hamilton Finlay: A Visual Primer* by Yves Abrioux (Reaktion Books, 1994). The notion of storyboarding is evinced by Kenneth Koch in his wonderful *The Art of the Possible: Comics Mainly Without Pictures* (Soft Skull Press, 2004). Here, Koch creates poems as comic strips or storyboards, finding surprising connections between the rhythms of poetry and comics, approaching language visually, something you might try yourself in class. Graphic narrative is epitomised in the work of Alan Moore, while graphic anti-narrative and graphic poetry is exemplified in Peter Blegvad's *The Book of Leviathan* (Sort Of Books, 2000). Shape poems reach something close to sublimity in *Calligrammes*, reprinted by Guillaume Apollinaire (University of California, 1991). The digital revolution continues rapidly; the landscape of its literature changes daily. For interesting and forward-looking ideas for writers and artists about hybrid electronic arts and transaesthetics, read Margot Lovejoy's *Digital Currents: Art in the*

Electronic Age (Routledge, 2004). Online literary journals and magazines are legion and vary greatly in quality. A good place to start is the superb *Jacket Magazine* (www.jacketmagazine.com), which has generous international links. The Electronic Literature Organisation (www.eliterature.org) is a nonprofit organisation initiated in 1999 to promote the creation and enjoyment of electronic literature. Since 2001, the organisation has been based at University of California at Los Angeles. They host the electronic literature directory, where you can access hypertext fiction and poetry; works of fiction published solely or initially on the World Wide Web that require its capabilities; kinetic poetry presented in Flash and using other platforms; computer art installations which ask viewers to read them or otherwise have literary aspects; interactive fiction; novels that take the form of e-mails, SMS messages or blogs; poems and stories that are generated by computers; collaborative writing projects that allow readers to contribute to the text of a work; and online literary performances that develop new ways of writing.

Chapter 10

Writing in the community and academy

All of us who write work out of a conviction that we are participating in some sort of communal activity. Whether my role is writing, or reading and responding, might not be very important. I take seriously Flaubert's statement that we must love one another in our art as the mystics love one another in God. By honoring one another's creation we honor something that deeply connects us all, and goes beyond us . . . Life is energy, and energy is creativity. And when we as individuals pass on, the energy is retained in the work of art, locked in it and awaiting release if only someone will take the time and the care to unlock it.

JOYCE CAROL OATES, *Paris Review* interview (Plimpton, 1989: 383–384)

Made well, shaped well, writing ceases to feel like artifice and becomes alive, and the moment that happens it ceases to be your own and becomes communal. There are creative writers who argue that you cannot be a good writer without also conducting your life with a degree of care, with a kindness, a kind of accounting for oneself within a larger community. William Carlos Williams went so far as saying that one reason to write was to become a better person. Richard Hugo reads this statement as a private understanding 'that a lifetime of writing was a slow, accumulative way of accepting one's life as valid . . . what dumb animals know by instinct and reveal in their behavior: my life is all I've got' (1979: 72). There are also writers who argue that the opposite suits their work better, but that too is a choice of conduct, of life as an artlessness or artfulness depending on your point of view. They may speak behind their hands, as it were, but that does not mean they do not intend their voice to be heard. How a writer reaches a balance between these private points of view is always revealing: it reveals itself in their work, and in how they position themselves and their writing within public arenas. In this final chapter, we explore two important and sometimes conflicting public arenas for creative writing students, writer-teachers and writers: community and academy.

Community as open space

As Joyce Carol Oates declares in *The Faith of a Writer*, 'Through the local or regional, through our individual voices, we work to create art that will speak to others who know nothing of us. In our very obliqueness to one another, an unexpected intimacy is born. The individual voice is the communal voice. The regional voice is the universal voice' (2004: 3). Chapter Two showed ways in which writers absorb lives and stories, how they are readers of the world and of people. In Chapter Five we discussed the many selves a writer might access, sometimes through imitation, the taking of personae, the creation of an Other, or even direct appropriation of lives and experience. The South American novelist Carlos Fuentes reminds us that 'The Book tells us that the Other exists, that others exist as well, that our persona does not exist in and of itself but has a compelling moral obligation to pay attention to others, who are never superfluous to our lives' (Fuentes, 2004: 221). In essence, a writer is a community whose story is told through their books. Writing is solitary work some of the time, but even writing can be a social process through the living of regular life, discussions and workshops. 'Work for most people is really very social, and the actual thinking is often done in community' – Tobias Wolff. What might Wolff mean by this?

Lights in the dark

Writing can be an act of community even if the writer does not stir from their room at all, even if they choose never to meet a reader or give a performance of their work. It creates an unexpected intimacy. Books, if they are made well, are communal – 'energy is retained in the work of art, locked in it and awaiting release if only someone will take the time and the care to unlock it'. Communication engenders community; and a creative communication implies a heightened regard for community, however unknown (or unknowing) that community may be. Creative writers might even prey and spy on a community for material, but they carry its message forwards even if the writer is underhand or duplicitous with them. The critic Harold Bloom argues that there are no ethics of reading, that it is a selfish pleasure. We could argue by extension (and as provocatively) that there are few, or no, ethics to writing. After all, isn't one of the principles of creative writing that writers write for themselves, and that only by writing for themselves can writers hope to please an audience beyond their own writing room? Some creative writers write for audience, but many do not. Instead, they set out to *create* an audience, to *challenge* one into existence, and you cannot create or challenge a community through inaction or silence.

This may all seem contradictory, but the very contradictoriness is symptomatic of the world of creative writing as we saw in Chapter One. It is why I call the discipline of creative writing an open space, and asked you to think of literature as a continent that contains many countries, languages and countless points of view. What we can agree is that it is impossible to deny that writing and speaking are forms of binding together. To do so would be to defy biology and even religion. As Barry Lopez writes, 'Each story is an act of trust between a writer and a reader; each story, in the end, is social. Whatever a writer sets down can harm or help the community of which he or she is a part' (1999: 15). Many people look to writers for their own voice and story; for a choice of conduct; and even for a way of thinking about our interpenetrating cultures. 'Literature must be our anthropology', argues the novelist Ian McEwan in *The Literary Animal*, who goes on to claim, 'That which binds us, our common nature, is what literature has always, knowingly and helplessly, given voice to' (Gottschall and Wilson, 2005: 19).

Think about it this way. How many times have you read books of fiction for answers about your own life, or found yourself and your dilemmas reflected in the mirror of a novel? How often have you seen people in grief turn to poetry as a form of consolation? Why, during crisis, do many people seek answers in nonfiction? They seek guidance from creative writing, even though what they find is art and artifice, symbols and patterns. Guidance may even take the form of escapism or fantasy: a book offers a reader, and its writer, a second chance at reality. 'Writing is a way of saying you and the world have a chance' – Richard Hugo (1979: 72). Even if that chanced reality is a fiction, it may hold the presence of life, in its language or story, more luminously than might be found in an actual life. For many people, books are lights in their dark, and creative writing is a means by which to see, hear and stay in touch. People sign up for creative writing courses to learn literary style, but many also sign up because they are seeking a quality of perception that we used to call truth. They have found it through reading, and they wish to discover it again through writing.

Writing Game

TELLING A COMMUNITY'S STORY

Write an extended work of creative nonfiction about a community for whom *you* are the 'carrier' of its story. Use the investigative techniques outlined in Chapter Seven such as interview and archival research in record offices. Include at least one legend of the area, and the life story of at least two people. Try to put yourself into the foreground for most of this piece.

AIM: Work of this type trains you to listen and watch your world carefully, seeing through the everyday smokescreens and filtering out falsehoods.

Community as open space

Writing as a public art is one way of being unequivocal about the place of writing in a peopled landscape. However, writing does not need books, monuments or sculptures to be *of* a community. Publishing houses, academies and literary festivals are the circuit, a kind of literary three-ring circus. There, the audience is already created, and they largely get what they want – even if what they want is to be challenged. But creative writing thrives in many open spaces, and new writers are often to be found in less visible spaces in which writing thrives just as openly, if less famously.

These spaces include public libraries, schools, community groups, reading groups, prisons, hospitals, nursing homes, refugee centres, YMCA organisations, adult education groups, some workplaces and, expanding exponentially, cyberspace. Writers have even found themselves plying their art in shopping malls, and teaching their discipline while on public transport, on mountain summits and at Antarctic research stations. There are even official and unofficial versions of writers working as graffiti and installation artists.

Probably the most super-official version of writing in the community is the Poet Laureate Consultant in Poetry to the Library of Congress in the United States. The laureate serves a fixed term, a procedure that now operates for the poet laureateship in the United Kingdom. As a community model, it works well, and has been imitated by states and cities in North America and throughout the world. The poet laureate's job is to raise national awareness of the reading and writing of poetry, and some of the projects are exceptionally inventive. Rita Dove brought together writers to explore the African diaspora; she also supported children's poetry and jazz events. Joseph Brodsky provided poetry in airports, supermarkets and hotel rooms. Maxine Kumin set up workshops for women writers.

Some writers are drawn to community writing because this is simply the milieu out of which they work. Leaving their physical community would mean killing their reason for writing, and being dishonest as artists and as human beings. In some cultures, the idea of a writer *not* being of a community would be simply bizarre, since the writer is the carrier of their community's story through history and times of change: its maker of tales, its memory-banker, its time-traveller.

Writing Game

As a class or writing group, devise a project for your local community. Remember you are part of that community, and you may wish to involve other members of it in its planning and delivery. Create a writing project that takes off from some issue that concerns or attracts many people. This might be something historical, political or social. It may even be sparked by something geographical, or special to your region like a dialect or the local names for things. Allow the project to run for one week at least, and work with as many people on their writing as possible using a site that is open and accessible, such as a public library. Try if you can to produce a small publication from the project. Share this with the participants and give it free to local people. Use the expertise of new people you have met to devise further local projects.

AIM: Such projects are locally empowering and can be fun. They can have far-reaching effects for the individuals involved, even to the point of making some of them reconsider their lives and become writers. The process will affect you, too; it will make you think even more clearly about your own writing and the kind of audience you might need to create for it.

The grassroots of creative writing

However, some people work as writers in a community because, unless they are very lucky or very ruthless, many find themselves needing to. Talent has nothing to do with luck, and being poorly paid for pursuing an art will not always be their fault. There are ways to get by during these stages, although for many writers these are not stages but entire lifestyles. A freelance writer can only earn so much by their writing, and working in schools and the community will allow you to earn time for your writing. However, teaching community writing will feed you, in more ways than you might expect, including your own creative work, a matter exemplified by the many contributors to *The Point: Where Teaching and Writing Intersect* (Shapiro and Padgett, 1983). Earning time for writing seems a fair payoff for a pursuit whose process is its own reward. Community writing makes you stay in touch with different audiences; it keeps your feet on the ground and your head in the world. That is why some creative writing programmes present opportunities to develop a project outside college, with a community group or in a workplace. The success of these projects is assessed as part of the degree course.

Community writing also returns creative writing to one of its first causes, pleasure. There is nothing so delightful as a class of eight-year-olds clamouring half-rhymes and triolets, or performing stories you have helped them to discover. However, this work is not simple – it requires training. You are not a teacher, but a writer in education. You will have to work to gain their respect, and the best way to do this is to be yourself, and prepare your workshops thoroughly, and above all unpatronisingly. If you let it, working with a community will feed your writing. It will open your eyes to things you may have missed in your own experience, or to matters you can expect to meet yourself, as a person and as a writer.

The poet Kenneth Koch taught creative writing regularly to schoolchildren, but also to older people in a nursing home in Rhode Island. He knew the obstacles of such a project, but he 'sensed possibility': he sensed how the pleasure of writing could itself be 'a serious thing for them to work at, something worth doing well and that engaged their abilities and their thoughts and feelings'. Even so:

> Most were in their seventies, eighties and nineties. Most were from the working class and had limited education. They had worked as dry cleaners, messengers, short-order cooks, domestic servants . . . Everyone was ill, some people sometimes in pain. Depression was frequent. A few were blind, and some had serious problems in hearing . . . To be added to all of this was their confinement.   (1997: 5)

Yet Koch, working with an assistant poet, arrived with no preconceptions aside from an idealistic view that, since he loved writing poetry so much, and gained so much pleasure from the process, he imagined everyone else would: 'it is such a pleasure to say things, and such a special kind of pleasure to say them as poetry' (1997: 6).

Writing Game

A ROOM OF YOUR OWN
This is not a writing project; it is a means to several projects. Try writing the story or poem that emerges from any Writing Game in this book, but write it in different places within a single morning. Try at the very least three places in which you have *never* written. These might include any of the following: a café, public transport such as a bus or train, a library, a park table or bench, a garden, a museum of art or history, a zoo, a hide in a nature reserve, the noisiest room in your home. Attempt to bring elements of the place into the poem or story.

AIM: You will discover that some places and locales suit your writing better. Dislocate your creative practice from the places you expect it to arise: the quiet study, the studio, the bedroom. You should adopt this new place as your 'writing room', a territory for your creativity. Going to work there will trigger ideas and faster writing on subsequent occasions. Serendipity is an important aspect of writing, and writing in an unusual place can bring unexpected material. Sometimes you need to leave home to find a *home* for your writing. Some writers leave their house, walk around the block and return home, simply to prompt the mental aim of 'going to work'!

Rooms of our own

Writing as an act of community is important; but the space in which you write, and the community writes, is vital. A seminar room can be helpful of course, but a housing project, a foreign city or a walk in the woods can be seminar rooms and writing houses too. T. S. Eliot wrote fifty lines of *The Waste Land* in a seaside shelter in Margate. J. K. Rowling wrote the first drafts for Harry Potter in an Edinburgh café. Writing needs seminar rooms, but it also needs more rooms of its own outside the arena of formal education, in the interstitial zones of society. Find these zones yourself, and write in them, and *from* them. Take the community to these spaces, and 'occupy' them for writing.

To this end, I suggest that creative writing students and teachers begin a campaign for every major city in the world to create a Writer's Room, a low-cost, writerly version of a painter's studio or atelier. These spaces will be installed in, or built on to, an existing public library. The space will be open for writing, for workshops, for performance. The room's walls will be covered with whiteboards to assist teaching and writing, as they are in some institutes of mathematics (ideas always arrive at inconvenient times). There will be audio and visual digital recording equipment; computers will be linked, at which writers will work individually or collaboratively. There will be Internet access, and computers with publishing programme software, so that publications can be created from that space.

Not only will every city have a room of its own, but it will also be the home of a small press or journal. Universities publish in-house quarterlies of new literature; cities should also. Free, pre-scheduled access is given to this room for any local writers who require space and time to work. This is exactly the kind of urban project enjoyed by filmmakers, digital artists, visual artists and photographers. Society needs to make more space for its creative writers, especially writers from non-traditional writing backgrounds, and we need to catch them young. Without resources like this, we risk becoming complicit in the perpetual re-creation of what Tillie Olsen called 'silences': 'the unnatural thwarting of what struggles to come into being, but cannot . . . the obvious parallels: when the seed strikes stone; the soil will not sustain; the spring is false; the time is drought or blight or infestation; the frost comes premature' (2003:

6). As a discipline, creative writing provides open spaces for re-engagement. In order to explore that engagement, and how academies become such open spaces, I need to talk a little more personally about why I wrote this book.

Creating writing in the creative academy

I began my working life as a scientist, one who also wrote creatively, and I would say that if what you do requires you at best to write clearly, then we are all writers. The Two Cultures, the division of knowledge systems into Arts and Science, was a splintering of the processes by which knowledge and language move and grow. There are no Two Cultures, and there never were. The debate between Science and Arts was based largely on prejudice, fear, and a kind of snobbery – a class war between disciplines, their teachers and their students. We might as well say there are a Million Cultures for all the illumination such a debate brings. Creative writing as a discipline may help to shift the debate into a more constructive set of engagements. This topic offers you a few genies escaping their lamps.

Creative writing across disciplines

As I said under 'Why we read' in Chapter One, reading nonfiction is as vital as reading fiction or poetry. Popular science provides you with research material for creative nonfiction, fiction and poetry. Reading science, or biographies of scientists, will present you with ideas, characters and situations. It will also give you new language: the terminology of science is gravid with metaphor, and is constantly inventing new usages. In my own university, undergraduate students take a three-year honours degree in Creative Writing, balancing the study of literature with its practice. In their second and third year, students tend to specialise in a genre, such as poetry, fiction, drama or creative nonfiction. Specialisation is a necessary prison, given the structures of the academy, but it is a falsification of how writers work in the world: it prizes focus above experience. This open prison needs to become open space.

Therefore, these students are also encouraged to take or audit courses outside humanities and creative writing – for example, in philosophy or psychology, but also in medicine, physics, mathematics, biology, chemistry or information technology. Obviously, they need to have some interest and experience of these subjects first, but what they are doing is ploughing a subject for language and material they might use later in creative writing. They are also developing a more rounded profile of qualifications that they can take usefully into the real world. And they are acting as ambassadors for creative thought and practice among students of science and social science; they gain experience of people and ideas they otherwise may not encounter.

There is two-way traffic. Some of the most enthusiastic students of creative writing at my own university come from physics, computing and mathematics. They borrow the concision and play of poetic technique to understand and communicate the concision and play of the languages of their own subjects. They use narrative fiction to tell science-based stories.

Are these 'practitioners' writers? Some of them become part-time writers while carrying out research in their disciplines. Most go on to become teachers of physics, computing and mathematics. They use creative Writing Games as a means to teach their subject. Entrepreneurial students from our business school have done the same. They understand that the industry of 'business games' as icebreakers, creativity exercises and meeting energisers is close in approach to that of the generative writing workshop or Writing Game. They parachute into our courses; steal ideas; and parachute out. Just like writers.

Creative writing with science

It is a fair, if flawed, perception that, somehow, the hypothesis-making part of the scientific process is creative, and the testing and experimental stage draws away from art. The act of drawing away is not entirely the case for those of us who have lived by science. Repeated experimentation and the process of scientific dissemination are precisely analogous to the processes of rewriting, publication and criticism. Some littérateurs like to live their lives in terminology; scientists leave it behind them in the lab; good writers leave it to the theorists. What writers call workshops, scientists call coffee-break discussions. Furthermore, it is not enough now for a talented scientist to be content with publication in an internationally refereed journal.

Popular science writing requires the same creative and technical skill as the writing of creative nonfiction. In fact, it *is* creative nonfiction, and the skill with which it is composed has been responsible for melting many of the falsehoods that have iced up between the arts and sciences, not least the idea that scientists cannot write. Scientists, such as the popular science writers Margaret Boden, Max Perutz, Steven Rose, Steven Pinker and Richard Dawkins, are *creative* writers. They learned technique, and found a voice. They prize imagination, energy of expression, style, and understand their own process of creativity. They show how the same processes underlie the ways in which science proceeds. An example – writing on the discoverers of DNA, Max Perutz observed:

> Like Leonardo, Crick and Watson . . . achieved most when they seemed
> to be working least . . . engaged in argument and apparently idle . . .
> attacking a problem that could be solved only by a tremendous leap of
> the imagination . . . Imagination comes first in both artistic and
> scientific creations.   (2003: 204)

Can the study and practice of creative writing make you a better scientist?
Courses in creative writing may encompass writing popular science; courses
in science may encompass writing creative nonfiction. Popular science is, after
all, the art of creative nonfiction. Just as many writing students do not become
serious writers, so not all students who sign up for science degrees become
scientists, but many could become clearer and more energetic communicators
of their disciplines, as journalists, or as mediators between the public sphere
and scientific endeavour. In the same way that many of our best creative writers
have also been among the more insightful critics, many of our best scientists are
its best communicators and critical exponents of science. The use of creative
writing in science courses might contribute to a greater public understanding
of science and technology.

Writing Game

ADVENTURES IN THE LABORATORY

As a group, or individual, arrange a visit to a scientific laboratory, with the request
that you work alongside scientists for one week. You will be surprised by how
flattered and curious many scientists will be by your presence. Discuss their work
with them every day, and write a story, poem or piece of creative nonfiction in
direct response to that conversation. Share your work with the scientists, and ask
them to respond with their own creative writing at the end of the week.

AIM: There is an atmosphere of experiment-at-play in a laboratory which you
rarely encounter anywhere else, except in a theatre company during
read-throughs and rehearsals. Tune in to this play of thought, and use the
language of your scientists innovatively and precisely within your own writing.

Creative writing as a crossover discipline

At my own university, creative writers and their students now work directly
with undergraduate students and postgraduate researchers in the departments
of medicine, business, biology, computing, engineering and physics. Their
presence is partly predicated on the need to help new scientists and businesspeople write more clearly and engagingly. We do not teach composition or
generic skills; we build on them, and work with exceptionally gifted students.

However, one underlying principle, agreed with departmental heads beforehand, is to help these students begin to think more laterally in language – even more wildly – and to conceive of ideas and paradigms via the unusual route of Writing Games and thought-experiments based on the creation of poems and fictions. What is striking is that, although some initial scepticism about these experiments in teaching and learning came from the scientists, they quickly realised that students were doing better in their writing, communicating their findings more clearly, and benefiting from human contact and creative play as researchers. Any residual scepticism was much more likely to reside within students and faculty in the humanities.

Our work was informed by an important movement called 'Writing Across the Curriculum'. This movement grew in response to a perceived deficiency in literacy among university students in the 1980s. It is now widespread – its advocates thinking of writing as a learning tool. Writing helps students synthesise, analyse and apply course content. Students often use logbooks and journals, and the idea, as in creative writing, is to become an active participant in your subject and that practice can create fluency. All this is coterminous with the discipline of creative writing, although it has to be said that, at some institutions, creative writing occupies a much more privileged position in terms of the status of both students and faculty. 'Writing in the Disciplines' is part of the movement of 'Writing Across the Curriculum'. It is based on the understanding that each discipline has its own conventions of language and style and that these conventions must be taught to students so that they might successfully participate in academic discourse. Reports, article reviews and research papers are the most commonly used assignments. At my own university, we experimented with using many creative writers and creative Writing Games to deliver these parts of the curriculum, and to do so with creative panache, teaching them as though they were performance art. External teaching tests have shown real progress, and a side-benefit of increased recruitment at a time when science is suffering in this respect.

In Britain in the early twenty-first century, the Royal Literary Fund went even further, and organised residencies for hundreds of creative writers to work at many UK universities. This imaginative enterprise was funded from royalties the author of *Winnie the Pooh*, A. A. Milne, had left to the Fund. The 'bear of little brain' bequeathed more than what might have been expected of him, for in this way creative writing and the teaching of advanced rhetoric rejoined each other through a bold experiment. The purpose was not to teach creative writing, but to work with students on their academic and expository writing. The thinking was rooted in the notion of not burning up the creative energy of creative writers on teaching poetry and fiction, but on focusing their skills of clear language and argument. The presence and work of these novelists, dramatists and poets were utilised as much by students from science, medicine and social science as they were by students of humanities. The discipline crossed over quite harmoniously into other forms of knowledge, for it helped *to tell the story of those forms of knowledge.* It is arguable that creative writing began finding some new, unusual, maybe historical, rooms of its own (some of which we explored in Chapter One). However, although the uses of creative language and creative reading are important for these new open spaces, sometimes we reach a space where language runs out.

Creative recognitions

I offer only two examples from personal experience as an environmental scientist working on freshwater insects in the Lake District of England. My research focused on a family of lake midges whose species number in their thousands, and new subspecies and variants evolve regularly like minute but dynamic elements of a lake's language. You identify these species by a carapace deposited on a lake surface on emergence as winged adults, and use a 'key', a book that explores and relates what you see under a powerful microscope to what has been seen by others in your field. This key represents current knowledge. Occasionally, you reach a zone where the current knowledge simply tapers to nothing, for the variant is completely new, unrecognisable. You stare at it, or part of it, not seen before by the human eye, and not described or drawn by the human mind. With the key, you reach the point where its lake runs dry.

When scientists reach this point, this moving edge of knowledge, they surf forwards by a combination of previous knowledge, guesswork and intuition. With a species, you describe and classify it according to its likeness to something already described: you use simile to compare it, and you use metaphor to name it. The Latin names of insects are a spectrum of metaphoric and descriptive acuity. They are little, related images which represent an entire life form, a species, however temporary its moment of evolved presence. Its *unseen* worlds are metaphorised into recognition; its *invisibility* released by simile. I always regarded science at this level as a form of creative and collaborative writing. The physicist Niels Bohr observed, 'When it comes to atoms, language can be used only as in poetry. The poet, too, is not nearly so concerned with describing facts as with creating images.'

My second example echoes Les Murray's 'painless headache' metaphor described in Chapter Four. The concentration of attention required for identifying species is heightened even further when the numerical presence of these species is factored alongside other data, such as oxygen level, acidity, and thirty or more other physico-chemical variants, all of which make up the natural, but invisible, world of that species. The final piece of data would be time itself – the measure of a season, say. To make any kind of testable judgement about these creatures required these data to be crunched by powerful multivariate statistical programmes. Depictions of correlation would unfold; thousands of permutations of relatable factors would be played against each other; and the significance of any connectivity (for example, the surface area of a lake and the diversity of species) might feed out. You begin to see the world is wider than your thought. The creative magic of numbers, not words, is the language of the natural world. This is why I made so much of this 'natural magic' earlier in this book.

When such data are swung across time, they seem to swarm like bees in a moving rope of migration. You hypothesise there must be a common purpose somewhere, but you would have to be a *bee* to understand the language of the movement, in this case the dance, noise and destination of the data. What you have to do is think yourself inside a natural ballroom of numbers, its walls and ceilings made up of moving and sliding micro-elements. Max Perutz names imagination as the first element of scientific creation. In understanding the multivariate nature of an invisible world, an intuition, strongly informed by practice, played a part that sometimes seemed as strong as the role given to statistical significance.

I have never felt closer to that balance of perception and imagination than when I am writing creatively, or watching students in a creative writing class making discoveries for themselves among the swarm, noise and dance of language. When I claimed earlier that in the discipline of creative writing we are all beginners, some of that tone of mind informs the natural process of scientific discovery: the design and making of pattern; the neural ravelling of understanding and perception.

As the immunologist and poet Miroslav Holub wrote, 'The emotional, aesthetic and existential value is the same . . . when looking into a microscope . . . and when looking into the nascent organism of the poem' (1990: 143). Reading that quotation, you can see that scientists can play the *scientiste* just as much as artists can play the *artiste*. In Chapter One, we discussed how the pleasure of creativity might illuminate aspects of knowledge that are apparently non-literary, and the findings of neuroscientists that '*Story* is a basic principle of mind', that 'parable is the root of the human mind – of thinking, knowing, acting, creating, and plausibly of speaking' (Turner, 1996: 1). The literary mind may prove to be the fundamental mind. The repercussions for the role of creative writing as a discipline speaking across disciplines could be tremendous. Since that interdisciplinary genie is out, we can seed a few wishes.

Academy as open space

Wishes

I wish that the discipline of creative writing saw itself even more as a natural landbridge to a far wider community of readers and writers. It should never become a drawbridge pulled high between academy and community. It is not in its nature. Writing in the community is not some worthy cause, neither is it some Claude Glass reflection of real life from which to compose. It is a way of life for many people who become writers, or wish to become writers but do not have financial or social resources to support them. Maybe more courses could be taught outside campus, as they are in adult and worker education programmes. Maybe more university writing workshops could take place in malls, community centres and places where people work and live. Maybe some mountains need moving. If a university will not go to the community, then the community could request space within the university. I suspect many institutions will be flattered to be asked. Community projects within writing courses are a small and necessary means universities can use to make these first steps.

I wish it were more clearly understood that, in some ways, higher education needs creative writing more than creative writing needs higher education. Colleges want student fees for one; they wish to answer student demand for another. However, higher education also desires the social, cultural and political relevance, and understanding, that writing and writers bring to higher education. These matters are priceless, for they have more to do with the outside reputation of an institution than in its ability to make money. 'Money culture recognizes no currency but its own . . . art offers an exchange in kind', says the novelist Jeanette Winterson. Reputation, of course, at bottom, is a kind of currency. Reputation is the wisest long-term investment, whether for a writer or an institution of learning. Reputation begins locally and grows globally: it must start within the local community, and writers are effective ambassadors *to* – and *of* – that community. I wish this were something writers and universities were learning and understanding about each other.

I wish we allowed ourselves to recognise that all good writers are creative, that even, say, textbooks of philosophy or zoology, when written clearly and entertainingly, with an eye on the audience, are acts of creative writing. On a good day, we can call ourselves – or overhear ourselves called – creative.

I have come to believe, reluctantly, that 'creative' is an abused word, abused to the point where it has become divisive. 'Imaginative writing' is at once more concise but more exclusive than creative writing. But do we really mean that some writers are creative and the rest of them are uncreative? Isn't the difference between creative and non-creative at this level largely the difference between good, thoughtful writing and bad, thoughtless writing? I see no division in the integrity of practice between our best novelists and poets and the best of our scientists or social scientists. Sometimes they are the same person. I wish we had greater freedom to create university degrees that in their turn created Renaissance people, and that did not encourage suspicion about our capacity for being good at more than one pursuit in our lives. The freedoms and opportunities of 'self-inclusive scholarship' (see Chapter Seven) ought to be extended to our students.

Writing Across the Disciplines is a hugely important movement; a lot of the energy for it came from people who cared about writing. 'Creative Writing Across the Disciplines' seems a natural step; the interdisciplinary energy and focus might come from the discipline of creative writing. The spectre of specialisation has now crept into many school curricula, and creativity is also under threat there. It is now as important for creative practice to be reintroduced in high schools as it is in universities. To this end, I wish writers could make themselves even more active on the borders between knowledge systems in universities and high schools. I see a division in many writers and would-be writers between desire and achievement, between promise and execution. Artistic insecurity emerges from that friction, and feeds the desire to keep the creative writing territory free of competitors from other non-literary fields, and even from younger writers. Our job is to close the fault line between a writer's perfectly natural velleity and their desired action. However, in doing this excellent work, I wish that writers would make an even greater effort to open our educational work to people from non-traditional literary backgrounds, such as science and business, and not reinforce prejudices born of mistrust or insecurity. Taking creative nonfiction teaching into science and business is the obvious way to get inside their respective Troys if that is where one wishes to create and challenge audiences.

Writing Game

MAKING A DRAMA OUT OF A CRISIS
Read aloud *Glengarry Glen Ross* by David Mamet (NA2: 2509); try to perform it as a group. Visit a business school and evolve a workshop with their students that looks at a particular crisis in commerce, using this play as a starting point. Note

the language of the play and its use of the terminology of business and real estate. Your theme might be the downfall of a major corporation, or fraud issues such as insider dealing. Improvise and act out a play that dramatises this crisis. Use the improvised drama as the platform for a short story of your own, or tell the story of this workshop and the personalities with whom you worked.

AIM: Although we like to reduce economics to numbers and market forces, every action in business is made up of people, and their adventures, personalities and human errors. A play can offer immediate insights into what goes wrong and what goes right at such moments of crisis. In this way, drama is a very insightful educational and social tool.

Chimeras

Academies are excellent patrons for us but may also be precarious territory. They are seductive and always have been for artists. They offer community not solitude; audience not neglect; money not privation; power not vulnerability; structures not chaos; publication not obscurity; assessment not opinion. There are chimeras. Some academies are like clubs and class systems: institutions with rules and concealed social codes. If some creative writers are *in*, then it follows that some are *out*. The continent of writing suddenly acquires its own petty class system. That goes for students and staff. Degrees in writing become passports to publication or teaching jobs. No qualification: no career. Closed space. Yet, if all colleges of writing vanished, we would not find ourselves suddenly short of writers.

Institutions protect themselves, and protect their captured icons. Writers can be paraded as cultural ornaments, used to justify, or paper over, less respectable activity. As we discussed in Chapter Two, sometimes teaching and writing feed negatively into each other, falsifying natural, intuitive practice; and a programmatic philosophy develops, ossifying into assertion or ideology, rather than inquiry and demonstration. The writer becomes ivory-towered, a tenured libertarian. Writers based in academies risk being insulated against the very milieu, the living and working communities, out of which they write. If the writer is insecure or depressive, the security and success of an institution can bring out their worst qualities. The writer swells into a fat fish in that small pond unaware the pond is a fish farm. They risk getting lost in corridors of power, or are too much at ease in the status-greedy structures of education, more toxic to creative thought and action because they are phantasmal. The risk is that they end up colluding too closely with those for whom literature is less important than their job title suggests it to be. As the novelist Russell Celyn Jones has written, some writer-teachers protect themselves from becoming institutionalised by 'developing a wilful amnesia towards the dreary language of administration,

"IF SOME CREATIVE WRITERS ARE *IN*, THEN IT FOLLOWS THAT SOME ARE *OUT*."

never writing about campuses . . . and maintaining associations with the gaol house, as a counterpoint to the asylum of the gifted that pays your salary'. Not everybody is as resourceful. Writing can be a desperate business. The seduction of a salary can lead to collusion.

The worst thing that can happen to the writers is their teaching begins to mess with their own writing. As Lynn Freed argued, their work sounds like a teacher writing – low risk or theory-driven or forced. It gets worse. The creative writing industry can also begin to look like a conspiracy of worthiness and mere competence. William Packard quotes the editor of the *New York Quarterly* remarking:

> most of the poets out there want to have their cake and eat it too – their cover letters boast of prestigious grants, cushy academic jobs, numerous publications in trendy mags . . . You can't live bunny lives and write tiger poetry, simultaneously. If anyone out there wants to write with originality and honesty and recklessness, then he or she may have to change a lot of things about the life they're living.   (1992: 27)

"THE WRITER SWELLS INTO A FAT FISH IN THAT SMALL POND UNAWARE THE POND IS A FISH FARM."

That reminds us again of Rilke – 'ask yourself in the most silent hour of your night: must I write? . . . then build your life in accordance with this necessity'. Packard continues, 'Our present era has been characterized by William Jay Smith as filled with a lot of 'creative writing writing' – competent, passionless stuff learned in workshop and seminars and published in Mickey Mouse magazines.' In the literary pages of newspapers, contemporary fiction writers who have attended courses suffer the same caricaturing and censure as poets, for there are those for whom the creative writing industry is a cartoon world, a cloud-cuckoo-land of fantasy accomplishment and vacuum-sealed reputation.

It is evidently much more open-ended. At best, the teaching of creative writing provides a moving edge for literary evolutions and language's revelations. The more we practise attending to *language* in our reading and writing, and the more we practise attending to the world in which language lives, the more experienced we become at translating our individual senses and our perceptions into writing, and being believed by readers who, it is worth remembering, live *in* this world, and whose attention we have to earn. However, if we do not continue to create and re-create our space, we stand accused of insularity and decadence. An open book of possibility, the creative academy is an open space, but it sometimes needs rewriting. Maybe, just sometimes, we need rewriting. As is the gardener, so is the garden.

Ideas

Most writers in education know these dangers. They acknowledge and combat them, or they confound them. Many writers seize the opportunities to build bridges across the disciplines and into local communities. Most educational institutions are more liberal and humanist than any of their governments, and do remarkable work both inside and outside their constituencies and communities; they are a front line of tolerance, outreach and inquiry. My view is that we must never get above ourselves – we are makers of language, of stories and poems, not makers or repackagers of hierarchy. However, we must never get *below* ourselves, either. For a writer, self-understanding takes priority over career and status. Self-understanding makes you want to *do* something, rather than just *be* something. What shall we do?

First, we can embrace the various origins, histories and contradictions of this discipline. Second, we can accept a parity of seriousness with other taught art forms. Third, we can work on equal terms within other fields of creative endeavour, including science, by raising public awareness of other knowledge systems through popular science and creative nonfiction. Fourth, we can cease having to justify our work as some pedagogical adjunct to literary studies or social work. It embraces those areas, of course, but is a discipline all of its own, and as ancient in its origins and purposes as the teaching of rhetoric and Greek drama. Finally, students and teachers can stop apologising for the academic discipline of creative writing. There is every reason to celebrate the pursuit and practice of creativity. If nothing else, I hope this book demonstrates that creative writing is above all a natural human activity.

Creative writing can be taught. Once upon a time it was taught through the writing and speaking exercises embedded in rhetoric and the dramatic arts. We lost this, but we have created a second chance. I possess this positive view of creative writing because of moving a long distance from a position of scepticism about it. I originally chose to be a scientist and, as somebody who veered from literary matters, I have felt a starvation for creative permission, as though I was standing outside a lit house with no permission to enter. Various writers let me through the door; they taught me to read as a writer, to write as an apprentice. I am pleased for writers; we are living in a time in which creativity is valued. Let us explore a new level for writing in education that investigates any false borders between community and academy. We seek to extend creative writing's franchise in education, and also extend our work into the communities, workplaces and schools outside the academy – to write with our door open on the world.

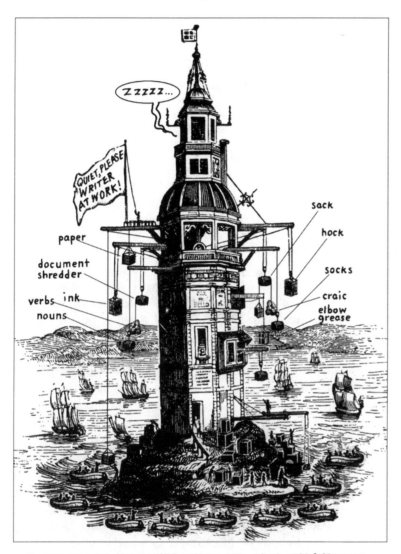

"...THERE ARE THOSE FOR WHOM THE CREATIVE WRITING
INDUSTRY IS A CARTOON WORLD, A CLOUDCUCKOOLAND
OF FANTASY ACCOMPLISHMENT AND VACUUM-SEALED
REPUTATION."

Writing Game

FINALLY, AGAIN WHO ARE YOU?
Why do you write and how do you write? Are there pressures in your life that force you into silence? Write a statement of no more than 800 words describing your current reasons and methods. What drives and what hinders you? How can you improve your writing conditions? Use these questions as headings from which to write quickly and without too much deliberation.

AIM: Compare your answers with those you wrote in the Writing Game on this theme in Chapter Two. If more progress is needed, then make some tough and practical decisions, based on some of the suggestions in this book, to change things so your life allows you greater fluency of practice as a writer.

The door and the abyss

Rilke wrote, 'No one can advise or help you – no one. There is only one thing you should do. Go into yourself. Find out the reason that commands you to write.' Rilke had rich patrons and safe space in which to write, the Duino castle for one. In many ways, he could afford to change his life, to write for angels. We live in real-time and open space. By all means, go into yourself; climb down to the invisible abyss from which your writing rises. But Rilke was wrong about the value of guidance once you get to that abyss. '*Andiam, chè la via lunga ne sospigne*', says Virgil, the poet's shade leading the living Dante through hell – 'Let us go, for the long way urges us'. Writers are nobody, and they are everybody. The light of writing allows us to find our way through, and recall Lawrence's 'Bavarian Gentians' from Chapter Eight: 'let me guide myself with the blue, forked torch of this flower / down the darker and darker stairs, where blue is darkened on blueness'.

We, as students, writers and teachers of writing, work and write within our social and educational communities – we are those communities. We play bit parts mostly; or we understudy on those stages. Our lives can be somewhat anarchic, not least because creative writing is a discipline that slides and slices across knowledge, thereby cutting across conformity. Writers are players on a stage; they are players in that society, and we do not always have to play the clowns. We do not have to take ourselves too seriously, of course, but we can take our discipline more seriously.

Fine writers and free thinkers choose the educational arena. They campaign by their very presence to make it a better space for creative thought and action. Writers work in education at all levels but, without being precious, writers must do so on their own terms, and not just out of necessity. The tonic effects of poverty on creativity are overrated; education offers at least the semblance of integrity, and the possibility of doing some good to someone at some time. What should be your first move?

Writers teach because they can, so the first and best thing you can do for yourself, as a new writer, is to apprentice yourself to a mentor who is a practising author, one who understands the fact that writing gets you lost, and who can help you sense the guide ropes that lead through the inferno's circles to and from your abyss. The personal history of literature is one of writers being taken on by other writers, of being welcomed and guided by somebody slightly further along 'the long way'. As an academic discipline, creative writing encourages these strange but life-changing meetings.

Joyce Carol Oates said, 'by honoring one another's creation we honor something that deeply connects us all, and goes beyond us'. We learn creative writing because we can, remembering that learning, like writing, is also an act of community. Writers carry a community's story in the voice of their memory. Think of creative writing as an open space, a continent of languages and memory. Too often, we hear and see each other at distance, or not at all. This allows us to ignore each other; skim across knowledge, language and understanding; and let our attention atrophy. Creative writing – even *clear* writing – closes these distances between us. It makes us wake up. Creative writing throws open doors to the world, and even to other worlds within us and beyond our own. It lets in the light of language. Without telling us what to think, it makes us see and hear each other. We understand ourselves better by writing with light. Go and open your door.

Recommended reading

Writing in the community has a huge literature all of its own but, unfortunately, much of it is perceived as so-called 'underground', 'worker' and 'community' literature, so it does not get picked up on academia's radar. Therefore, these recommendations represent a tiny slice of some of the more mainstream examples. In New York, the Teachers and Writers Collaborative, founded in 1967, is a salutary example. A nonprofit organisation, its members believe that writers can make a unique contribution to the teaching of writing and literature (www.twc.org). In many ways, the members of this collaborative are the invisible heroes of *The Cambridge Introduction to Creative Writing*. The work of the American poet Kenneth Koch is cited throughout this book, and Teachers and Writers helped him in his community and schools projects. When Koch entered a classroom, the children would clap and shout with pleasure. His playful but scrupulously planned pedagogy is captured in *Wishes, Lies and Dreams: Teaching Children to Write Poetry* (HarperPerennial, 1999). This is as important a book for new creative writers wishing to adventure into the community as it is for teachers seeking new ways to get children writing. It contains games, poems and practical advice. Koch also worked in nursing homes, encouraging creative writing, and *I Never Told Anybody: Teaching Poetry Writing to Old People* (Teachers and Writers Collaborative, 1997) is another satisfying teaching book for community writers. Creative writing in health care is an association with a powerful tradition among writers and medical practitioners. A number of creative writers explore this tradition as practice in Fiona Sampson's *Creative Writing in Health and Social Care* (Jessica Kingsley, 2004). David Morley's *The Gift: New Writing for the National Health Service* (Stride, 2002) brings together creative writing by authors and healthcare workers in a unique community writing project coordinated by the author, the purpose of which was to explore 'the art of medicine and the medicine of art'. *Our Thoughts are Bees: Working with Writers and Schools* by Mandy Coe and Jean Sprackland (Wordplay Press, 2005) provides advice about British schools placements. Creative writing's role within therapy and personal development is explored in Celia Hunt's *Therapeutic Dimensions of Autobiography in Creative Writing* (Jessica Kingsley, 2000). In Britain, the National Association of Writers in Education provides a focus for standards, training and good practice (www.nawe.co.uk). The scientist Max Perutz challenges received ideas about the place of the imagination in science in *I Wish I'd Made You Angry Earlier* (Cold Spring Harbor Laboratory Press, 2003). This is also a fine example of popular science as an act of creative writing. For readers interested in writing, imagination and science, they might consult the writings of the sociobiologist E. O. Wilson, especially his synthesis *Consilience: The Unity of Knowledge* (Abacus, 2003), in which he argues that 'We are learning the fundamental principle that ethics is everything. Human social existence . . . is based on the genetic propensity to form long-term contracts that evolve by culture into moral precepts and law.' Wilson's teaching is partly invoked within the final part of this book. *The Literary Animal*, edited by Jonathan Gottschall and David Wilson (Northwestern University Press, 2005), is a fascinating collection of essays by scholars at the forefront of evolutionary literary analysis: by scientists who take a serious interest in creative writing; and by literary analysts who have made evolution their explanatory framework. It seems clear to me, as a scientist and as a poet, that the synthesis of the humanities and what Steven Pinker calls the 'new sciences of human nature' is an open space in which the discipline of creative writing finds ever-stronger purpose.

Writing Game

IN YOUR BEGINNING IS YOUR END

Write a 500-word afterword to your own imaginary collected poems, complete stories or the final edition of your creative nonfiction. Assume your working life has glowed with success, and your readership is widespread and uncritical. Knowing that this is probably your final opportunity in print to say something *true* about yourself to your readers, write a brief account of what you think your weaknesses were, and why your audience may have missed them. In the final sentence, state what you think were the lessons you might pass on to younger writers just starting out.

AIM: Sometimes telling yourself the truth is the hardest thing to do, like drawing something accurately and seeming to do so without art. Describing your own weaknesses is necessary to the development of writerly honesty, but also necessary to your development and integrity.

Illustrative bibliography

Abbott, H. Porter, *The Cambridge Introduction to Narrative*, Cambridge: Cambridge University Press, 2002.

Abrioux, Yves, *Ian Hamilton Finlay: A Visual Primer*, London: Reaktion Books, 1994.

Addonizio, Kim and Laux, Dorianne, *The Poet's Companion*, New York: Norton, 1997.

Allen, Walter, *Writers on Writing*, London: Dent, 1948.

Alvarez, Al, *The Writer's Voice*, London: Bloomsbury, 2005.

Amis, Martin, *Experience*, London: Vintage, 2001.

Anderson, Linda (ed.), *Creative Writing: A Workbook with Readings*, London: Routledge, 2006.

Apollinaire, Guillaume, *Caligrammes*, Berkeley: University of California Press, 1991.

Attridge, Derek, *Poetic Rhythm: An Introduction*, Cambridge: Cambridge University Press, 1995.

Atwood, Margaret, interview BBC 4, bbc.co.uk/bbcfour/audiointerviews/profilepages/atwood, November 1996.

Atwood, Margaret, *Negotiating with the Dead: A Writer on Writing*, Cambridge: Cambridge University Press, 2002.

Barry, Elaine (ed.), *Robert Frost on Writing*, New Brunswick: Rutgers University Press, 1973.

Beard, Richard, *X20*, London: Flamingo, 1996.

Behn, Robin and Twichell, Chase (eds), *The Practice of Poetry: Writing Exercises from Poets who Teach*, New York: HarperResource, 1992.

Bell, Julia and Magrs, Paul, *The Creative Writing Coursebook*, London: Macmillan, 2001.

Bell, Madison Smartt, *Narrative Design: A Writer's Guide to Structure*, New York: Norton, 1997.

Bernays, Anne and Painter, Pamela, *What If? Writing Exercises for Fiction Writers*, New York: Quill, 1991.

Berry, Cicely, *Your Voice and How to Use It*, London: Virgin Books, 2003.

Bishop, Elizabeth, *The Complete Poems*, New York: The Noonday Press, 1979.

Blake, Carole, *From Pitch to Publication*, Basingstoke: Macmillan, 1999.

Blegvad, Peter, *The Book of Leviathan*, London: Sort Of Books, 2000.

Bloom, Harold, *The Anxiety of Influence*, 2nd edition, Oxford: Oxford University Press, 1997.

Bloom, Harold, *How to Read and Why*, London: Fourth Estate, 2000.

Bly, Carol, *Beyond the Writers' Workshop*, New York: Anchor, 2001.

Boden, Margaret A., *The Creative Mind: Myths and Mechanisms*, London: Routledge, 2004.

Boisseau, Michelle and Wallace, Robert, *Writing Poems*, 6th edition, New York: Longman Pearson, 2004.

Booker, Christopher, *The Seven Basic Plots*, London: Continuum, 2004.

Bradbury, Malcolm (ed.), *The Penguin Book of Modern British Short Stories*, London: Penguin Books, 1988.

Brande, Dorothea, *Becoming a Writer*, New York: Harcourt and Brace, 1934; reprint New York: Tarcher Penguin, 1981.

Brook, Peter, *The Empty Space*, Harmondsworth: Penguin, 1990.

Brower, Reuben, *Mirror on Mirror: Translation Imitation Parody*, Cambridge, MA: Harvard University Press, 1975.

Brown, Clare and Paterson, Don (eds), *Don't Ask Me What I Mean: Poets in Their Own Words*, London: Picador, 2003.

Browne, Renni and King, Dave, *Self-Editing for Fiction Writers: How to Edit Yourself into Print*, New York: HarperResource, 2004.

Burke, Sean (ed.), *Authorship: From Plato to the Postmodern*, Edinburgh: Edinburgh University Press, 1995.

Burnshaw, Stanley, *The Poem Itself*, Harmondsworth: Penguin, 1960.

Burroway, Janet, *Writing Fiction*, New York: Longman, 2003.

Burroway, Janet, *Imaginative Writing*, 2nd edition, New York: Longman, 2006.

Calder, Nigel, *The Magic Universe*, Oxford: University Press, 2003.

Carver, Raymond, *Fires*, London: Picador, 1986.

Coe, Mandy and Sprackland, Jean, *Our Thoughts are Bees: Working with Writers and Schools*, Southport: Wordplay Press, 2005.

Connolly, Cyril, *Enemies of Promise*, London: Penguin, revised edition 1961.

Cox, Ailsa, *Writing Short Stories*, London: Routledge, 2005.

Curtis, Tony (ed.), *As the Poet Said . . .* , Dublin: Poetry Ireland, 1997.

Dawson, Paul, *Creative Writing and the New Humanities*, London: Routledge, 2005.

Dillard, Annie, *The Writing Life*, New York: HarperCollins, 1989.

Eshleman, Clayton, *Companion Spider*, Middletown: Wesleyan University Press, 2001.

Fenton, James, *An Introduction to English Poetry*, London: Penguin, 2002.

Ford, Richard (ed.), *The Granta Book of the American Short Story*, London: Granta, 1992.

Freed, Lynn, 'Doing Time: My Years in the Creative Writing Gulag', *Harper's Magazine*, July 2005, pp. 65–72.

Freedman, Diane and Frey, Olivia (eds), *Autobiographical Writing Across the Disciplines*, Durham: Duke, 2003.

Fuentes, Carlos, *This I Believe*, London: Bloomsbury, 2004.

Fussell, Paul, *Poetic Meter and Poetic Form*, New York: Random House, revised edition 1979.

Gardner, John, *The Art of Fiction*, New York: Vintage Books, 1983.

Gardner, John, *On Becoming a Novelist*, New York: HarperPerennial, 1985.

Gerard, Philip, *Creative Nonfiction*, Cincinnati: Story Press, 1996.

Gottschall, Jonathan and Wilson, David (eds), *The Literary Animal*, Illinois: Northwestern University Press, 2005.

Gutkind, Lee, *The Art of Creative Nonfiction*, New York: John Wiley & Sons, 1997.

Haffenden, John, *Viewpoints: Poets in Conversation*, London: Faber and Faber, 1981.

Hamilton, Ian, *Robert Lowell: A Biography*, London: Faber and Faber, 1982.

Harmon, William (ed.), *Classic Writings on Poetry*, New York: Columbia University Press, 2003.

Heaney, Seamus, *Finders Keepers: Selected Prose 1971–2001*, London: Faber and Faber, 2002.

Herbert, W. N. and Hollis, Matthew (eds.), *Strong Words: Modern Poets on Modern Poetry*, Newcastle: Bloodaxe Books, 2000.

Hershman, D. Jablow and Lieb, Julian, *Manic Depression and Creativity*, New York: Prometheus Books, 1998.

Hollander, John, *The Gazer's Spirit*, Chicago: University of Chicago Press, 1995.

Hollander, John, *Rhyme's Reason*, New Haven: Yale Nota Bene, 2001.

Holub, Miroslav, *The Dimension of the Present Moment*, London: Faber and Faber, 1990.

Hughes, Ted, *Poetry in the Making*, London: Faber and Faber, 1967.

Hughes, Ted, *Winter Pollen*, London: Faber and Faber, 1994.

Hughes, Ted, *By Heart*, London: Faber and Faber, 1997.

Hugo, Richard, *The Triggering Town: Lectures and Essays on Poetry and Writing*, New York: Norton, 1979.

Hunt, Celia, *Therapeutic Dimensions of Autobiography in Creative Writing*, London: Jessica Kingsley, 2000.

Hunt, Celia, 'Assessing Personal Writing', *Auto/Biography* 9 (1–2), 2001, pp. 89–94.

Hunt, Celia and Sampson, Fiona, *Writing: Self and Reflexivity*, London: Palgrave, 2006.

Jack, Ian (ed.), *The Granta Book of Reportage*, London: Granta, 2006.

Kennedy, X. J. and Gioia, Dana, *An Introduction to Poetry*, New York: Longman, 1998.

King, Stephen, *On Writing*, London: Hodder, 2000.

Kinzie, Mary, *A Poet's Guide to Writing Poetry*, Chicago: Chicago University Press, 1999.

Koch, Kenneth, *Rose, Where Did You Get That Red?*, New York: Vintage, 1990.

Koch, Kenneth, *I Never Told Anybody: Teaching Poetry Writing to Old People*, New York: Teachers and Writers Collaborative, 1997.

Koch, Kenneth, *Wishes, Lies and Dreams: Teaching Children to Write Poetry*, New York: HarperPerennial, 1999.

Koch, Kenneth, *The Art of the Possible: Comics Mainly Without Pictures*, New York: Soft Skull Press, 2004.

Koestler, Arthur, *The Act of Creation*, London: Picador, 1975.

Kundera, Milan, *The Art of the Novel*, New York: FirstHarperPerennial, 2000.

Lakoff, George and Johnson, Mark, *Metaphors We Live By*, Chicago: University of Chicago Press, 1980.

Lamott, Anne, *Bird by Bird: Some Instructions on Writing and Life*, New York: Anchor, 1995.

Le Guin, Ursula, *Steering the Craft*, Portland: Eighth Mountain Press, 1998.

Leahy, Anna (ed.), *Power and Identity in the Creative Writing Classroom*, Clevedon: Multilingual Matters, 2005.

Lennard, John, *The Poetry Handbook*, Oxford: Oxford University Press, 1996.

Lodge, David, *The Art of Fiction*, London: Penguin Books, 1992.

Lodge, David, *The Practice of Writing*, London: Penguin, 1997.

Logan, William, *The Undiscovered Country: Poetry in the Age of Tin*, New York: Columbia University Press, 2005.

Lopez, Barry, *Arctic Dreams*, New York: Scribner, 1986.

Lopez, Barry, *About This Life*, London: Harvill Press, 1999.

Lovejoy, Margot, *Digital Currents: Art in the Electronic Age*, London: Routledge, 2004.

MacCarthy, Fiona, *Byron: Life and Legend*, London: John Murray, 2002.

Mahon, Derek, *Collected Poems*, Loughcrew: Gallery Press, 1999.

Malcolm, Janet, *The Journalist and the Murderer*, London: Granta, 2004.

Mandelstam, Nadezhda, *Hope Against Hope*, London: Collins and Harvill Press, 1971.

Mandelstam, Osip, *The Noise of Time: Selected Prose*, trans. Clarence Brown, Evanston: Northwestern University Press, 2002.

Matthews, Harry and Brotchie, Alastair, *OuLiPo Compendium*, London: Atlas, 1998.

Mills, Paul, *The Routledge Creative Writing Coursebook*, London: Routledge, 2006.

Moore, Alan, *Writing for Comics*, Urbana: Avatar, 2005.

Moore, Marianne, *Complete Poems*, London: Faber and Faber, 1968.

Morley, David, *The Gift: New Writing for the National Health Service*, Exeter: Stride, 2002.

Murray, Les, *Translations from the Natural World*, Manchester: Carcanet Press, 2003.

Myers, D. G., *The Elephants Teach: Creative Writing Since 1880*, New Jersey: Prentice Hall, 1995.

Nabokov, Vladimir, *Speak, Memory: An Autobiography Revisited*, London: Penguin, 2000.

Novakovich, Josip, *Fiction Writers Workshop*, Cincinnati: Story Press, 1995.

Oates, Joyce Carol, *The Faith of a Writer*, New York: HarperCollins, 2004.

Oliver, Mary, *A Poetry Handbook*, San Diego: Harvest, 1994.

Olsen, Tillie, *Silences*, New York: The Feminist Press, 2003.

Ostrom, Hans, Bishop, Wendy and Haake, Katherine, *Metro: Journeys in Writing Creatively*, New York: Addison-Wesley, 2001.

Packard, William, *The Art of Poetry Writing*, New York: St Martin's Press, 1992.

Padgett, Ron, (ed.), *Handbook of Poetic Forms*, 2nd edition, New York: Teachers and Writers Collaborative, 2000.

Paterson, Don, *The Eyes*, London: Faber and Faber, 1999.

Paterson, Don, *The Book of Shadows*, London: Picador, 2004.

Perutz, Max, *I Wish I'd Made You Angry Earlier*, New York: Cold Spring Harbor Laboratory Press, 2003.

Pessoa, Fernando, *Selected Poems*, London: Penguin Books, 1974.

Pfenninger, Karl H. and Shubik, Valerie R. (eds), *The Origins of Creativity*, Oxford University Press, 2001.

Phillips, Larry W. (ed.), *Ernest Hemingway on Writing*, New York: Scribner, 1984.

Plimpton, George (ed.), *Women Writers at Work: The Paris Review Interviews*, New York: Penguin Books, 1989.

Pope, Rob, *Creativity: Theory, History, Practice*, Abingdon: Routledge, 2005.

Pound, Ezra, *The ABC of Reading*, New York: New Directions, 1934, reissued 1960.

Preminger, Alex and Brogan, T., *The New Princeton Encyclopedia of Poetry and Poetics*, Princeton: Princeton University Press, 1993.

Pullman, Philip, 'Introduction' to *Paradise Lost*, Oxford: Oxford University Press, 2005.

Queneau, Raymond, *Cent Mille Milliards de poèmes*, Paris: Editions Gallimard, 1961.

Queneau, Raymond, *Exercises in Style*, Paris: Editions Gallimard, 1947.

Redmond, John, *How to Write a Poem*, Oxford: Blackwell, 2006.

Rodenburg, Patsy, *The Right to Speak: Working with the Voice*, London: Methuen, 1992.

Rodden, John (ed.), *Conversations with Isabel Allende*, trans. Virginia Invernizzi, Austin: University of Texas Press, 1999.

Said, Edward, *On Late Style*, London: Bloomsbury, 2006.

Sampson, Fiona (ed.), *Creative Writing in Health and Social Care*, London: Jessica Kingsley, 2004.

Sansom, Peter, *Writing Poems*, Newcastle: Bloodaxe Books, 1994.

Schaefer, Candace and Diamond, Rick, *The Creative Writing Guide*, New York: Addison-Wesley, 1998.

Schmidt, Michael, *Lives of the Poets*, London: Phoenix, 1999.

Scully, James (ed.), *Modern Poets on Modern Poetry*, London: Fontana, 1966.

Shapard, Robert and Thomas, James, *Sudden Fiction International*, New York: Norton, 1989.

Shapiro, Nancy and Padgett, Ron (eds), *The Point: Where Teaching and Writing Intersect*, New York: Teachers and Writers Collaborative, 1983.

Sheeler, Jessie, *Little Sparta: The Garden of Ian Hamilton Finlay*, London: Frances Lincoln, 2003.

Showalter, Elaine, *Teaching Literature*, Oxford: Blackwell, 2003.

Sinclair, John D. (trans.), *The Divine Comedy*, 3 vols, New York: Oxford
    University Press, 1961.
Smith, Frank, *Writing and the Writer*, London: Heinemann, 1982.
Spiegelman, Art, *MAUS: A Survivor's Tale*, New York: Random House, 1986.
Steegmuller, Francis, *Cocteau: A Biography*, Boston: Atlantic/Little Brown, 1970.
Steele, Timothy, *All the Fun's in How You Say a Thing: An Explanation of Meter
    and Versification*, Athens: Ohio University Press, 1999.
Stein, Sol, *Stein on Writing*, New York: St Martin's Press, 1995.
Strand, Mark and Boland, Eavan, *The Making of a Poem: A Norton Anthology of
    Poetic Forms*, New York: Norton, 2000.
Strunk, William and White, E. B., *The Elements of Style*, Massachusetts: Allyn and
    Bacon, 2000.
Szymborska, Wisława, *People on a Bridge*, trans. Adam Czerniawski, London:
    Forest, 1996.
Thomas, Edward, *Collected Poems*, Oxford: Oxford University Press, 1978.
Treglown, Jeremy, *V. S. Pritchett: A Working Life*, London: Chatto and Windus,
    2004.
Turner, Mark, *The Literary Mind*, Oxford: Oxford University Press, 1996.
Wainwright, Jeffrey, *Poetry: The Basics*, London: Routledge, 2004.
Wilson, E. O., *Consilience: The Unity of Knowledge*, New York: Abacus, 2003.
Wolff, Tobias, *Old School*, London: Bloomsbury, 2005.
Wood, James, 'The Last Word', *Guardian Review*, 11 June 2005, p. 7.
Wright, C. D., *Cooling Time*, Washington: Copper Canyon Press, 2005.
Zinsser, William, *On Writing Well*, New York: Collins, 2005.

Index